意大利文化与景观遗产法典

国家文物局　编译

文物出版社

封面设计：周小玮

责任印制：陆　联

责任编辑：许海意

图书在版编目（CIP）数据

意大利文化与景观遗产法典/国家文物局编译. —北
京：文物出版社，2009.9
ISBN 978－7－5010－2817－7

Ⅰ.意…　Ⅱ.国…　Ⅲ.文化遗产－保护－法典－
意大利　Ⅳ.D954.621

中国版本图书馆 CIP 数据核字（2009）第 153183 号

意大利文化与景观遗产法典

国家文物局　编译

*

文 物 出 版 社 出 版 发 行

（北京市东直门内北小街 2 号楼）

http://www.wenwu.com

E-mail：web@wenwu.com

北京燕泰美术印刷有限公司印刷

新 华 书 店 经 销

787×1092　1/16　印张：19.5

2009 年 9 月第 1 版　　2009 年 9 月第 1 次印刷

ISBN 978－7－5010－2817－7　定价：180.00 元

立 法 令

考虑到《意大利共和国宪法》第 76 条、87 条、117 条和 118 条的规定；

考虑到 1988 年 8 月 23 日第 400 号法律第 14 条的规定；

考虑到 1998 年 10 月 20 日第 368 号立法令的规定，该法令根据 1997 年 3 月 15 日第 59 号法律第 11 条及其后续修订与补充建立了文化遗产与活动部；

考虑到 1999 年 10 月 29 日第 490 号立法令的规定，该法令根据 1997 年 10 月 8 日第 352 号法律第 1 条对相关文化和环境遗产立法加以汇编；

考虑到 2002 年 7 月 6 日第 137 号法律第 10 条的规定；

考虑到 2003 年 9 月 29 日内阁会议通过的初步决议；

听取了根据 1997 年 8 月 28 日第 281 号立法令组建的联席会议的意见；

听取了意大利共和国参议院和众议院主管委员会的意见；

考虑到 2004 年 1 月 16 日内阁会议通过的决议；

按照文化遗产和活动部部长与大区事务部部长达成一致的建议，

意大利共和国总统特发布以下立法令：

第 1 条

1. 由 184 条和附件 A 组成的《文化与景观遗产法典》业经部长提议和副署通过。

本法令经中央政府盖章后纳入意大利共和国官方法规大全。所有意大利人必须根据自己的义务遵守本法并确保本法的贯彻落实。

总　　统　钱皮
总　　理　贝卢斯科尼
文化遗产与活动部部长　乌尔巴尼
大区事务部部长　拉·洛基亚

2004 年 1 月 22 日于罗马

核准人：司法部部长　卡斯泰利

目　录

CONTENTS

LEGISLATIVE DECREE no. 42 of 22 January 2004   Code of the Cultural and
Landscape Heritage, pursuant to article 10 of law no. 137 of 6 July 2002

FOURTH PART – SANCTIONS ·············· 223

TITLE I – *ADMINISTRATIVE SANCTIONS* ·········· 224

TITLE II – *PENAL SANCTIONS* ·············· 228

第一部分　总　则

第1条 原 则

1. 在执行宪法第9条时，意大利共和国应按照宪法第117条所确定的权限和本法各项规定保护和强化文化遗产。
2. 文化遗产的保护和强化应致力于保持全体国民对历史文化遗产及其国土的记忆，致力于推动文化的发展。
3. 国家、大区、自治市、省和城市应确保文化遗产的持续保存，并努力促进文化遗产的公众享用和强化。
4. 其他政府部门在开展各自活动的过程中应确保文化遗产的保存和公众享用。
5. 属于文化遗产之物品的所有者、占有者或持有者均必须确保其物品的保存。
6. 第3款、第4款和第5款所述文化遗产的保存、公众享用和强化工作应根据文化遗产保护法律实施。

第2条 文化遗产

1. 文化遗产由文化财产和景观资产组成。
2. 根据第10条和第11条的定义，文化财产包括具有艺术、历史、考古、人种－人类学、档案和目录学价值的可移动和不可移动物品，以及其他由法律确定为或根据法律证明具有历史文化价值的物品。
3. 自然景观资产包括第134条所述具有体现某地区历史、文化、自然、形态学、审美学价值的建筑物和区域，及由法律或根据法律认定为具有上述价值的资产。
4. 属于政府的文化遗产在满足政府使用需要的情况下，并且在符合保护需要的条件下，应供公众享用。

第3条 文化遗产的保护

1. 文化遗产的保护工作包括行使相关职能和规范相关活动，以便在充分调查的基础上对构成文化遗产的物品进行鉴定和识别，确保为了公众享用之目的而对所述遗产进行保护和保存。
2. 保护职能的行使还可以通过统一或规范文化遗产领域固有权利和行为的手段进行。

第4条 国家在文化遗产保护中的职能

1. 为了确保文化遗产保护职能的统一行使，根据宪法第118条，文化遗产保护职能统归文化遗产与活动部（以下简称"文化遗产部"）直接行使。文化遗产部也可以根据第5条第3款和第4款的规定，通过协议和协调，将保护职能移交给大区行使。根据第5条第2款和第6款已经移交给大区的职能不再变动。

2. 文化遗产部对属于国家的文化财产行使保护职能，即使这些文化财产一直在其他政府部门或实体的保管之下或已经同意交由他们使用。

第5条　大区和其他地方政府部门在文化遗产保护中的合作

1. 大区和自治市、大都市区及省（以下称"其他地方政府部门"），根据本法第二部分第一编的规定行使文化遗产保护职能时应与文化遗产部合作。

2. 本法规定的有关非国家所有和保护的书稿、手迹、文献、资料、古籍和藏书，以及非国家所有的书籍、出版物、雕版画等的保护职能由大区负责。

3. 根据相关协议或安排，按照国家、大区和特伦托、博尔扎诺两自治省相互关系常务会议（以下称"国家－大区会议"）的意见，大区也可以行使对私人藏书及其他非国家所有的带有相应底片和铸模的地图、乐谱、照片、影片或音像资料的保护职能。

4. 除第3款规定的形式外，根据差异性和相适应性原则，也可以视保护工作的需要认定与大区之间进行协调的其他形式。

5. 可通过协议或安排确定与其他地方政府部门进行合作的特殊形式。

6. 根据本法第3部分的规定，景观资产保护的行政管理职能应授予大区。

7. 对于第2款、第3款、第4款、第5款和第6款所述的职能，文化遗产部有权进行指导和监督；对长期不作为、长期不履行职责的部门，文化遗产部有权取而代之。

第6条　文化遗产的强化

1. 文化遗产的强化工作包括行使保护职能和规范相关活动，以便促进文化遗产知识的传播，确保为遗产的利用和公众享用创造最佳条件。强化工作还包括促进和支持文化遗产的保存工作。

2. 文化遗产的强化形式应与保护措施相辅相成，不得影响保护工作的重点任务。

3. 意大利共和国鼓励和支持国民以个体或组织形式参与强化文化遗产的工作。

第7条　与强化文化遗产相关的职能和任务

1. 本法制定与强化文化遗产有关的基本原则。大区要根据这些原则行使其法定权力。

2. 文化遗产部、大区和其他地方政府部门要在强化文化遗产的活动中努力做到通力协作，步调一致。

第 8 条　特别自治区和特别自治省

1. 在处理属本法管理的事务时，根据制定法和相关执行条例授予特别自治区和特伦托、博尔扎诺两自治省的权力保持不变。

第 9 条　具有宗教价值的文化财产

1. 根据宗教活动的需要，经与相关当局协调一致，文化遗产部应参与处理属于基督教和其他宗教派别的团体和机构的具有宗教价值的文化财产的紧迫事宜。在适当的情况下，大区也应参与此类事宜的处理。
2. 同样地，在处理此类事务时需要遵守根据 1984 年 2 月 18 日签订、1985 年 3 月 25 日第 121 号法律修订实施的《拉特兰条约修订协议》第 12 条缔结的有关协议，或根据宪法第 8 条第 3 款在与基督教以外的其他宗教派别签署协议的基础上发布的法律各项规定。

第二部分 文化财产

第一编　保　护

第一章　保护的对象

第 10 条　文化财产

1. 文化财产包括属于国家、大区、其他地方政府部门、其他任何公共团体和机构及民间非赢利社团所有的，具有艺术、历史、考古或人种－人类学价值的可移动和不可移动物品。

2. 文化财产还包括：

   a) 博物馆、画廊、美术馆及国家、大区、其他地方政府部门及其他任何政府部门和机构的展览场所的收藏品；

   b) 国家、大区、其他地方政府部门及其他任何政府部门和机构的档案和单份文件；

   c) 国家、大区、其他地方政府部门及其他任何政府部门和机构的图书馆藏书。

3. 在根据第 13 条进行了公示的情况下，文化财产还包括：

   a) 属于第 1 款所述机构之外的主体的具有特别重要的艺术、历史、考古或人种－人类学价值的可移动和不可移动物品；

   b) 属个人私有的，具有特别重要的历史价值的档案和单份文件；

   c) 属个人私有的，具有特殊文化价值的藏书；

   d) 由于从总体上涉及政治或军事历史，以及文学、艺术和文化历史，或对于证明公共、集体或宗教机构身份和历史而言具有特别重要价值的可移动和不可移动物品，不管这些物品属于谁；

   e) 从传承、知名度和特殊环境特征角度看，整体上具有特殊艺术或历史价值的收藏品或系列物品，不管这些物品属于谁。

4. 第 1 款和第 3 款 a) 项所列的物品，包括：

   a) 涉及古生物学、史前学和原始文明的物品；

   b) 具有古钱币研究价值的物品；

   c) 稀有或珍贵的书稿、手迹、文件、古籍，以及书籍、印刷品、雕版画及其铸模；

   d) 稀有和珍贵的地图和乐谱；

e) 稀有和珍贵的照片及其底片和铸模、电影摄影胶片和音像载体；

f) 具有艺术或历史价值的别墅、公园和花园；

g) 具有艺术或历史价值的公共广场、街道、道路及其他城市室外空间；

h) 具有历史和人类学价值的采矿点；

i) 具有艺术、历史和人种－人类学价值的船舶和漂浮物；

j) 具有历史或人类学价值，可作为乡村经济传承见证的乡村建筑物。

5. 第 1 款及第 3 款 a）项和 e）项所列物品，如属在世作者的作品，或其生成时间不超过 50 年，在不违反第 64 条和第 178 条规定的情况下，不属本编规定的保护范围。

第 11 条　特定保护的文化财产

1. 在不影响第 10 条适用的情况下，下列物品，只要属于本编规定的特定保护对象，不论有何前提和条件，都应视为文化遗产：

　a）第 50 条第 1 款所述的壁画、铭牌、涂鸦、牌匾、碑文、壁龛和其他建筑装饰物，不管是否向公众展示；

　b）第 51 条所述的艺术家工作室；

　c）第 52 条所述的公共区域；

　d）第 64 条和第 65 条所述的在世作者创作的绘画、雕刻、书画艺术及其他艺术品，或生成时间不超过 50 年的任何艺术品；

　e）第 37 条所述的具有特殊艺术价值的当代建筑师的建筑作品；

　f）第 65 条所述的以任何手段生成的，生成时间超过 25 年的照片及其底片和铸模、电影摄影作品的样品、音像材料或动画系列图像，以及事件的口头或文字记录；

　g）第 65 条和第 67 条第 2 款所述的超过 75 年的运输工具；

　h）第 65 条所述的具有科学技术发展史价值的超过 55 年的物品和工具；

　i）第 50 条第 2 款所述的由法律认定的第一次世界大战历史遗迹。

第 12 条　文化价值的鉴定

1. 第 10 条第 1 款所述的可移动和不可移动物品，如系已过世艺术家作品或其生成时间超过 50 年，在进行第 2 款所述的鉴定之前，属于本编规定的保护范围。

2. 文化遗产部主管机构依据职权，或根据物品所有者在提供有关证明材料的前提下提出的申请，根据文化遗产部为确保评估标准的一致性提出的总体原则对第 1 款所述物品进行鉴定，以确定其是否具有艺术、历史、考古和人种－人类学价值；

3. 对国家所有的不可移动物品，第 2 款所述申请应包括物品清单和相应说明的信息单。

准备物品清单的标准、填写信息清单的格式及两个表单的传送方式由国有财产局通过发布部长令的办法确定。如涉及转让给国防部门使用的建筑物，还要与负责工程和国有财产的主管部门取得一致意见。文化遗产部应发布法令，确定准备和提交鉴定申请的标准和程序，及第 1 款所述的申请人提交有关证明文件的标准和程序。

4. 如果待鉴定物品不具有第 2 款所述的价值，该物品则不属于本编规定的保护范围。

5. 属于国家、大区和其他地方政府部门所有的物品，如对其价值做出否定的评估，应将相关信息的档案送交主管机构，如果没有理由相信会违背公共利益的话，主管机构应根据文化遗产部的评估放弃该物品的国家所有权。

6. 第 3 款和第 4 款所述物品，如已被放弃国家所有权，按照本法之宗旨，可自由转让。

7. 根据第 2 款所述的总体指导原则对物品的艺术、历史、考古或人种 – 人类学价值的确认过程构成第 13 条所述公示的内容，确认过程中使用的相关标准应以第 15 条第 2 款规定的方式登记。被确认物品需无限期地纳入本编规定的保护范围。

8. 属于国家所有的不可移动物品如获得肯定的评估，其说明性信息清单应与第 7 款所述鉴定标准一起存入电子档案，以便文化遗产部和国有财产局根据他们各自的法定权限用于对不可移动物品进行监管和制订工作计划。

9. 本条规定适用于第 1 款所述的物品，不论其所有者的法律地位发生怎样的变化。

10. 2003 年 9 月 30 日第 269 号法令第 27 条第 8 款、10 款、12 款、13 款及 13 之 2 款的规定经修改并入 2003 年 11 月 24 日第 326 法律，仍然有效。

第 13 条 文化价值的公示

1. 鉴定结果公示应确认被鉴定物品具有第 10 条第 3 款所要求的价值。

2. 第 10 条第 2 款所述物品不需要公示。不管作为其所有者的主体在法律地位上发生怎样的变化，这些物品都要接受保护。

第 14 条 公示程序

1. 文化价值鉴定结果的公示程序应由监管人主动启动，也可以由监管人所在大区或其他任何相关地方政府部门提出要求时启动，同时要通知被鉴定物品的合法所有者、占有者或持有者。

2. 通知的内容应包括通过初步调查确定的物品鉴定和评估要素、执行第 4 款所述各项规定的情况，及有关提供观察结果的期限说明。提供观察结果的期限在任何情况下都应不少于 30 天。

3. 如果公示程序关系到建筑群，通知还要发送到自治市或都市区。

4. 为稳妥起见，公示的通知要按本编第二章、第三章第一节和第四章第一节的各项规定落实。

5. 第 4 款所述有关规定在文化遗产部根据 1990 年 8 月 7 日第 241 号法律第 2 条第 2 款规定的公示程序结束时停止执行。

6. 文化价值鉴定结果的公示需经文化遗产部批准。

第 15 条 公示的通知

1. 第 13 条所述鉴定结果公示应通过信使或有回执的挂号信件通知被鉴定物品的合法所有者、占有者或持有者。

2. 如果涉及的可移动或不可移动物品必须公告，鉴定结果公示方法应根据监管人的要求在相关登记机构备案，并对其后的合法所有者、拥有者或持有者具有法律效力。

第 16 条 公示的行政复议

1. 如对第 13 条所述鉴定结果公示的合法性和法律依据有异仪，可在接到通知后 30 天内向文化遗产部提起行政复议。

2. 提出行政复议意味着有争议的措施中止法律效力。作为一种防范措施，本编第二章、第三章第一节和第四章第一节的相关规定依然适用。

3. 文化遗产部应在收到行政复议后 90 天内，经与主管咨询机构协商后对此做出裁决。

4. 如果行政复议得到认可，文化遗产部应废除或修改有争议的措施。

5. 1971 年 11 月 24 日的意大利共和国总统第 1199 号令的有关规定适用于本法。

第 17 条 编 目

1. 文化遗产部应在大区和其他地方政府部门的参与下做好文化财产的编目工作并协调相关活动。

2. 编目的程序和方式将由部长令制定。为此，文化遗产部应在大区的协作下，确定国家层次上通用的数据收集、交换、获取、使用和处理及通过计算机将这些数据集成到国家、大区和其他地方政府部门数据库的方法。

3. 文化遗产部和大区，可以在大学的协作下共同努力，确定有关文化财产编目方法的学习、研究和创新规划。

4. 文化遗产部、大区和其他地方政府部门应按照第 2 款所述部长令规定的方式负责为自己占有的文化财产编目，并在与所有者取得一致的前提下负责其他文化财产的编目工作。

5. 本条中提到的数据应汇总到国家文化财产目录。

6. 对根据第 13 条规定发布的有关鉴定结果公示的信息进行咨询应该规范，以确保文化财产和秘密信息的安全。

第二章 监管与检查

第 18 条 监 管

1. 对文化财产的监管是文化遗产部的任务。

2. 第 12 条第 1 款所述的国有文化财产，不管其使用或保管单位是谁，均由文化遗产部直接监管。为对第 12 条第 1 款所述的大区和其他地方公共机构所有的文化财产行使监管权，文化遗产部还要与大区进行协商和协调。

第 19 条 检 查

1. 监管人可随时对文化财产保存与保管的落实情况和现状进行检查。除特别紧急情况之外，检查应至少提前 5 天通知。

第三章　保护与保存

第一节　保护措施

第 20 条　禁止行为

1. 不得破坏和损害文化财产，不得将文化财产用于与其历史或艺术特性不符的目的，对文化财产的使用不得影响其保存。
2. 文化财产档案不能分散流失。

第 21 条　需要批准的活动

1. 下列活动需经文化遗产部批准：
   a) 拆除文化财产的构件，即使事后经过修复的；
   b) 移动文化财产，即使不违反第 2 款和第 3 款规定的暂时移动；
   c) 收藏品及系列文化财产分割；
   d) 根据第 13 条已公示过的，且已存入公、私档案的文件的抛弃；
   e) 向其他法人实体转让属于公共档案和私人档案的成套文件。
2. 由于持有人住所或经营场所的变更需移动文化财产应提前通告监管者。监管人可在接到通告后 30 天内提出防止文化财产在运输过程中受损的必要措施。
3. 国家、政府部门和机构现有档案的移动无需批准。
4. 除上述各项所述情况外，其他各种涉及文化财产的工程活动均需监管人批准。
5. 批准相关活动的依据是项目的施工图纸或申请人提供的工程技术说明。批准的同时可以提出某些建议。

第 22 条　建筑项目的批准程序

1. 除第 25 条和第 26 条所述情况外，第 21 条第 4 款所述的涉及公、私建筑工程的批准，监管人应在接到申请之后 120 天内做出。
2. 如果监管人要求澄清或提供补充材料，第 1 款所述的批准期限应暂时中止计算直到收到要求的文件为止。

3. 如果监管者要进行技术性鉴定，且已事先通知申请人，则第 1 款所述的期限应暂时中止计算直到获得正式鉴定结果，但无论如何推迟时间不能超过 30 天。

4. 如果第 2 和第 3 款规定的期限已过又无回音，申请人可要求行政部门采取行动。如果行政部门在收到申请人的要求之后 30 天内不作为，应将申请视为得到批准。

第 23 条　简化的建筑施工许可程序

1. 如果根据第 21 条规定已获得批准的工程尚需申请建筑施工许可，根据本法规定可通过开工公示的方式进行。有关方面应在开工公示的同时将批准书连同相关的工程设计一起递交自治市政府。

第 24 条　公共文化财产工程

1. 对于代表国家、大区、其他地方政府部门及其他任何政府部门和机构进行的公共文化财产工程，第 21 条所述的必要批准可通过文化遗产部和相关政府部门之间签署的协议表述。

第 25 条　业务协调会议

1. 在影响文化财产的项目和工程中，要召开业务协调会议，由文化遗产部的主管部门在会议期间做出根据第 21 条所述的必要批准，并进行合理公示。批准书应列入会议记录，并包括为实施工程项目而做出的任何建议。

2. 如果文化遗产部的主管部门提出正当的异议，负责项目的行政部门可要求内阁总理在内阁审议的基础上做出裁决。

3. 业务协调会议上做出的有利决定的接受方应将会议提出的建议的执行情况通报文化遗产部。

第 26 条　环境影响评估

1. 如涉及需要进行环境影响评估的工程项目，第 21 条规定的批准应由文化遗产部在政府部门研究环境适应性的联合会议上，根据为评估而提交的最终工程规划做出。

2. 如果根据第 1 款要求对工程规划进行的审查表明，工程与受到影响之文化财产的保护紧迫性不符，文化遗产部可否决该工程项目，并通报环境与土地保护部。因此，环境影响评估程序应视为已予以否定。

3. 如果工程进行中出现与第 1 款所述批准相冲突的情况，而且使受保护文化财产的完整性面临风险，监管人应下令中止施工。

第 27 条　紧急情况

1. 遇到确系紧急情况，可采取为避免被保护文化财产受损而必不可少的临时措施，并立即通知监管人。所确定的工程设计必须及时提交监管人以便得到必要的批准。

第 28 条　预防性措施

1. 对违反第 20 条、第 21 条、第 25 条、第 26 条和第 27 条规定开工的工程或没按批准书要求施工的工程，监管人可责令其停工。
2. 对涉及第 10 条所述文化财产的工程，监管人有权责令停工，甚至可以在第 12 条第 2 款所述的评估尚未完成，或第 13 条所述的鉴定结果公示还没有发出的时候行使这种权力。
3. 如果第 2 款所述的停工命令在收到开始评估或鉴定结果公示程序的通知后 30 天内未能传达，应视为已经取消。
4. 如果在具有考古价值的地段进行市政工程施工，监管人甚至可以在第 12 条第 2 款所述的评估工作还没有进行或第 13 条所述的鉴定结果公示还没有发布时要求在上述地段进行预防性考古取样分析，费用由市政工程的施工方承担。

第二节　保存措施

第 29 条　保　存

1. 文化遗产的保存工作靠一贯的、协调的和有计划的研究、预防、维护和修复工作加以保障。
2. "预防"是指可将与文化财产有关的风险限制在一定范围之内的系列活动。
3. "维护"是指为控制文化财产的状态、保持文化财产及其组成部分的完整性、功能性和独特性而从事的所有活动和工作。
4. "修复"是指为实现文化财产的完整性、恢复其本来状态、保护和传播其文化价值而通过一系列活动对其进行的直接干预。根据现行法律法规，对于那些位于已宣布存在地震风险的地区的不可移动文化财产，其修复工作应包括结构上的加固。

5. 文化遗产部应规定文化财产保存的指导原则、技术规则、标准和模式。在行使这些职能时可争取大区的参与及大学和有资质的科研机构协作。

6. 根据有关在建筑物上进行工程设计和作业的现行法律法规的规定，建筑物中的可移动文化财产和表面装饰的维护与修复工作应由有资质的文化财产修复人员根据有关法规承担。

7. 为建筑物中的可移动文化财产和表面装饰的修复及其他保存活动提供补充性作业的修复人员和其他工作人员的操作规程，由文化遗产部根据 1988 年 8 月 23 日第 400 号法律第 17 条第 3 款的规定以部长令的形式制定，并取得国家 – 大区会议同意。

8. 通过文化财产修复培训要达到的标准和质量管理水平，由文化遗产部在与国家 – 大区会议事先协商的基础上根据 1988 年第 400 号法律第 17 条第 3 款的规定以部长令的制定，并应与教育、大学和科研部部长保持一致。

9. 文化财产修复指南由根据 1998 年 10 月 20 日第 368 号立法令规定成立的高级教育与培训学校及第 11 款所述的中心和国家认可的其他公、私机构提供。文化遗产部在与国家 – 大区会议事先协商的基础上，根据 1988 年第 400 号法律第 17 条第 3 款的规定，并与教育、大学和科研部保持一致，以部长令确定培训委托程序、对本款所述教育机构的组织与职能的最低要求、教学活动和结业考试的监督程序，这些教学培训活动必须至少有一个文化遗产部的代表参与以及相关教育专业人员的参与。

10. 从事文化财产修复或其他保存活动的辅助性工作的专业人员培训由公、私机构根据大区的相关规章进行。相关课程需达到 1997 年 8 月 28 日第 281 号立法令第 4 条确定的标准和质量管理水平。

11. 文化遗产部和大区可通过专门的安排和协议，在大学和其他公、私机构的参与下，联合成立培训中心。这些中心可以是跨大区的，可以赋予法人资格，受托从事与文化财产保存和修复有关的具有特殊复杂性的科研、实验、分析、文献整理和恢复工作。根据第 9 款规定，在这些中心可以设立从事文化财产修复教学的高级培训学校。

第 30 条　保存义务

1. 国家、大区、其他地方政府部门及其他任何政府部门和机构必须做好其所占有的文化财产的保存工作，并保证其安全。

2. 第 1 款所述的机构，还有民间非赢利性社团，除现有档案外，应按监管人规定的方式将他们所占有的文化财产放置在规定的位置。

3. 文化财产的私人所有者、占有者或持有者必须做好他们所有、占有或持有的文化财产的保存工作。

4. 第 1 款所述的机构必须做好其档案保存和整理工作，保持它们的完整性，并为它们的历史档案编写目录。历史档案包括 40 年以前形成的相关文献资料。根据第 13 条的规定已公示的私人档案的不论所有者、占有者或是持有者都要承担同样的义务。

第 31 条   志愿保存

1. 无论文化财产的所有者、占有者或持有者主动从事文化财产的修复和其他保存工作都应根据第 21 条规定获得批准。
2. 在批准过程中,监管人应根据有关方面的要求就上述工作有无资格根据第 35 条和第 37 条的规定获得国家资助发表意见。为了确定其享受法律规定的减免税待遇的资格,监管人还可对上述工作的必要性予以证明。

第 32 条   强制保存

1. 文化遗产部可强制文化财产的合法所有人、占有人或持有人从事为确保文化财产受到妥善保存而必须的工作,也可以采取直接的保护行动。
2. 第 1 款的规定也适用于第 30 条第 4 款规定的义务。

第 33 条   强制保护工作的执行程序

1. 为执行第 32 条的规定,监管人需编制技术报告,并说明有待采取措施的必要性。
2. 技术报告应与程序启动通知一起送交文化财产的所有者、占有者或持有者。文化财产的所有者、占有者或持有者可在收到通知后 30 天内提交其反馈意见。
3. 如果监管人认为没必要直接采取措施,应在执行和落实技术报告的过程中给文化财产的所有者、占有者或持有者规定一个期限,指定他们如期提交执行保存任务的计划。
4. 计划应由监管人批准,并附有必要的说明和确定的开工期限。如涉及不可移动文化财产,监管人应将计划递交自治市或都市区。后者可在收到通知后 30 天内提出合理的意见。
5. 如果文化财产的所有者、占有者或持有者没能履行提交计划的义务,没在监管人规定的期限内按监管人的提示对计划进行修改,或者拒绝承担义务,文化遗产部应直接执行。
6. 在紧急情况下,监管人可立即采取必要的保存措施。

第 34 条　强制保存工作的费用

1. 因采取文化财产保护措施而涉及的费用，不论是用于文化遗产部根据第 32 条规定指定的保护措施还是直接实行的措施，均由文化财产的所有者、占有者或持有者支付。但是，如果所采取的保护措施特别重要，或作为保护对象的文化财产已获准由公众使用或享用，文化遗产部可承担全部或部分费用。在这种情况下，文化遗产部要确定其打算承担的费用额度，并通知相关当事人。
2. 如果因采取文化财产保护措施而产生的费用已由文化财产的所有者、占有者或持有者承担，文化遗产部应给予补偿或根据第 36 条第 2 款和第 3 款的规定分期退还部分资金，但数量要保持在第 1 款所确定额度之内。
3. 对于因文化遗产部直接采取保护措施而产生的费用，文化遗产部应确定向所有者、占有者或持有者收取的额度，并设法按照有关强制性征缴政府财产税的现行法律规定的方式收回这部分开支。

第 35 条　文化遗产部的资金发放

1. 文化遗产部可分担文化财产所有者、占有者或持有者在采取第 31 条第 1 款所述的保护措施的过程中涉及的开支，额度不超过实际开支的二分之一。如果所采取的措施特别重要或关系到公众使用或享用的物品，文化遗产部可以考虑全额拨款。
2. 第 1 款的规定也适用于第 30 条第 4 款所述为保护历史档案而采取的措施。
3. 在确定第 1 款所述拨款比例时，其他享受税收优惠的公、私资金也应加以考虑。

第 36 条　资金的发放

1. 文化财产保护资金在文化财产保护工作完成和受益人实际承担的费用核清之后由文化遗产部发放。
2. 在对保护工作的进度定期评估的基础上可预付资金。
3. 如果保护工作没有完成，或仅部分完成，受益人应将预付资金退还。相关资金的回收工作应按照有关强制性征缴政府财产税的现行法律规定的程序完成。

第 37 条　利息补贴

1. 无论不可移动文化财产的所有者、占有者还是持有者为从事经批准的保存工作而从信贷机构获得抵押贷款，文化遗产部均可提供利息补贴。

2．利息补贴的最高额度按抵押贷款年利率的六个百分点计算。

3．补贴金将根据协议规定的程序直接拨放给信贷机构。

4．第1款所述的资金，也适用于监管人根据业主的申请已承认其具有特殊艺术价值的当代建筑物的保护。

第 38 条　向公众开放已采取保存措施的建筑物

1．由政府全部或部分出资或提供利息补贴进行了修复或采取了其他保护措施的建筑物，文化遗产部和个体所有者应在分析第 34 条所述的开支负担和第 35 条所述的资金发放的基础上做出专门安排，或达成专门协议，视每座建筑物的具体情况向公众开放。

2．上述安排和协议应在对保护工作的类型、建筑物的艺术与历史价值以及建筑物中保存的文化财产进行考虑后确定向公众开放义务的期限。安排和协议应由监管人通报建筑物所在的自治市或都市区。

第 39 条　国有文化财产的保存

1．文化遗产部应确定国有文化财产的保存工作要求。若这些文化财产已由其他政府部门或机构保管或使用，保存工作要求应与其协商后确定。

2．除非达成别的协议，第 1 款所述保存措施的计划及实施若涉及不可移动文化财产，应由上述政府部门或机构负责，文化遗产部保留批准保存项目和监督的权力。

3．第 1 款所述保存工作的实施若涉及可移动文化财产，文化遗产部应将其计划和开工安排通知自治市或都市区。

第 40 条　属大区和其他地方政府部门所有的文化财产的保存

1．属于大区和其他地方政府部门所有的文化财产，第 32 条所述的保存措施应与该文化财产的所属部门达成协议后确定，在特别紧急的情况下除外。

2．该协议还可包括第 30 条第 2 款规定的内容。

3．涉及国家、大区或其他地方政府部门及其他公、私机构的文化财产保存措施通常是预防性规划协议的主要内容。

第 41 条　政府部门将其持有的档案存入国家档案馆的义务

1．国家司法与行政机构应将 40 年以前已办结的事务的有关文件连同其查阅工具一起存入国家中央档案馆或国家档案馆。服役和军职名单应在生成 70 年之后存入。公证档案馆应收存 100 年以前已退出公证业务的公证文书。

2. 国家中央档案馆馆长和国家档案馆的负责人可以收存生成时间比较短但却面临散失或损坏危险的文献。

3. 档案只有在生成单位做出注销决定后才能由档案馆收存。存档费用由送存单位承担。

4. 已取消的政府部门或已解散的公共机构的档案应存入国家中央档案馆或国家档案馆，除非档案需要全部或部分移交给其他部门。

5. 第 1 款所述机构和部门应成立有文化遗产部和内政部的代表参加的委员会，负责监督现用和入库档案的合理保存，共同确定文件的整编、管理和保存标准，对第 3 款所述的档案注销提出建议，管理第 1 款所述的存档工作，鉴定文件的机密性。委员会的构成和职能由文化遗产部在与内政部协商一致的情况下根据 1988 年 8 月 23 日第 400 号法律第 17 条第 3 款的要求以发布法令的方式确定。注销档案应由文化遗产部批准。

6. 本条规定不适用于外交部。考虑到有些文件的军事和作战性质，本条规定也不适用于陆、海、空三军参谋部。

第 42 条　宪政机关历史档案的保存

1. 意大利共和国总统府应根据由总统令做出的规章和条例，在总统府秘书长的建议下，将其文件存入总统府历史档案室。查阅和接触意大利共和国总统府历史档案室所存文件的程序由总统令确定。

2. 众议院和参议院应根据各自议长办公厅的规章和条例将其文件存入各自的历史档案室。

3. 宪法法院根据有关宪法法院的组成与职能的现行法律做出的条例将其文件存入自己的历史档案室。

第 43 条　强制性保管

1. 为保障文化财产的安全并根据第 29 条的规定做好保存工作，文化遗产部有权将可移动文化财产移交给或暂时保存于公共机构。

第 44 条　无偿贷款和文化财产保存

1. 管理或存放艺术、考古学、目录学和科学收藏品的档案馆和机构的负责人可以在文化遗产部主管部门的许可下用无偿贷款从私人所有者手中接收可移动文化财产，条件是：接收文化财产的目的是为了供公众享用；接收的文化财产具有特殊重要性或系公共收藏品的重要补充；事实证明保存这些收藏品不会给公共机构带来特别沉重的负担。

2. 无偿贷款的期限不能少于 5 年。借贷双方任何一方如在贷款期满前至少两个月未通知对方取消贷款合同，则视为事实上再顺延一个同样时间的贷款期。借贷双方也可在自愿的基础上提前解除无偿贷款合同。

3. 档案馆和收藏机构的负责人可以采取任何必要的措施保存用无偿贷款接收的文化财产，并通知出贷方。相关开支由文化遗产部承担。

4. 应在文化遗产部的出资下为这些文化财产办理适当险别的保险。

5. 档案馆和收藏机构负责人还可在文化遗产部主管部门事先认可的情况下收存属于政府机构的文化财产，用于保存和监管这些文化财产的专项费用由送存单位承担。

6. 本条没有明确规定的事项，按有关无偿贷款和存放的规定处理。

第三节　其他保护形式

第 45 条　间接保护指令

1. 为防止可移动文化财产的完整性遭遇威胁，其透视或自然照明受到损害，或者建筑物的镶嵌或装饰面被改变，文化遗产部有权对保护距离、保管方法和其他规则做出指令性规定。

2. 根据第 46 条和第 47 条的规定做出第 1 款所述的指令经公告后立即生效。有关当地政府部门应将这些指令纳入建筑规则和城市规划指导文件。

第 46 条　间接保护程序

1. 监管人应主动规定间接保护程序，也可应大区或其他相关地方政府部门的要求规定间接保护程序，并通知指令涉及的建筑物所有者、占有者或持有者。如果需要通知的人太多，不可能按人头通知或工作量太大，监管人可用适当的广告形式将启动程序的通知公布于众。

2. 启动间接保护程序的通知应指明将要实施间接保护指令的建筑物，并说明指令的主要内容。

3. 如涉及建筑群，通知还要送达自治市或都市区。

4. 作为一种预防措施，通知还要根据上述指令中的相关事项，提出暂时禁止变动建筑物的要求。

5. 第4款所述措施应执行至文化遗产部根据1990年8月7日第241号法第2条第2款制定的相关程序期满。

第47条 间接保护指令的通知和行政复议

1. 间接保护指令应通过信使或以有回执的挂号邮件方式送达对相关建筑物享有合法权利的所有者、占有者和持有者。

2. 指令应在建筑注册部门备案，并对其所涉建筑物的合法后继所有者、占有者和持有者均有效。

3. 针对有关间接保护指令提出的行政复议应根据第16条予以受理，但复议的提出不应导致有争议的指令效力的中止。

第48条 展览和陈列的批准

1. 暂借下列文化财产用于展出和陈列需要批准：
   a) 第12条第1款所述可移动文化财产；
   b) 第10条第1款所述可移动文化财产；
   c) 第10条第3款a) 项和e) 项所述文化财产；
   d) 第10条第2款a) 项所述收藏品和单件文化财产；第10条第2款c) 项和第3款c) 项所述藏书；第10条第2款b) 项和第3款b) 项所述档案和单份文件。

2. 如批准涉及属于国家或在国家保护下的文化财产，申请需在展览和陈列活动开始前至少4个月提交文化遗产部，并说明负责暂借物品安全的责任方。

3. 批准时应考虑文化财产保存的紧迫性，属于国家的文化财产，还要考虑公众享用的紧迫性。批准还应以采取必要措施确保文化财产的完整性为前提。批准的标准、程序和方式由文化遗产部以部长令的形式加以规定。

4. 获得批准还需要申请方根据申请书中标明的价值，由文化遗产部事先核定，为文化财产进行投保。

5. 如果展览或陈列活动是由文化遗产部发起，或有国家或政府部门或机构参与，可由国家承担相关风险，而不必采取第4款所述的保险。政府担保的程序、方式和条件由文化遗产部与经济和财政部协商后以部长令形式确定。相关费用通过动用经济和财政部开支核定表中所列用于法定开支和日常开支的准备金加以解决。

6. 为申请享受税法规定的减免税待遇，文化遗产部有权根据有关方面的要求宣告文化财产展览或展示及其他文化创意活动的重要文化价值或科学价值。

第 49 条　广告和广告牌

1. 禁止在作为文化财产保护的建筑物或场所张贴广告或安装广告牌或其他广告媒体。但不会对所述建筑物或场所的外观、体面和公众享用造成损害，经监管人批准则可以张贴广告或安装广告牌。广告的批准需报送市政当局以便其根据权限授予批准。
2. 禁止在第 1 款所述文化财产建筑群内或附近的道路两旁设置广告牌或其他广告媒体，除非根据有关道路交通及街道车辆广告的法律法规给予批准，且监管人事先确定广告媒体的设置及类型不影响受保护文化财产的外观、体面和公众享用。
3. 在对广告与第 1 款所述建筑物之艺术或历史价值的兼容性进行评估后，监管人可授权或批准在一定时间内将为从事文化财产建筑保存或修复作业而搭建的脚手架掩盖物用于广告目的，时间不超过作业工期。为此，上述工程的投标合同必须附在要求批准或同意做广告的申请书上。

第 50 条　文化财产的拆除

1. 未经监管人批准，禁止拆除和下令拆除壁画、铭牌、涂鸦、牌匾、碑文、壁龛和其他建筑装饰物，不管其是否向公众展示；
2. 未经监管人批准，禁止拆除和下令拆除铭牌、涂鸦、牌匾、碑文、壁龛，移除经有关法律法规确定为第一次世界大战遗迹的碑石和遗址。

第 51 条　艺术家工作室

1. 禁止改变艺术家工作室的指定用途；禁止移动从整体上属于工作室组成部分，并根据第 13 条被公示为具有特别重要的历史价值的作品、文件、遗物及其他类似物品等。
2. 带天窗的传统工作室被用作艺术家工作室至少 20 年者，其指定用途也不得改变。

第 52 条　有文化价值区域的商业活动

1. 根据有关改造商业区域的法律规定，市政当局应与监管人协商确定禁止从事 商业活动或特殊条件下才能从事商业活动的具有考古、历史、艺术和环境价值的区域。

第四章 国内流转

第一节 转让和其他流转形式

第 53 条 国家文化财产

1. 符合《民法典》第 922 条所述类型特征，属于国家、大区和其他政府部门的文化财产构成国家文化财产。
2. 除本法规定的特殊方式外，属国家文化遗产的财产不得转让，也不得成为以第三方为受益人的权利客体。

第 54 条 不可转让的文化财产

1. 属于国家的下列文化财产不得转让：
   a）具有考古价值的建筑物和区域；
   b）根据现行法律规定的方法被认定为国家历史遗迹的建筑物；
   c）博物馆、美术馆、艺术画廊和图书馆收藏品；
   d）档案。
2. 下列物品同样不得转让：
   a）所有者为第 10 条第 1 款所述主体，属于已过世艺术家作品，生成时间超过 50 年，国家尚未根据需要按第 12 条规定的认证程序放弃所有权的可移动和不可移动物品；
   b）属于在世艺术家作品或其生成时间不超过 50 年但已被第 53 条所述机构收藏的物品；
   c）第 53 条所述机构的单份文件和属于第 53 条所述机构以外的政府部门和机构的档案和单份文件；
   d）属第 53 条所述机构所有且已根据第 10 条第 3 款 a）项规定公示为具有特别重要价值，可用以证明公众、集体或宗教机构的性质和历史的不可移动物品。
3. 第 1 款和第 2 款所述物品可以在国家、大区和其他地方政府部门之间流转。
4. 第 1 款和第 2 款所述物品只可根据其特征并按本部分第一编所述目的加以使用。

第 55 条　属于国家文化财产的建筑物的转让

1. 属于国家文化财产的一部分但又没有列入第 54 条第 1 款和第 2 款所列清单的不可移动文化财产未经文化遗产部批准不得转让。

2. 符合下列条件可获得第 1 款所述的批准：

   a）流转过程中必须确保文化财产的保护和强化，在任何情况下都不能影响公众享用；

   b）批准文件必须明确指定建筑物的用途，该用途必须与建筑物的历史与艺术性质相一致，并且肯定不会影响文化财产保存。

3. 批准转让意味着该文化财产脱离了国家所有权。转让后的文化财产仍要受到第 12 条第 7 款的保护。

第 56 条　需要批准的其他类型转让

1. 转让下列文化财产也需要经文化遗产部批准：

   a）第 54 条第 1 款和第 2 款及第 55 条第 1 款所述范围之外属于国家、大区和其他地方政府部门的文化财产；

   b）a）项所述范围之外属于政府部门的文化财产或除第 54 条第 2 款 a）项和 c）项所述物品之外属于民间非赢利社团的文化财产。

2. 第 1 款 b）项所述部门或团体部分出售收藏品、系列物品和藏书也需要获得批准。

3. 上述各款的规定同样适用于抵押和质押，以及其中可能造成文化财产转让的合法交易。

4. 向国家转让文化财产，包括以文化财产转让充抵应缴税款，无需批准。

第 57 条　转让批准规则

1. 转让文化财产需由财产所有者提出转让批准申请，并附有待转让财产当前的指定用途和必要的保存计划。

2. 第 55 条第 1 款所述财产的转让批准可由文化遗产部根据监管人的建议，经与大区协商，并通过大区与其他地方政府部门协商之后，按照第 55 条第 2 款规定的条件发布。批准规定的有关指令和条件应写入转让契据。

3. 不得进行针对被转让文化财产的任何工程活动，除非相关工程项目已根据第 21 条第 4 款事先获得批准。

4. 第 56 条第 1 款 a）项所述的文化财产、第 56 款第 1 款 b）项和第 2 款所述政府部门和机构的文化财产，在其不涉及公共收藏利益，且转让不影响其保存，也不影响公众享用的情况下，可批准转让。

5. 第 56 条第 1 款 b）项和第 2 款所述民间非赢利社团的文化财产，在转让不会对其保存或公众享用造成严重影响的情况下，可批准转让。

第 58 条　交换文化财产的批准

1. 第 55 条和第 56 条所述的文化财产、属于政府收藏品的单件文化财产，与属于政府部门、机构和个人的其他文化财产，包括属于外国政府部门、机构和个人的文化财产进行交换，如其交换可以增加国家的文化遗产或丰富公共收藏，文化遗产部可予批准。

第 59 条　转让的公示

1. 任何依法全部或部分转让文化财产或转让文化财产占有的契据，均需向文化遗产部报告。

2. 转让应在 30 天内按下列规定通报：

   a）如转让活动考虑的是金钱而不是价值，或属于占有的转让，由文化财产占有权的出让方或转让人通报；

   b）如转让属于强制性或破产销售，或由法院对未定转让合同的判决生效而引起的，由购买者通报；

   c）如属死者遗产转让，由继承人或遗产受赠人通报。继承人通报期限从接受遗产之日开始计算，或从到税务主管部门申报遗产税时开始计算；遗产受赠人通报期限从遗嘱公布之日算起，除非根据《民法典》的规定放弃继承权。

3. 通报应递交于财产所在地的主管监管人。

4. 通报内容应包括：

   a）转让各方的证明及其本人或法定代理人签字；

   b）文化财产的鉴定材料；

   c）文化财产所在地说明；

   d）转让的性质和条件说明；

   e）本编规定的用于通信联系的有关各方在意大利的常住地说明。

5. 如果第 4 款规定的通报内容不全或表述不完整、不准确，则视同没有通报。

第二节 优先购买权

第 60 条 根据优先购买权购买

1. 文化遗产部，或在第 62 条第 3 款所述情况下的大区或其他地方政府部门，有权按转让交易中确定的价格优先购买出于金钱考虑而转让的文化财产。

2. 如文化财产与其他物品一起出于单纯的金钱考虑而转让，或非从金钱上考虑而转让，或仅仅是交换，根据第 1 款所述由优先购买的一方正式确定其货币价值。

3. 如出让方不愿接受第 2 款所述的估价，财产的货币价值应由出让方和优先购买方通过协议指定的第三方确定。如双方在第三方的指定问题上达不成一致，或在被指定者不愿或不能接受委托时指定替换者方面也未能达成一致，应由合同缔结地的法院院长根据一方的要求指定第三方。相关费用由出让方承担。

4. 如果第三方的估价有差错或明显不公正，可以争论。

5. 如果文化财产依合法权利在市场上以现金出售，也可优先购买。

第 61 条 优先购买的条件

1. 优先购买权应在收到第 59 条所述转让通报之后 60 天内行使。

2. 如通报没有提交，或提交不及时，或不完整，优先购买权可在文化遗产部收到迟到通报，或获知第 59 条第 4 款所述通报的全部内容之后 180 天内行使。

3. 优先购买的规定应在第 1 款和第 2 款所述的期限内通知出让人和购买人。文化财产应从最后一个通知日起归属国家。

4. 在第 1 款所述期限内，优先购买权行使之前，财产转让契据的效力中止，出让人禁止交付文化财产。

5. 国家不受转让合同条款的约束。

6. 如果文化遗产部行使优先购买权而购买了部分转让物品，原买方有权废除合同。

第 62 条 优先购买的程序

1. 一旦收到涉及优先购买权的转让通报，监管人应立即通知文化财产所在的大区和其他地方政府部门。如涉及可移动财产，大区应通过自己的官方告知公众，并且可能的话，通过国家层面的其他合适的广告手段告知公众，对所涉物品及其价格进行说明。

2. 大区和其他地方政府部门应在接到通报后 30 天内向文化遗产部提出优先购买建议，并附上主管部门做出的关于通过该部门为购买提供必要费用的预算的决定。

3. 如文化遗产部不愿行使优先购买权，应在收到通报之后 40 天内通知其他感兴趣的部门。感兴趣的部门应承担有关费用，根据优先购买规定，在收到上述通报后最多不超过 70 天通知出让人和购买人。从通知期限的最后一天起，相关财产的所有权移交给行使了优先购买权的部门。

4. 在第 61 条第 2 款所述情况下，本条第 2 款和第 3 款第 1、第 2 句所述期限分别为从收到通报或获得通报主要内容之日起 90 天、120 天和 180 天①。

第三节 商业活动

第 63 条 商业活动的报告和登记义务，文献资料交易的通告义务

1. 地方公共安全部门应根据相关法律接受本法令附件 1 第 1 项所列物品的经营商提交的古旧物品商业经营活动预防性通报，并将经营通报副本报送监管人和大区。

2. 第 1 款所述物品的经营商应根据公共安全方面的规定将每天完成的经营活动项目登记入册，并注明所涉物品的特点。交易物品的价值上限由文化遗产部在与内政部协调一致的基础上以部长令确定，超过价值上限的交易物品必须有详细记述。

3. 监管人要对第 2 款第 2 句所述义务的履行情况定期进行检查核实。检查工作也可由其委派的官员去做。在开展第 5 条第 2 款、第 3 款和第 4 款所述保护工作的地方，核查工作应由大区派官员去完成。核查报告应通知相关当事人和地方公共安全部门。

4. 文件资料经营者、拍卖行所有者、负责房地产销售的政府官员必须将待出售的具有历史价值的文献资料清单送交监管人。无论以何种合法权利拥有档案的私人所有者、占有者或持有者收购具有上述价值的文献资料，应在获得资料后 90 内履行同样的通报义务。监管人可在接到通报后 90 天内启动第 13 条所述的鉴定程序。

5. 监管人在任何情况下都可依职权查明由私人合法所有、占有或持有的，或推测可能具有特别重要历史价值的档案或单份文件的现存情况。

第 64 条 真实性和出处证明

1. 根据有关行政管理文件的法规，任何人从事有关画作、雕塑、书画作品或古董，或

---

① 此处英文误为 "80 天"，经意大利使馆据意大利文原件校改为 "180 天"。

具有历史和考古价值物品的公开销售、商业展览或展销活动，或经常出售上述作品或物品，必须向买主提供物品真实性的证明文件，或至少要有大概来源和出处的证明文件；如无此类文件，则必须提供能够说明有关作品或物品的真实性或其大概来源和出处的所有相关信息的申明。根据作品或物品的性质，此类声明应附上该作品或物品的照片。

第五章　国际范围内的流转

第一节　出口和进口

第65条　永久性出口

1. 第10条第1、第2和第3款所述可移动文化财产禁止从意大利共和国领土永久出口。
2. 下列物品也禁止出口：
   a) 第10条第1款所述主体拥有的属于过世艺术家作品且生成时间在进行第12条所述鉴定之前已超过50年的可移动物品。
   b) 第10条第3款所述类型的，文化遗产部与相关咨询机构协商后做出预防性认定的，因可能会在客观特性、出处和存在环境等方面对文化遗产造成损害而在规定时间段内不准出口的物品，不管它们的所有者是谁。
3. 除第1款和第2款所述情况之外，下列物品从意大利共和国领土永久出口需按本章第1节和第2节规定的程序获得批准：
   a) 具有文化价值，属于过世艺术家作品，且生成时间超过50年的物品，不管属谁所有；
   b) 属个人所有的具有文化价值的档案和单份文件；
   c) 第11条第1款 f) 项、g) 项和 h) 项所述类型的物品，不管属谁所有；
4. 出口第11条第1款 d) 项所述物品无需批准。但有关当事人必须按照部长令规定的程序和方式向出口主管部门表明向境外转让的是在世艺术家的作品，或其生成时间不超过50年。

第66条　参加展出活动的临时出口

1. 为参加艺术活动、展览会或重要文化价值展示活动从意大利共和国领土临时出口第

65 条第 1 款、第 2 款 a）项和第 3 款所述物品和文化财产，在确保物品完整性和安全性的条件下可以获得批准。

2．下列物品在任何情况下都不得移出国家的领土：

　　a）在运输过程中或在不利的环境条件下容易受到损坏的文化财产；

　　b）构成博物馆、美术馆、艺术画廊、档案馆、图书馆、艺术或文献学收藏的 决定性和不可分割的主要收藏品的文化财产。

<h3 style="text-align:center">第 67 条　其他临时出口</h3>

1．下列情况下，第 65 条第 1 款、第 2 款 a）项和第 3 款所述物品和文化财产的可准予临时出口：

　　a）在使领馆、欧盟机构或国际组织担任职务，工作要求移居国外的意大利公民在任期内作为家具使用；

　　b）用作驻外使领馆的内部装饰；

　　c）必要的分析、调查或保护工作必须在国外进行；

　　d）其出境是根据互惠协议履行与国外博物馆机构签订的文化协定的需要，协定的有效期不超过 4 年，而文化财产的出境期限与协定有效期相同。

2．历史超过 75 年的交通工具临时离开意大利共和国领土参加国际展览和国际会议无需批准。已根据第 13 条规定做出公示者除外。

<h3 style="text-align:center">第 68 条　自由流转证书</h3>

1．任何人希望将第 65 条第 3 款所述物品和文化财产从意大利共和国领土永久性移出，必须向出口主管部门做出明确的申报并提交这些物品和财产，同时说明每件物品的市场价值，以获得自由流转证书。

2．出口主管部门应在物品和文化财产提交之后 3 天内通知文化遗产部主管机构。文化遗产部主管机构应在随后的 10 天内向出口主管部门提供欲永久出口物品的辨识要素。

3．确定了所申报价值的公平性之后，出口主管部门应根据得到的信息，做出合理的决定，发放或拒绝发放自由流转证书，并在 40 天内将决定通知提交物品或财产的相关当事人。

4．出口主管部门应按文化遗产部在与相关咨询机构协商后确定的指导原则判定要不要发放自由流转证书。

5．自由流转证书的有效期为 3 年，原件一式三份：第一份归入官方文件档案；第二份交给相关当事人，同时必须附上物品的流转情况；第三份交文化遗产部，作官方证书登记之用。

6. 拒绝发证意味着第 14 条所述公示程序的开始。为此，在拒绝发证的同时，应将第 14 条第 2 款所述鉴定评估要素通知有关当事人，相关物品或文化财产应受第 14 条第 4 款规定的约束。

7. 对于大区所属机构所有的物品和财产，出口主管部门应与大区协商。大区应在收到要求之后 30 天的期限内提出自己的意见。如果大区反对发给自由流转证书，则这种反对具有约束力。

第 69 条　对拒发证书的行政复议

1. 如对拒绝发放证书有异议，允许在 30 天内基于合法性或事实向文化遗产部提出行政复议。

2. 文化遗产部应在接到复议申请 90 天内与相关咨询机构协商后做出裁决。

3. 从提出行政复议之日起到第 2 款所述的 90 天期限结束之前，停止鉴定结果公示程序，但相关文化财产仍受第 14 条第 4 款规定的约束。

4. 如确认复议有效，文化遗产部应将相关文件退回出口主管部门，后者应在随后的 20 天内采取相应行动。

5. 1971 年 11 月 24 日意大利共和国总统第 1199 号令的规定适用于本条。

第 70 条　强制性收购

1. 在第 68 条第 3 款所述期限内，出口主管部门可建议文化遗产部强制性收购已申请自由流转证书的物品或财产，同时通知大区和相关当事人，并声明建议强制收购的物品在履行相关收购手续之前仍需由出口主管部门保管。在这种情况下，发放证书的期限延长到 60 天。

2. 文化遗产部有权根据自由流转申报中所述的价值有选择地收购相关物品或文化财产。收购规定应在申报后 90 天内通知相关当事人。在收购通知发出之前，相关当事人可以决定不出口或设法撤销出口。

3. 如文化遗产部不要求收购，应在自由流转申报提出后 60 天内通知提出收购建议的出口主管部门所在的大区。该大区有权按照第 62 条第 2 款和第 3 款的规定，根据自己的资金实力和购买承诺有选择地收购相关物品或文化财产。有关收购规定应在申报提交后 90 天内通知相关方。

第 71 条　临时流转证书

1. 任何人有意根据第 66 条和第 67 条的规定临时从意大利共和国领土出口该两条所述的物品和文化财产，都必须申明这种意图，将物品提交出口主管部门，并同时说明各件物品的市场价值和保证物品境外安全的责任方，以获得临时流转证书。

2. 确定所申报价值的公平性之后，出口主管部门应在有关物品和文化财产提交后 40 天内做出合理决定，发放或拒绝发放临时流转证书，做出必要指示并通知相关当事人。对拒绝临时流转的决定应允许根据第 69 条规定的程序提出行政申诉。

3. 如果申请临时出口的物品或文化财产具有第 10 条所述的价值，应将第 14 条第 2 款所述的要素告知相关当事人，同时做出同意或不同意出口的决定。若做出不同意决定则启动公示程序，有关物品或财产将受第 14 条第 4 款规定的措施的约束。

4. 出口主管部门应遵照文化遗产部在与相关咨询机构协商后规定的指导原则，判定要不要发放自由流转证书。如系第 66 条和第 67 条第 1 款 b）项和 c）项所述的临时出口，证书的发放还需获得第 48 条所述的批准。

5. 证书还需说明物品或财产回国的期限。回国期限可以根据相关当事人的要求延长，但最长不能超过从离开本国领土之日起 18 个月，符合第 8 款规定者除外。

6. 发放证书必须以相关当事人根据申请书中所示价值为相关文化财产投保为前提条件。如果展览或相关活动是由文化遗产部发起的，或在国家参与下，由政府部门、意大利驻外文化机构或超国家组织发起的，可由国家按第 48 条第 5 款的规定承担相关风险，从而不需保险。

7. 第 65 条第 1 款所述文化财产和第 3 款所述物品或财产的临时出境应以保证金的方式进行担保。保证条款可以由银行或保险公司签发，其金额应超出发放证书时核定的财产或物品价值的 10％。若被批准临时出口的物品不能在规定的期限内返回本国领土，保证金归政府所有。属于国家和市政当局的文化财产无需保证金。对具有特别重要性的文化机构，文化遗产部可免除其提供保证的义务。

8. 第 5 款和第 6 款的规定不适用于第 67 条第 1 款所述的临时出口。

第 72 条　进　口

1. 由欧盟成员国输入或从其他第三国进口第 65 条第 3 款所述物品或文化财产到意大利，应由出口主管部门根据申请核发证书。

2. 对输入和进口的物品或财产核发证书的依据是物品或财产的鉴定文件及原产地证明文件，证明该物品或财产系从欧盟成员国或其他第三国领土被运输或进口至意大利。

3. 输入和进口的证书有效期为 5 年，可根据相关当事人的要求延长。

4. 批准和延长证书有效期的条件、方式和程序由部长令规定，特别是在涉及输入或进口物品或文化财产的原产地认定问题时。

第二节　从欧盟成员国领土出口

第 73 条　名　称

1. 本章本节和第三节使用的下列名词的含义是：

a) "欧共体条例"（EEC Regulation）指 1992 年 12 月 9 日欧共体第 3911/92 号条例，由 1996 年 12 月 16 日欧盟第 2469/96 号条例和 2001 年 3 月 14 日欧盟第 974/01 号条例修改。

b) "欧共体指令"（EEC Directive）指 1993 年 3 月 15 日欧共体第 93/7 号指令，由 1997 年 2 月 17 日欧洲议会和欧盟委员会第 96/100 号指令和 2001 年 6 月 5 日欧洲议会和欧盟委员会第 200/38 号指令修改。

c) "请求国"指根据第三节发起要求归还原物的诉讼的欧盟成员国。

第 74 条　从欧盟成员国出口文化财产

1. 向欧盟成员国领土以外出口本法附件 A 所述的文化财产受"欧共体条例"和本条管辖。

2. "欧共体条例"第 2 条规定的出口许可证由出口主管部门连同自由流转证书一起核发，或在自由流转证书发出后最多 30 个月内核发。出口许可证的有效期为 6 个月。

3. 如系本法附件 A 所列文化财产的临时出口，出口主管部门应根据第 66 条、第 67 条和第 71 条规定的条件和方式核发临时出口许可证。

4. 本章第一节的规定不适用于持有其他欧盟成员国按"欧共体条例"第 2 条核发的许可证，且在许可证有效期内进入本国领土的文化财产。

5. 根据"欧共体条例"，文化遗产部出口主管部门负责核发文化财产的出口许可证。文化遗产部应将已核发的出口许可证汇总并列单保存，如有变化，应在两个月内通知欧共体委员会。

第三节　从欧盟成员国领土非法出境的文化财产的归还

第 75 条　归　还

1.1992 年 12 月 31 日之后从欧盟成员国领土非法出境的文化财产应根据本节规定归还。

2.此处所说的文化财产即由请求国现行法律定义为属于国家文化遗产的财产，即便这种定义是在这些财产从请求国出境之后做出的。请求国法律必须符合《欧洲经济共同体条约》第 30 条的规定，该规定已由《阿姆斯特丹条约》第 6 条和有关批准和执行法律所取代。

3.属于下列类别之一的文化财产允许归还：

　a）附件 A 所列文化财产；

　b）属于编入博物馆、档案馆和有保存价值的藏书目录的公共收藏品组成部分的文化财产。公共收藏品定义为属国家、大区、其他地方政府部门和其他公共部门和机构所有的收藏品，以及国家、大区或其他地方政府部门大力资助的收藏品；

　c）列入宗教藏品目录的文化财产。

4.违反"欧共体条例"或请求国关于保护国家文化遗产的法律规定出口文化财产，或文化财产在临时出境或出口期满之后仍不返还，视为非法。

5.经批准临时出境或出口的文化财产出境，若违反第 71 条第 2 款所述指示，也视为非法。

6.若提出申请，满足第 4 款和第 5 款所述条件，得允许归还。

第 76 条　对欧盟成员国的帮助与协作

1.对意大利来说，"欧共体指令"第 3 条所述的中央主管当局是文化遗产部。在执行该指令规定的各项任务时，文化遗产部要发挥好核心机构和所属分支机构的作用，也要争取其他各部及国家、大区和其他地方政府部门所属机构的合作。

2.为发现和归还属于欧盟其他成员国遗产的文化财产，文化遗产部要：

　a）确保与其他成员国主管当局合作；

　b）安排在本国领土范围内进行调查，以找到文化财产的所在位置并确定其占有人或持有人。调查任务要根据请求国的申请下达，请求国的申请应附上有助于调查的有用资料或文献，尤其是有关文化财产所在位置方面的资料和文件；

c) 将在本国领土上发现的，根据准确、一致的证据判定为从某一成员国非法出口的文化财产的有关情况通知相关成员国；

d) 帮助相关成员国在 c) 项所述通知发出后两个月内针对通知所述的文化财产开展的工作，以查证第 75 条所述前提和条件的存在。如在上述期限内未能开展查证工作，则 e) 项所述规定不适用；

e) 必要时下令将所述文化财产及其临时保管工作和确保其保存的其他必要措施转移到公共机构，但要防止在归还过程中转移；

f) 协助解决请求国和对文化财产享有无论哪种合法权利的占有人或持有人之间在归还问题上产生的争端。为此目的，也考虑到相关各方的特点和文化财产的性质，文化遗产部可建议请求国和财产占有人或持有人在双方一致同意的情况下，根据意大利法律通过仲裁解决争端。

第 77 条　归还诉讼

1. 根据第 75 条规定，对于非法从他们国家领土移出的文化财产，欧盟成员国可向普通法院提起要求归还的诉讼。

2. 诉讼应提交到相关文化财产所在地区有司法管辖权的法院。

3. 除了《民事诉讼法典》第 163 条规定的条件之外，法院的传票必须包括：

a) 说明所涉及财产为文化财产的证明文件；

b) 请求国主管当局有关文化财产从其国家领土非法出境的声明。

4. 除了通知对文化财产享有无论哪种合法权利的占有人或持有人之外，传票还要通知文化遗产部，以便归入要求归还的诉讼专项登记档案。

5. 传票一经归档，文化遗产部应及时通知其他成员国的中央主管当局。

第 78 条　归还诉讼期限的终止

1. 归还诉讼必须在请求国得知被非法移出其领土的文化财产的确切下落，并且确认对该财产享有无论哪种合法权利的占有人或持有人身份的 1 年期限内提起。

2. 在任何情况下，归还诉讼都要限制在文化财产被非法移出请求国领土之日起 30 年的期限之内。

3. 第 75 条第 3 款 b) 项和 c) 项所述文化财产的归还诉讼没有时间限制。

第 79 条　补　偿

1. 在下达文化财产归还令的同时，法院可根据相关当事人的要求按公平标准给予补偿。

2．为获得第 1 款所述的补偿，相关当事人必须证明其在实施购买行动时履行了适当的注意义务。

3．通过捐赠、继承和遗赠等渠道获得文化财产的占有人不能享有超过财产授予人的有利地位。

4．承担补偿义务的请求国可要求对财产在意大利的非法流转负有责任的当事人弥补自己的损失。

第 80 条　补偿的支付

1．补偿款项在归还文化财产的同时由请求国支付。

2．补偿支付和文化财产交接情况由文化遗产部指定的公证人、法官或公职人员制作一份官方记录。文化遗产部应收藏一份官方记录的副本。

3．官方记录的形成即意味着要求归还的诉讼登记的取消。

第 81 条　帮助与协作的费用

1．查找、转移和保管待归还文化财产时出现的相关费用，落实第 76 条所述工作的其他开支，和执行法院归还命令所必不可少的开支，均由请求国承担。

第 82 条　意大利提起的归还诉讼

1．归还从意大利领土非法出境的文化财产的诉讼由文化遗产部在外交部的协同下，在相关文化财产被发现的欧盟成员国法院提起。

2．文化遗产部要争取获得本国司法官员的帮助。

第 83 条　被归还文化财产的归属

1．如果归还的文化财产不属于国家，文化遗产部应对其加以保管，直到它被交付给对其享有合法权利的人。

2．交付文化财产时应追还国家在归还和保管过程中发生的费用。

3．如无法确定究竟谁有权利接受归还的文化财产，文化遗产部应通过在意大利共和国《官方公报》上发布公告或其他广告形式将归还诉讼公布于众。

4．如果有权接受归还文化财产者从第 3 款所述《官方公报》发布通知之日起五年内没有提出交付要求，该文化财产归国家所有。经与相关咨询机构和大区协商之后，文化遗产部应下令将该文化财产分配给国家、大区或其他地方政府部门的博物馆、图书馆或档案馆，以确保其得到最佳保护，并在最合适的文化环境中供公众享用。

第 84 条　通知欧共体委员会和国会

1. 文化遗产部应将意大利为执行"欧共体条例"而采取的措施通知欧洲共同体委员会，并接受其他成员国向委员会提供的相应信息。
2. 文化遗产部应在该部年度预算开支核定的附件中向国会提交一份有关本章执行情况及"欧共体条例"和"欧共体指令"在意大利和其他欧盟成员国落实情况的报告。
3. 文化遗产部每三年要在与相关咨询机构协商之后向欧共体委员会提交一份关于第 1 款所述"欧共体条例"和"欧共体指令"施行情况的报告。该报告还要抄送给国会。

第 85 条　被盗文化财产数据库

1. 按照部长令规定的方式在文化遗产部内建立被盗文化财产数据库。

第 86 条　与其他欧盟成员国的协议

1. 为鼓励和推动人们对其他欧盟成员国的文化遗产及相关法规和保护工作组织方法的了解，文化遗产部应努力与其他成员国的对口部门达成适当的协议。

第四节　国际统一私法协会公约

第 87 条　被盗或非法出口的文化财产

1. 国际统一私法协会《关于被盗或非法出口文化财产公约》附件所述文化财产的国际返还工作受《公约》及其批准与执行法的管辖。

第六章 探查和发现

第一节 在本国领土的探查和偶然发现

第 88 条 探查活动

1. 在本国领土任何一部分进行的考古探查和第 10 条所述物品的发现活动由文化遗产部统一负责。

2. 文化遗产部可下令临时占用第 1 款所述探查和发现活动所在地的建筑物。

3. 建筑物的业主有资格获得占用补偿，补偿方式按公共征用的一般规定确定。补偿可以用货币，也可以根据业主的要求用对国家没有收藏价值的全部或部分发现物品抵偿。

第 89 条 探查特许

1. 文化遗产部可以将从事第 88 条所述探查活动的特许权授予公共部门或私营机构，并代表他们下达占用施工场所建筑物的命令。

2. 除了遵守授予特许权时所做的指示之外，获得特许权的部门或机构还必须遵守文化遗产部视为必要的其他一切指示。如果获得特许权的部门或机构不遵守这些指示，特许权将被收回。

3. 如果文化遗产部要求接管探查工作，也可以收回特许权。在这种情况下，特许权获得者在特许权被收回前从事探查活动所发生的费用应予补偿。补偿金额由文化遗产部确定。

4. 如特许权获得者决定不接受文化遗产部确定的金额，补偿金额应由仲裁主席任命有资格的估价员确定。相关费用先由特许权获得者垫付。

5. 第 1 款规定的特许权也可以授予探查工作所在建筑物的所有人。

6. 文化遗产部可根据申请，准许为展览之目的而将发现的物品全部或部分留给大区或其他地方政府部门，条件是所述部门应拥有合适的场所，确保发现物品得到保存和监护。

第 90 条　偶然发现

1. 任何人偶然发现第 10 条所述不可移动或可移动物品，应在 24 小时内报告文化财产监管人、市长或公共安全部门，并采取临时保存措施，让其在原发现地保持原状。
2. 如果发现的是可移动物品，而且没有别的监护措施可以采取，发现人有权为了确保其安全和保存之目的而将其转移，等待主管部门的到访。如有必要，发现人可请求公共安全部门协助。
3. 被偶然发现的物品的每一位持有者都必须遵守第 1 款和第 2 款有关保存和监护的规定。
4. 监护和移动过程中发生的费用由文化遗产部补偿。

第 91 条　对被发现物品的所有权和资格

1. 根据《民法典》第 822 条和第 826 条之规定，任何人以任何方式在地下或海床发现的第 10 条所述文化财产，均属国家所有，不管是可移动的还是不可移动的，都将成为政府财产和政府不可剥夺资产的一部分。
2. 任何时候代表国家、大区、其他地方政府部门或其他公共部门或机构拆除建筑物，根据合同可由拆除公司保留的拆除物不包括在拆除过程中发现的具有第 10 条第 3 款 a）项所述价值的物品。任何与此相反的协议都将是无效的。

第 92 条　发现奖励

1. 文化遗产部应给予下列人员不超过发现物本身价值四分之一的奖励：
   a）在其中发现文化财产的建筑物所有人；
   b）按第 89 条规定获得探查特许权者；
   c）履行了第 90 条规定的义务的意外发现者。
2. 建筑物所有人获得第 89 条所述探查特许权，或者建筑物所有人就是相关物品的发现者，有权得到不超过被发现物品本身价值二分之一的奖励。
3. 未经所有人或持有人同意进入他人地产并进行探查的发现者没有资格享受奖励。
4. 奖励可以是货币，也可以是部分被发现的物品。根据经济和财政部会同文化遗产部按照 1988 年 8 月 23 日第 400 号法律第 17 条第 3 款确定的方式和限度，有关当事人可以在提出申请的情况下享受相当于奖金数额的课税减免，以代替奖励。

第 93 条 奖励的核定

1. 对发现物价值的核定完成之后，文化遗产部要根据第 96 条规定对有资格的个人或团体的奖励进行核定。
2. 有资格的个人或团体都可得到部分奖励。其数额不超过被发现物品临时核定价值的五分之一。
3. 如果有资格接受奖励的个人或团体不接受文化遗产部的最后评估，被发现物品的价值应由相关各方在协商一致基础上指定的第三方确定。如果在第三方指定，或在被指定者不愿或不能接受任务时指定替换者方面不能达成一致，应由对物品发现地拥有司法管辖权的法院院长根据一方的要求指定第三方。相关费用由有资格接受奖励的个人或团体承担。
4. 如果第三方的评估结果存在差错或明显的不公平，可以争论。

第二节 在毗邻国家水域地区的探查和发现

第 94 条 联合国教科文组织公约

1. 在国家水域边界向外延伸 12 海里范围内海域的海床发现的具有考古和历史价值的物品，根据 2001 年 11 月 2 日在巴黎通过的联合国教科文组织《保护水下文化遗产公约》附件《有关开发水下文化遗产之活动的规章》加以保护。

第七章 征 用

第 95 条 文化财产的征用

1. 如属改善保护条件以满足公众享用之必需，可移动和不可移动文化财产可由政府以公用理由征用。
2. 文化遗产部可根据要求授权大区、其他地方政府部门及其他公共团体和机构从事第 1 款所述的征用工作。在征用工作中，由文化遗产部宣布征用的公共用途，并将相关契据移交给从事征用工作的有关团体。

3. 文化遗产部还可以代表公共非赢利团体下达征用命令，对相关程序担负直接责任。

第 96 条　手段性征用

1. 当征用属于实现下列目的所必须时，建筑物和区域可以公用理由征用：隔离或恢复遗迹、确保自然光线或景观、保护或修缮装饰面、增加公众享用、提高利用率。

第 97 条　考古征用

1. 文化遗产部可征用建筑物用于从事考古工作或开展第 10 条所述文化财产的探查活动。

第 98 条　公共用途公告

1. 公共用途通过部长令加以公告，或在第 96 条所述情况下由大区通过有关规定公告并通报文化遗产部。

2. 对第 96 条和第 97 条所述征用的批准视同于公共用途的公告。

第 99 条　文化财产征用的补偿

1. 对第 95 条所述征用的补偿按所涉财产若在国内自由买卖合同中可能获得的公平价格计算。

2. 补偿按公共用途征用一般性规定确定的方式支付。

第 100 条　一般法律的参照

1. 有关公共用途征用的一般法律规定在与本法相容的前提下适用于第 96 条和第 97 条所述的征用。

第二编 享用和强化

第一章 文化财产的享用

第一节 总 则

第101条 文化机构和文化场所

1. 在本法中，博物馆、图书馆、档案馆、考古公园和考古区、纪念性建筑群被视为文化机构和文化场所。
2. 定义：
    a）"博物馆"：为教育和研究之目的而获得、保存、整理和展出文化财产的永久性设施；
    b）"图书馆"：为促进阅读和研究之目的而收集和保存书写或刊印在任何基底上的系列藏书、资料及信息以供查阅的永久性设施；
    c）"档案馆"：为研究和调查之目的而收集、编目和保存具有历史价值的原始文件以供查阅的永久性设施；
    d）"考古区"：以存在化石或人造物遗迹，或史前或古代建筑遗迹为特色的遗址；
    e）"考古公园"：以具有重要考古证据和历史、景观或环境价值为特色，被当作露天博物馆的一片区域；
    f）"纪念性建筑群"：建成于不同时代，且随着时间的推移自然而然地具有艺术、历史或人种－人类学重要价值的诸多建筑物的集合。
3. 第1款所述文化机构和场所，属于政府部门的，被指定为公众享用并为公众提供服务。
4. 属于私人所有且向公众开放的展览和咨询设施及第1款所述场所，提供私人的社会公益服务。

第102条 公有文化机构与场所的享用

1. 国家、大区、其他地方政府部门和任何其他公共部门和机构要确保存在于第101条所述文化机构和场所的文化财产的享用符合本法规定的基本原则。

2．根据第 1 款所述原则，非属国家所有或国家已根据现行法律将使用权交出的存在于文化机构和场所的文化财产的享用受大区法律管辖。

3．第 101 条所述文化机构和场所以外的公共文化财产的享用应根据本编规定，在符合为上述财产确定的法定用途的情况下做好享用工作。

4．为协调和促进与公有文化机构和场所有关的文化财产的享用，国家、代表国家的文化遗产部、大区和其他地方政府部门应按照第 112 条规定的程序制定相关协议。在没有制定协议的地方，各公共团体必须保证文化财产的享用处于其管辖之下。

5．为确保当地文化财产的充分享用和强化，文化遗产部还可通过第 4 款所述的协议根据补偿原则将文化机构和场所的管辖权转让给大区和其他地方政府部门。

第 103 条　进入文化机构和场所

1．进入公共文化机构和场所可以免费，也可以收费。文化遗产部、大区和其他地方政府部门可以通过协议对进入文化机构和场所的事宜进行协调。

2．为阅读、学习和研究之目的进入公共图书馆免费。

3．如进入文化机构和场所涉及收费问题，文化遗产部、大区和其他地方政府部门应确定：

　　a）什么情况下可以免费进入；

　　b）用以确定相关价格的门票种类和标准。门票价格应包括制定 c）项所述协议时衍生出的费用；

　　c）门票发行、分配和销售及收取相关费用的方式，还可以通过与公共团体或个人协议确定。新的计算机技术可用于处理门票业务。在签订协议的基础上，还可以办理门票预售和第三方销售；

　　d）分配给全国画家、雕刻家、音乐家、作家和剧作家社会援助和养老金协会的门票销售收入百分比。

4．必须对特殊入场收费进行监管，以防发生对其他欧盟成员国公民的不公正歧视现象。

第 104 条　私有文化财产的享用

1．下列物品可接受公众出于文化目的的参观：

　　a）第 10 条第 3 款 a）项和 d）项所述具有特殊价值的不可移动文化财产；

　　b）第 13 条所述已公告的收藏品。

2．第 1 款 a）项所述不可移动文化财产的特殊价值由文化遗产部与所有人协商后以法令形式公告。

3. 参观程序由所有人和监管人协议确定，并通知该财产所在的自治市或都市区。

4. 第38条所述规定将继续适用。

第 105 条 使用权和公众享用权

1. 文化遗产部和大区在各自的职权范围内确保公众在遵守本部分各项规定的前提下获得文化财产的使用权和享用权。

第二节 文化财产的使用

第 106 条 文化财产的个人使用

1. 文化遗产部、大区和其他地方政府部门可批准个人申请者将其保管的文化财产用于与其原有文化用途相符的目的。

2. 对于交由文化遗产部保管的文化财产的使用，监管人应制定付费标准和相应的操作程序。

第 107 条 文化财产的手段性、临时性使用和复制

1. 在不违反第2款和有关著作权规定的情况下，文化遗产部、大区和其他地方政府部门可批准复制和手段性、临时性使用他们所保管的文化财产。

2. 如果是用雕刻作品或浮雕作品的原件制作模件，这样的文化财产复制通常是禁止的，不管这些作品用的是什么材料。用已有的原件复制品制作模件通常是允许的，但要有监管人的批准。复制模件的程序由部长令调整。

第 108 条 特许权费、复制费、风险抵押金

1. 特许使用费和与文化财产复制相关的费用由承担财产保管义务的当局确定。确定上述费用时还要考虑下列因素：

   a）特许使用活动的性质；

   b）生产复制品的方式方法；

   c）使用的场所和财产及使用时间；

d）复制品的用途和复制目的及其给申请者带来的经济利益。

2．费用通常应提前支付。

3．个人为自己学习之目的申请复制或公共团体为强化文化财产之目的申请复制不收费。不管发生多少费用，申请者都无需为行政部门给予特许权而提供补偿。

4．鉴于特许内的活动可能会损坏文化财产，承担财产保管义务的部门应通过银行或保险系统建立一定数额的保证金。在免费情况下，出于同样的考虑，也需要建立保证金。

5．当确认被特许使用的文化财产没有受到损坏，使用过程中产生的费用已经结清的时候，保证金予以退还。

6．文化财产使用费和复制费的最低限额由给予特许的行政部门规定。

第 109 条　文化财产的图像资料和胶片的编目

1．如特许使用权涉及出于图像和胶片收集、编目之目的的复制，给予特许权时应规定：
   a）提交每张胶片或照片的一份原始复制件；
   b）用后归还带有相关编码的彩色照片原件。

第 110 条　现金收入和收益分配

1．在第 115 条第 2 款所述情况下，销售文化机构和场所门票所得收入及文化财产特许使用费和复制费，应根据各自的会计业务规定，交给文化机构和场所或文化财产所属的政府部门或承担保管义务的政府部门。

2．如文化机构、场所或文化财产属国家所有或归国家保管，第 1 款所述收益应上交省级国库，也可以存入一个在上述国库注册的邮政往来账户，或存入各文化机构和场所官员在信贷机构开立的往来账户。在后一种情况下，银行机构在收到上述款项后五天内将其打入省级国库。经济和财政部应根据该部制定的标准和方法把收到的资金重新分配给有资格的基本预算单位作为该部的开支预算。

3．属国家所有或归国家管理的文化机构和场所的门票收入根据第 29 条用于上述机构和场所的安全与保存工作，也可以用于文化财产的征用和收购。征用和收购时可以行使优先购买权。

4．其他政府部门所有或归其管理的文化机构和场所的门票收入用于文化遗产的增加和强化。

第二章 强化文化遗产的原则

第 111 条 强化活动

1. 文化遗产的强化活动包括为履行职能、实现第 6 条所述目标，实现资源、设施或网络的稳定建构和组织，提供专门技能、资金或媒介资源。国民也可以赞同、配合或参与这类活动。

2. 强化文化遗产的活动可以由国家也可以由私人发起进行。

3. 国家发起的强化文化遗产活动应符合参与自由、主体多元、活动连续、待遇平等、经济可行和管理透明的原则。

4. 私人发起的强化文化遗产活动视同于社会公益活动，其目的是增进社会团结。

第 112 条 公有文化财产的强化

1. 国家、大区和其他地方政府部门要确保强化活动在第 101 条所述的文化机构和场所进行，并遵守本法规定的基本原则。

2. 根据第 1 款所述的原则，在非属国家所有的或国家已经根据现行法律将使用权交出的文化机构和场所举办的文化财产强化活动受大区法律约束。

3. 根据本编规定，第 1 款所述文化机构和场所以外的公有文化财产的强化活动要确保符合业已明确的文化财产的法定用途。

4. 为了协调、配合和补充构成政府所有之文化遗产的文化财产的强化工作，国家应通过文化遗产部、大区和其他地方政府部门形成地区性协议，确定目标，制定实现目标的时间表和方法。根据第 115 条的要求，应通过这些协议明确适当的管理形式。

5. 如果主管部门之间在规定的期限内未能达成第 4 款所述的协议，国家应通过文化遗产部与大区首脑、省长和相关市长一起，共同做出决定。在没有协议的情况下，各政府部门必须将文化财产强化活动置于自己的管辖之下。

6. 国家可通过文化遗产部与大区和其他地方政府部门在联席会议上为在全国范围内达成第 4 款所述协议制定总体指导方针和程序。

7. 私人也可以参与第 4 款所述的协议，并且在得到相关方面同意的情况下，协议可涉及私有文化财产。

8. 有兴趣的公共团体也可以与文化团体或志愿团体达成特别协议，共同开展旨在提高和传播文化财产知识的工作。

第 113 条　私有文化财产的强化

1. 私人为强化私有文化财产而发起相关活动和建立相关设施可得到国家、大区和其他地方政府部门的资助。
2. 资助的程度要视所涉及的文化财产的重要性而定。
3. 采取资助措施时，应与文化财产的所有者、占有者或持有者达成协议，共同确定强化方式。
4. 大区和其他地方政府部门也可以通过参与第 3 款所述的协议对第 104 条第 1 款所述的文化财产强化活动表示赞同。

第 114 条　强化的质量控制

1. 文化遗产部、大区和其他地方政府部门应尽可能在大学的参与下制定衡量强化活动质量的标准。此标准应定期修改。
2. 第 1 款所述质量控制标准将在联席会议上达成一致后由文化遗产部部长令通过。
3. 根据第 115 条负责强化活动管理的有关当事人必须确保已确定的质量控制标准的执行。

第 115 条　管理形式

1. 对私人发起进行的文化财产强化活动实行直接或间接管理。
2. 直接管理由行政管理部门成立专门机构负责。这些机构在科技、组织和财会方面拥有自主权，并配有适当的技术人员。
3. 间接管理执行方式是：
   a) 将管理工作直接委派给在很大程度上由公共管理部门组成的、拥有文化财产或公共管理部门有较大利益存在其中的机构、基金会、协会、财团、公司或其他实体；
   b) 根据第 4 款和第 5 款所述的标准将管理特许权交给第三方。
4. 国家和大区可以采取间接管理的做法，以确保文化财产的强化工作达到令人满意的水平。第 3 款 a) 项和 b) 项所述的两种管理形式的选择应在对效率、效力、要达到的目标、相关方式方法和时间表进行对比分析的基础上做出。
5. 在进行了第 4 款所述的对此分析之后，如果倾向于将管理特许权交给第三方，则第三方同样要在对比分析的基础上通过公开竞争产生。

6. 其他地方政府部门一般采取第 3 款 a)项所述的间接管理，除非出于强化活动范围与类型上的考虑，认为直接管理具有经济优势或更为合适。

7. 通过拥有合法资格从事强化活动的各方事先协议，第 3 款所述管理工作的委派或特许可以在分担和联合的基础上做出安排。

8. 活动主办方与管理受托或受权方之间的关系由一份服务合同确定。合同要特别明确所提供服务的质量水平和业务人员的专业水平，以及活动主办方和服务提供方保留的指导权和控制权。

9. 活动主办方可以分担第 3 款 a)项所述各方的资产或资金，后者的参与可能被授予待强化文化财产的特许使用权。如果活动主办方或服务方分担的工作全部结束，或者参与方撤出，或不管何种原因停止活动或服务的委派，则特许使用权无条件失效。除了其自身的经济价值之外，被批准使用的文化财产无需特殊的经济担保。

10. 待强化文化财产的特许使用权可与第 3 款所述的委派管理或特许管理权联系起来。一旦委派或特许的服务或活动结束，特许权无条件失效。

第 116 条　特许使用的文化财产的保护

1. 第 115 条第 9 款和第 10 款所述处于特许使用状态的文化财产仍要不折不扣地根据相关法规加以保护。文化遗产部行使保护职能，也可根据已经获得特许使用权的当事人的要求提供保护。

第 117 条　附加服务

1. 面向公众的文化援助和接待服务可以在第 101 条所述的文化机构和场所开展。

2. 第 1 款所述的服务包括：

　　a) 与目录及其编制、声像和计算机援助、其他所有相关信息资料和文化财产的复制等有关的出版与销售服务；

　　b) 与书籍和档案资料的复制和图书借阅投递有关的服务；

　　c) 录音档案、幻灯片和博物馆藏品管理；

　　d) 文化财产复制品的销售渠道和商业利用管理；

　　e) 公关服务，包括儿童资助与娱乐、信息与教育指导及援助服务、会议场所提供等；

　　f) 自助餐厅、饭馆、行李暂存等服务；

　　g) 文化展览和文化活动的组织与促进工作。

3. 第 1 款所述的服务可与保洁、保安和售票服务协力进行。

4. 上述服务工作的管理应按第 115 条规定的方式进行。

5. 服务特许费按第 110 条规定收取和分配。

第 118 条　学习和研究活动的促进

1. 文化遗产部、大区和其他地方政府部门应尽可能在大学和其他公、私实体的参与下，开展、促进和资助与文化遗产有关的研究、学习及其他认知性活动，也可以与他们联合开展这方面的活动。

2. 为了确保有系统地汇总和传播第 1 款所述研究、学习及包括编目在内的其他活动的成果，文化遗产部和大区可达成协议，共同创建地区或跨地区的永久性文化遗产研究与记录中心，并欢迎大学和其他公、私实体参加。

第 119 条　文化遗产知识在学校的传播

1. 文化遗产部、教育大学与研究部、大区和其他相关地方政府部门可通过协议传播文化遗产知识，促进学生对文化遗产的享用。

2. 在第 1 款所述协议的基础上，第 101 条所述文化机构和场所的主管人员可与隶属国家教育系统的各级各类学校签订课程开发、音像资料和教具准备、教师教育与培训的专门协议。课程、资料与教具要考虑到申请学校的特殊性和因残疾学生的参与而产生的特殊需求。

第 120 条　文化财产保护与强化活动的赞助

1. 文化财产保护和强化活动的赞助定义为国民为了提升自己名字、品牌、形象、活动或产品的知名度，以实物或服务的形式赞助文化遗产部、大区和其他地方政府部门或者其他国民在保护和强化文化遗产方面的相关活动的计划和实施。

2. 第 1 款所述知名度的提升要通过将赞助主体的名字、品牌、形象、活动或产品与被保护或强化的文化财产的艺术性、历史性和外观造型相协调的创意相结合而得以实现，并且要通过赞助合同加以确定。

3. 赞助合同还要明确资金支付方式和出资方监督被资助创意实现情况的形式。

第 121 条　与银行基金会的协议

1. 文化遗产部、大区和其他地方政府部门可以在各自职权范围内，也可联手与信用机构重组和监管规定中所述的，依法在艺术、文化遗产及相关活动中寻求旨在有益社会的基金会签订谅解备忘录，以协调文化遗产的强化工作，并在此框架内确保可用资金的平衡利用。为了实现备忘录中规定的目标，政府可以加入自己的资金。

第三章　档案文件的查阅与保密

第122条　国家档案和公共部门历史档案：文件查阅

1. 保存在国家档案馆和大区、其他地方政府部门及其他公共部门和机构历史档案室的文件可以自由查阅，但下列情况除外：

   a) 涉及国家内政或外交事务的，根据第125条之规定确定为机密的文件，在生成50年之后方可查阅；

   b) 含有敏感信息和涉及在有关个人信息使用的法律中明示的刑罚性措施的信息的文件，在生成40年后方可查阅。如所含信息反映当事人健康状况、性经历或个人家庭关系等情况，查阅期限延长至生成后70年。

2. 在第1款规定的禁止查阅期限结束之前，相关文件仍可根据行政文件使用规定查阅。归档或存档之前的查阅请求由持有文件的行政部门受理。

3. 第1款所述之规定同样适用于存入国家档案馆或公共团体历史档案室，或已经捐赠、出售或作为遗产或遗赠物遗留给上述档案馆或档案室的私人档案和文件。存档人和捐赠、出售以及作为遗产或遗赠物遗留这些文件的人也可以提出禁止查阅最近70年内生成的全部或部分文件的条件。这种限制与第1款规定的限制一样不适用于存档人、捐赠人、出售人和他们指定的其他任何人。如果与文化财产有关的文件涉及购买权的利益关系，所述时间限制也不适用于存档人、捐赠人和出售人的代理人。

第123条　国家档案和公共部门历史档案：保密文件查阅

1. 即使在第122条第1款规定的禁止查阅期限结束之前，内政部也可以在咨询了国家档案主管官员的意见和听取了内政部保密档案文件查阅委员会的意见之后，批准出于历史研究之目的的查阅保存在国家档案馆的保密文件。批准查阅保密文件的条件对所有申请者一律平等。

2. 根据第1款规定批准查阅的文件得保持其机密性，不得传播。

3. 出于历史研究之目的查阅保存在大区、其他地方政府部门及其他任何公共部门和机构档案室的机密性文件，同样需要遵守第 1 款和第 2 款的规定。第 1 款所述的意见由档案监管人提供。

第 124 条　为了解历史之目的查阅现行档案

1. 在不违背有关公共行政文件使用的现行法律的情况下，国家、大区和其他地方政府部门应制定出于历史研究之目的查阅现行档案和存档档案的条例。
2. 为第 1 款所述之目的查阅其他公共部门和机构的现行档案和存档档案，由档案所属的部门和机构在文化遗产部规定的总指导方针下自行管理。

第 125 条　机密性的宣布

1. 第 122 条和第 127 条所述不可自由查阅之文件的存在和性质由内政部协同文化遗产部确定。

第 126 条　个人资料的保护

1. 在个人资料的所有者行使了有关个人资料使用的法定权利之后，历史档案文件应受到保护，查阅时需参考涉及这些权利行使的文件。
2. 如果个人资料的使用确实存在对相关个人的尊严、隐私或身份造成伤害的风险，可随时根据资料所有者的要求下令冻结那些不具有重大公共利益的个人资料。
3. 为了解历史之目的查阅包括个人资料的文件，还要遵守有关个人资料使用的法律规定的道德行为规范。

第 127 条　个人资料的查阅

1. 根据第 13 条被公示为文化财产的档案或单份文件的所有者、占有者或持有者，应允许学者通过档案监管人提出的正当要求，按有关当事人与监管人达成一致的程序进行查阅。相关费用由学者承担。
2. 被宣布为具有第 125 条所述之机密性质的单份文件不在允许查阅之列。根据第 122 条第 3 款被确定为符合禁止查阅条件的文件也不在可查阅之列。
3. 第 123 条第 3 款和第 126 条第 3 款之规定适用于为历史目的查阅个人档案，即使这些档案没有根据第 13 条的要求公示为文化财产。

第三编　过渡性规定和最后规定

第 128 条　按以前法规送达的通知

1. 第 10 条第 3 款所述文化财产，若根据 1909 年 6 月 20 日第 364 号法律和 1922 年 6 月 11 日第 778 号法律送达的通知尚未更新或注册，现按第 14 条规定的程序办理。在手续办完之前，原通知依然有效。

2. 根据 1939 年 6 月 1 日第 1089 号法律第 2 条、第 3 条、第 5 条和第 21 条送达的通知和根据 1963 年 9 月 30 日意大利共和国总统第 1409 号令第 36 条和 1999 年 10 月 29 日第 490 号法令第 6 条、第 7 条、第 8 条和第 49 条通过并送达的宣告仍然有效。

3. 如果发现后来生成的新要素或以前不为人知或不曾评估过的要素，文化遗产部可以根据自己的职权，或根据相关所有者、占有者或持有者的要求，更新曾属第 2 款所述通知对象的文化财产的公示程序，以证明该财产应根据有关规定加以保护的属性仍然存在。

4. 如根据第 3 款提出更新公告程序的申请遭到拒绝，允许根据第 16 条对拒绝申请的决定提出行政申诉，或对程序的最后公示提出行政申诉，即使最后公示是依职权进行的。

第 129 条　特定立法

1. 针对单个城市或其中的某些地区、建筑群、国家历史纪念地和具有历史、艺术或考古价值的遗址的法律继续有效。

2. 根据 1871 年 6 月 28 日第 286 号法律、1883 年 7 月 8 日第 1461 号法律、1891 年 11 月 23 日第 653 号敕令和 1892 年 2 月 7 日第 31 号法律做出的涉及遗产信托的艺术收藏品的规定继续有效。

第 130 条　以前的条例

1. 根据本法制定的各项法令、条例发布之前，1911 年 10 月 2 日第 1163 号敕令和 1913 年 1 月 30 日第 363 号敕令批准的条例及本部分法律所含其他条例性规定，凡可适用者继续有效。

第三部分　景观资产

第一编　保护和强化①

第一章　总　则

第 131 条　景观价值的保护

1. 在本法中，"景观"定义为：以反映自然和人文历史及两者间相互关系为特色的国家领土的一部分。
2. 景观的保护与强化就是要保护景观以显而易见的标志所表达出的价值。

第 132 条　公共管理部门间的合作

1. 公共管理部门应在景观保护、规划、改造、改进和强化活动的指导方针和标准的制定及相关工作的管理方面加强合作。
2. 指导方针和标准还要从可持续发展的角度考虑保护和整合景观环境的价值。
3. 为了宣传和增强景观知识，公共管理部门应开展培训和教育活动。
4. 文化遗产部和大区应制定景观保护与强化政策，同时还要考虑根据部长令设立的国家景观质量观察台以及在各大区基于同样目的设立的观察台的研究、分析和建议。

第 133 条　国际协议

1. 景观环境的保护与强化工作要符合国际协议规定的国与国之间的合作义务与原则。

第 134 条　景观资产

1. 景观资产包括：
   a) 第 136 条所述，并由第 138 条到第 141 条确认的不可移动财产和区域；
   b) 第 142 条所述的区域；

---

① 本部分仅列此一编，意大利文原件亦如此，已经意大利使馆核实。

c）受第 143 条和第 156 条所述景观规划保护的任何不可移动财产和区域。

第 135 条　景观规划

1. 大区应确保景观受到适当的保护和强化。为此，各大区应按照合适的分区法律管理各自的辖区，批准景观规划或城市用地规划时应具体考虑景观价值和所辖区域整体状况。景观规划和城市用地规划以下统称"景观规划"。

2. 针对第 134 条所述的资产，景观规划应明确规定与景观价值相符的改造措施、不可移动景观和受保护区域的改造和改进创意、景观强化措施，以及可持续发展前景。

第二章　景观资产的鉴别

第 136 条　具有显著公共价值的建筑和区域

1. 下列财产由于其显著公共价值而适用于本编规定：
    a）具有突出的自然美或地质奇观的不可移动财产；
    b）非属本法第二部分所述保护对象，但却因其非凡的美景而著名的别墅、花园和公园；
    c）以体现美学和传统价值为特色的不可移动物体群；
    d）被视为具有独特品质的美丽景观及公众可以前往观赏美景的观景点和观景楼。

第 137 条　省级景观资产委员会

1. 各省根据大区规定的方法成立一个委员会，负责提出公示第 136 条 a）项和 b）项所述不可移动财产及 c）[①] 项和 d）项所述地区之显著公共价值的建议。

2. 大区行政长官、建筑财产和景观监管人及主管各地区考古财产的监管人属于委员会的法定成员。其他成员人数不超过 6 人，由大区从具有景观保护特殊专业知识和经验的人中选择任命。委员会要注意倾听相关市长的意见，也可向专家咨询。

---

① 此处英文误为"a)"，经意大利使馆据意大利文原件校改为"c)"。

第 138 条　显著公共价值的公示建议

1. 第 137 条所述的委员会，应根据大区行政长官、大区或其他相关地方政府部门的倡议，通过监管人及大区和省级办事处获得必要的信息，评估第 136 条所述不可移动财产和区域是否存在显著的公共价值，并提出公示显著公共价值的建议。提出公示建议时应提供公示的依据，包括：相关不可移动财产和区域的历史、文化、自然、形态学和审美学特点已被证明对所在地区具有重要意义和价值，并且已被当地民众认识到。建议还要包括针对第 143 条第 3 款所述管理的指示、措施和标准。

2. 显著公共价值公示建议的目的在于建立具体的保护和强化规章。建议要突出景观环境的独特要素和价值，并成为景观规划中所规定的规章制度的组成部分。

第 139 条　显著公共价值公示程序的参与

1. 委员会关于公示不可移动财产和区域的显著公共价值的建议应附上比例适当便于识别的平面图，在市政公告牌上公示 90 天，并保存以备公众向相关市政办事机构查询。

2. 建议通知和市政公告牌上的相关公告事项应及时在至少两家发行面广的当地日报和一家全国发行的日报上公布。如已建立网站，应在对受保护的不可移动财产和区域具有司法管辖权的大区和其他地方政府部门的网站上公布。

3. 委员会的建议在市政公告牌上公示 60 天之后，自治市、都市区、省、根据 1986 年 7 月 8 日第 349 号法律第 13 条确认拥有共同利益关系的团体和其他任何有关当事人都可以向大区提供他们的观察材料。大区也有权下令进行公众调查。

4. 对于第 136 条 a）项和 b）项所述不可移动财产，在第 1 款、第 2 款和第 3 款所述的步骤完成之后，大区应将公示程序开始的信息通知财产的所有者、占有者或持有者及相关都市区或自治市。

5. 第 4 款所述通知的内容应包括地标等不可移动财产的识别要素，并提出所有者、占有者或持有者应尽的后续义务。

6. 从收到第 4 款所述通知之日起 60 天内，不可移动财产的所有者、占有者或持有者可向大区提出自己的观察资料。

第 140 条　显著公共价值的公示和相关认知措施

1. 根据委员会的建议，在审阅了观察资料和考虑了公众调查结果之后，大区应发布关

于第 136 条 a）、b）项所述不可移动财产和 c）、d）项所述区域的显著公共价值的
公示。

2. 关于公示第 136 条 a）、b）项所述不可移动财产的规定同样要通知财产的所有者、占
有者或持有者，存入市政档案，并在大区土地登记处登记。

3. 显著公共价值公示在意大利共和国《官方公报》和大区《官方公报》上公布。

4.《官方公报》的副本应在所有相关市政部门的公告牌上公示 90 天。显著公共价值公
示书副本和相关平面图应保存，供公众向相关市政办事机构查询。

第 141 条　文化遗产部的措施

1. 如果委员会在接到根据第 138 条提出的申请后 60 天内没能做出评估，或大区在上述
申请提出后一年内未能做出有关显著公共价值公示，大区行政长官可申请由文化遗
产部接手。

2. 在收到省级委员会可能已经获得的文件副本之后，文化遗产部主管部门应为提出显
著公共价值公示建议展开初步调查。

3. 文化遗产部应将建议送交相关市政当局，以便市政部门履行第 139 条第 1 款所述的
义务，而文化遗产部得直接履行第 139 条第 2 款、第 4 款和第 5 款所述的义务。

4. 文化遗产部应对根据第 139 条第 3 款和第 6 款规定提出的观察材料进行评估，并通
过法令做出相关规定。显著公共价值公示法令应以第 140 条第 2 款、第 3 款和第 4
款所述的方式通知、保存、登记和发布。

5. 前款规定也适用于有关第 143 条第 3 款 e）和 f）项所述内容的显著公共价值公示现
行规定一体化的建议。

第 142 条　受法律保护的区域

1. 在景观规划根据第 156 条规定获得批准之前，出于景观价值的考虑，下列区域在任
何情况下都适用于本编之规定：

　　a）沿海地域，包括伸入水线以下 300 米深的狭长地带和高出海平面的陆地；

　　b）与湖泊相连的地域，包括伸入水线以下 300 米深的狭长地带和高出水平面的
陆地；

　　c）根据 1933 年 12 月 11 日第 1775 号敕令批准的合并法规定列为水厂和发电厂用地
的河流、溪流和水道，以及宽度为 150 米的相关堤岸或坝基；

　　d）阿尔卑斯山脉海拔超过 1600 米的山区、亚平宁山脉海拔超过 1200 米的山区和
岛屿；

e）冰川和冰川谷地；

f）公园和国家或大区自然保护区，及公园外围保护区；

g）2001年5月18日第227号立法令第2条第2款和第6款确定的森林覆盖地域，包括受到火灾破坏和有待恢复的林地；

h）已经划定的农业院校建设用地和市政用地；

i）根据1976年3月13日共和国总统第448号令列入清单的沼泽地；

j）火山；

k）本法生效时被鉴定为具有考古价值的区域。

2. 第1款的规定不适用于：

a）1985年9月6日在城市规划中被确定为A类地区和B类地区的地段；

b）在根据1968年4月2日第1444号部长令制定的1985年城市规划中没有被列为a）项所述的地区，而仅为多年实施计划之一部分的地段，以及在没有城市规划的城市中根据1971年10月22日第865号法律第18条被确定为位于建筑群中心且周界固定的地段。

3. 第1款的规定不适用于虽列入c）项，但其整体或部分可被考虑用于景观目的，且已被相关大区列入特殊清单并加以公布的地区。文化遗产部可通过第141条规定的程序确认上述资产的景观价值。

4. 由第157条所述行动和措施衍生出来的各项规章在任何情况下将继续有效。

第三章　景观规划

第143条　景观规划

1. 景观规划应根据自然与历史特点，从景观价值的相关性和完整性程度出发，对地域进行同质分类，明确哪些地域具有高景观价值，哪些地域的景观价值已经受到破坏或严重下降。

2. 规划应为不同景观价值水平已被认知的各地域确定景观环境价值目标，特别是下列活动的景观质量目标：

a）保持景观的特征、构成要素和表面形态，还要考虑建筑类型、建筑材料和建筑技术；

b）制订与已经认识到的不同价值水平相适应的，不损害地域景观价值的城市和建筑发展纲要，特别注意保护已列入联合国教科文组织世界遗产名录的景点和农业区；

c）改造和改进需要保护但却处于危机状态或已经退化的建筑物和区域，目的在于恢复原有的价值或生成与原有价值相辅相成的新的景观价值。

3. 景观规划应有描述和说明性内容，包括意见和建议。规划的制订分为以下阶段：

a）通过分析地域的历史特性、自然特性和审美特性以及他们之间的相互关系，并给需要保护、改造、改进和强化的景观价值进行界定，对整个地域进行一次全面调查；

b）在明确风险因素和景观脆弱性的基础上，通过与其他土地规划、计划和保护活动的比较，分析土地改造的力度；

c）确定景观区域及相关的景观质量目标；

d）对已明确区域的土地保护与使用做出总体界定与操作指示；

e）明确受法律保护区域的独有特征的保护方法和措施，在必要的情况下，还要明确针对已公示为具有显著公共价值的建筑物和区域开展景观强化工作的管理标准和作业活动；

f）确定在受到严重危害和严重退化地域开展的改造和改进工作。

g）确定必要的措施，确保改变地域外貌的工作与当地景观保护工作协调一致。为相关地域的可持续发展而进行建设活动和投资，要以采取上述措施为前提。

h）根据第134条c）项要求，确定与第136条和第142条所述不同的、需要有具体的保护和使用措施的建筑物和区域的目录。

4. 如涉及不同类型的地域改造项目和工程，景观规划要清楚地说明哪些区域的工程和项目是在查明其符合景观规划根据第3款d）、e）、f）和g）项提出的指示、措施和管理标准的基础上获得批准的；还要清楚地说明在实行第145条所述的协调和调整要求时为哪些区域确定了要引入土地规划的限制性因素。

5. 规划同时还可以确定：

a）在哪些受第142条规定保护的区域，经批准的项目和工程的实施，出于景观价值水平或对规划规模影响进行评估的合理性的考虑，必须事先得到第146条、第147条和第159条所述当局的认可；

b）在哪些区域，第138条、第140条、第141条和第157条所述的活动和措施不适用。在那里，项目和工程可以在证明符合景观规划和城市规划规定的基础上，按照建筑许可程序和相关规章明确的方式实施，而无需申请第146条、第147条和第159条所述的批准。

c）在哪些景观受到严重危害或退化的区域，改造和改进工作无需申请第146条、第147条和第159条所述的批准。

6. 第5款b) 项规定的生效应以根据第145条所述景观规划进行协调的城市规划获得批准为前提条件。要得到上面所说的批准，需要对第157条、第140条和第141条规定的效果进行更改，并对列入第142条所述清单的区域类别进行修改。

7. 规划可以将一段监控期内获得的积极结果，即证明其有效地遵守了有关地域改造的现行规定，作为许可第5款b) 项所述工程和项目的生效条件。

8. 规划在任何情况下都要规定：在第5款b) 项所述的区域对完成的工程进行抽查，发现严重违反现行规定的情况，应在发现违规现象的自治市重新实行第146条、第147条和第159条所述的批准制度。

9. 景观规划还要明确大区景观保存、改造、改进、强化和管理的优先项目，说明要采用的方法，包括激励措施。

10. 大区、文化遗产部和环境与土地保护部可达成制订景观发展联合规划的协议。协议要规定制订联合规划的期限和大区批准规划的期限。如联合规划没有被大区规定接受，则应由文化遗产部与环境和土地保护部磋商后以部长令的形式代为批准。

11. 第10款所述协议还要确定对规划进行定期修改的条件、程序和时间表，特别是增加第140条和141条所述的补充规定。

12. 如果不能达成第10款所述的协议，或达成协议后没有制订联合规划的行动，则第5款、第6款、第7款、第8款所述规定不适用。

第144条　宣传和参与

1. 景观规划的批准程序要确保政府行动的协调一致，相关当事人和社会团体的参与，及宣传方式的广泛性和多样性。前述社会团体系出于保护由1986年7月8日第349号法律第13条所认定的共同公共价值之目的而形成。

2. 如因执行第143条第3、4、5款的规定而发生对第157条、第140条和第141条所述行动和规定效果的修改，景观规划中相关规定的生效以完成第140条第3款和第4款所述形式的宣传为条件。

第145条　景观规划与其他规划的协调

1. 根据1998年3月31日第112号立法令第52条，文化遗产部应确定旨在明确规划方向的全国范围景观保护工作基本纲领。

2. 景观规划要规定与土地和行业规划及全国和大区经济发展规划相协调的措施。

3. 第143条和第156条所述景观规划的规定对自治市、都市区和省的城市规划文件具有强制性；城市规划文件中所含任何规定与景观规划的规定不一致时，直接以景观规划的规定为准；在城市规划文件与景观规划取得一致之前，景观规划确立的规章可一直有效；景观规划的规定对行业的干预也具有约束力。在环境保护方面，景观规划的规定在任何情况下都高于其他规划文件中所含的规定。

4. 在景观规划规定的期限内，无论如何都不能超过批准后两年，自治市、都市区、省和自然保护区管理机构应使土地和城市规划文件与景观规划的规定协调一致，在必要的情况下，还要增加一些符合景观规划的、根据地域的具体特点证明有助于确保对规划中确认的景观价值提供最佳保护的规定。因这些规定而形成的对财产的限制不构成补偿条件。

5. 大区要对城市规划文件与景观规划规定的协调和调整程序进行规范，确保文化遗产部的相关机构参与其中。

第四章　受保护财产的监督与管理

第 146 条　批　准

1. 不可移动财产和区域的合法所有者、占有者或持有者，如需采取第 157 条所列的行动和措施，或采取依照第 138 条和第 141 条提出的建议，或其财产和区域属于第 142条或景观规划规定的保护范围，不得毁坏这些财产或区域，也不得进行有损受保护景观价值的变更活动。

2. 为了得到预先批准，第 1 款所述财产的合法所有者、占有者或持有者需向大区或大区委托的主管当局提交他们欲开展工程的计划，并附上必需的相关文件。

3. 在本立法令施行 6 个月内，内阁总理应在与国家－大区会议取得一致的基础上通过法令明确规定证明拟进行的工程与景观价值相适所必需的文件。

4. 工程批准申请书应说明相关财产的现状、现有景观价值的要素、拟进行的变更对景观的影响、必要的缓解和补偿措施等。

5. 在审查待批准的申请时，主管当局要核实工程活动与景观规划中所含规定的相适性，并确定：

　　a）与强制性命令所认可的景观价值的相适性；

　　b）与建筑或区域管理标准的协调性；

　　c）与景观质量目标的一致性。

6. 在明确了工程活动与景观的相适性并征求了景观委员会的意见之后，行政当局应在收到申请之后 40 天内将批准建议并附工程规划和相关文件送主管监管部门，并通知有关当事人。给有关当事人的通知相当于根据 1990 年 8 月 7 日第 241 号法律启动有关程序的通知。如果行政当局查明所附文件不符合第 3 款的要求，应要求提供必要的补充文件。在这种情况下，上面所说的期限从提出要求之日开始顺延。如果行政当局认为有必要为第 3 款规定的文件获得补充文件，或有必要对文件进行核实，上述期限应从提出要求之日延长至收到文件之日，或从发出有必要进行核实的通知之日延长至核实进行之日。延长期限只能有一次，且无论如何不能超过 30 天。

7. 监管部门应在收到第 6 款所述建议之后 60 天的强制性期限内发表自己的意见。如果监管部门在规定期限内没有拿出自己的意见，行政当局必须对批准申请进行裁夺。

8. 行政当局应在收到监管人的意见之后 20 天内做出给予批准或拒绝批准的决定。能否获得批准决定着截然不同的后续行动，也是能否取得特许或获得其他合法施工权利的前提。得不到批准，不能开工。

9. 如果在第 8 款规定的期限内没有做出是否批准的决定，有关当事人有权向大区申请批准。大区也可指定一名专员在收到申请之后 60 天内做出答复。如果认为获得补充文件或进行核实确有必要，答复期限可延长至收到要求的文件之日或进行核实之日，但只能延长一次。如果大区没有将批准权委托给当地主管部门，批准申请应提交给主管监管部门。

10. 景观工程批准书：

   a）在发出 20 天后生效。

   b）应及时送交在办理过程中发表过意见的监管部门，连同意见一起送交大区和省；如果工程涉及，还要送交工程项目所在的山区社团和受强制性命令保护的建筑物或区域所在的公园管理部门。

   c）不得以事后补救的法规为依据为已完成的工程发放，即使是部分完成的工程。

11. 为保护 1986 年 7 月 8 日第 349 号法律第 13 条确定的共同公共利益而成立的环境组织及对此有利害关系的公、私实体若对景观工程的批准有异议，可向大区行政法院提出申诉，也可向共和国总统提出特别申诉。即使在申诉提出之后或在申诉程序进行之中申诉方宣布撤诉或不再感兴趣，也要对申诉做出裁定。对于大区行政法庭发布的决定和命令，有权对景观工程的批准提出申诉的任何一方都可提出异议，即使该方当初并没有提出申诉。

12. 每个自治市都要建立一个清单，列明每一项景观工程批准书的发放日期，简要描述所涉及的相关财产，并说明批准书的发放是否与监管人的意见相反。清单每七天更新一次，可以自由查阅。每季度向大区和监管部门报送一份清单副本，以供他们根据第 155 条行使督察职能。

13. 前款规定也适用于与探矿和采矿活动有关的事项。

14. 本条规定不适用于在采石场和泥炭沼地进行农事活动的批准。根据相关法律，环境和土地保护部对这类农事活动行使管理权，但在行使权力的过程中要考虑主管监管部门从景观角度提出的评估意见。

第 147 条　国家行政部门所从事的工程的批准

1. 如果第 146 条所述的待批准的申请涉及国家行政部门从事的工程，包括军队人员住房建设项目，应根据 1990 年 8 月 7 日第 241 号法律第 14 条及以下条文，以及后续修改和补充规定召开的军队会议的决定发放批准书。
2. 根据 1986 年 7 月 8 日第 349 号法律第 6 条规定必须要接受环境影响评估的政府行政部门从事的工程项目，第 1 款所述的批准书应按第 26 条规定的程序发放。
3. 如国防工程影响到需执行景观保护规定的建筑物和区域，其预防性联合评估方式，应在本法生效后 6 个月内由内阁总理根据文化遗产部的建议，在与国防部和其他相关国家行政部门取得一致的基础上通过法令确定。

第 148 条　景观委员会

1. 本法生效后 1 年之内，各大区应采取行动在已被委任行使景观工程审批权的当地部门内成立景观委员会。
2. 委员会由在景观保护方面被公认为具有特殊经验的人组成。
3. 对第 146 条、第 147 条和第 159 条所述景观工程批准事宜表达意见是委员会义不容辞的责任。
4. 大区和文化遗产部可以通过协议共同确定文化遗产部参与景观委员会活动的方式。在这种情况下，第 146 条第 7 款所述的意见应根据协议中确定的方式在会上表述。第 146 条第 10 款、第 11 款和第 12 款的规定依然有效。

第 149 条　无需批准的工程

1. 在不影响第 143 条第 5 款 b）项和第 156 条第 4 款执行的情况下，下列工程活动无需得到第 146 条、第 147 条和第 156 条所要求的批准：
   a）不改变景点的周围环境和建筑物外观，以保存为目的的日常或临时维护、加固和修复工程；
   b）不会造成带有建筑物和土建工程的景点环境发生永久性变动的，以不改变当地水文地质系统为条件的，与农业、林业和牧业活动有关的工程；

c）根据相关法律的规定并得到相关法律授权的情况下，为植树造林、土地开垦、预防火灾等目的，在第 142 条第 1 款 g）项所述的森林地带进行去除植被的作业。

第 150 条　工程的禁止和中止

1. 不管第 139 条和第 141 条所述的市政公告牌上有没有公布，也不管有没有第 139 条第 4 款所述的通知，大区或文化遗产部都有权：
   a）阻止未经批准的或以任何方式对文化财产造成损害的施工活动；
   b）下令中止已经开始的施工活动，即使尚未采取 a）项所述的阻止行动。
2. 如果在 90 天的期限内，第 138 条所述的委员会建议或第 141 条所述的文化遗产部主管部门的建议没有在市政公告牌上公示，或第 139 条第 4 款所述的通知没有被相关方面收到，则针对在未被公示为具有显著公共价值的建筑物或区域进行的施工活动的阻禁令不再有效。
3. 如果在 90 天的期限内，大区未将为了不妨碍景观规划的落实而在施工中应该遵守的指示通知有关方面，有关禁止或中止损害了景观规划中预计要采取改造或改进措施的景观财产的施工活动的规定不再有效。
4. 以上各款所述规定还需通报相关自治市。

第 151 条　停工后所需开支的补偿

1. 如涉及环境资产的施工活动以前不在第 138 条和第 141 条所述规定的适用范围，或不曾被公示为具有显著公共价值，被责令停工之前没有见到第 150 条第 1 款所述的禁止令，则有关方面在接到停工通知之前发生的开支可以得到补偿。拆除已完成工程的费用由下令停工的权力部门承担。

第 152 条　需有特殊指示的工程

1. 如要在 136 条 c）项和 d）项所述区域内或其周围，或在该条 a）项和 b）项所述建筑附近开辟道路、开发采石场或为工厂开挖沟渠，大区有权为实施中的工程项目指定距离、施工方法，并做出相应变更，在充分考虑已完成工程的经济效用的同时努力防止对受本编保护的文化财产造成伤害。文化遗产部也拥有同样的权力，但在行使这种权力之前需与大区协商。

第 153 条　广告牌

1. 未经大区确定的主管部门批准，第 134 条所述景观资产内部或其附近禁止设置广告牌或其他广告媒体。
2. 第 1 款所述景观资产内部或其附近的道路两侧禁止设置广告牌或其他广告媒体，除非根据 1992 年 4 月 30 日第 285 号立法令第 23 条第 4 款及其后来的修改获得批准，并有大区确定的主管部门事先发表赞成意见，说明广告媒体的设置及类型与受保护的建筑群和区域的景观价值相适应。

第 154 条　建筑物外表的颜色

1. 大区确定的主管部门可下令在第 136 条 c）项和 d）项规定的区域内对颜色与整体美不一致的建筑物外表面更换新的颜色，使其与整体美趋于协调。
2. 第 1 款所述规定不适用于第 10 条第 3 款 a）项和 d）项所述的，并根据第 13 条规定公示的建筑物。
3. 属于第 136 条 c）项或第 139 条第 1 款 m）项所列具有考古价值的区域的建筑物，为稳妥起见，其外表面颜色的处理应由主管部门与主管监管部门协商确定。
4. 如建筑物的所有者、占有者或持有者方面不按规定办事，主管行政部门应在其职权范围内执行法律。

第 155 条　监　督

1. 受本编保护的景观资产的监督职能由文化遗产部和大区行使。
2. 大区要对它所确定的景观保护主管部门执行现行立法令的情况实施监督。对不服从法律规定或长期不积极履行职责者，大区可行使更换权。

第五章　第一次应用和过渡性条款

第 156 条　景观规划的审核与调整

1. 本立法令生效后 4 年内，根据 1999 年 10 月 29 日第 490 号立法令第 149 条规定拟定了景观规划的大区应对规划中的条款与第 143 条中的条款的一致性进行审核。如缺乏一致性，要进行必要的调整。

2. 本法生效后 180 天内，文化遗产部应在与国家－大区会议达成一致的基础上拟定与大区的总体协议方案，共同确定对受保护建筑物和区域进行调查、分析、普查和编目的方法与程序，包括最适于在不同计算机系统间运行的制图技术和特点分析技术。

3. 大区和文化遗产部应达成协议，根据第 2 款所述总体协议方案，共同管理审核和调整土地规划的联合行动。对调整过的规划，协议应规定大区批准的期限。如在联合行动结束之后大区没有提出什么规定，则土地规划通过部长令代为批准。

4. 如在审核和调整过程中发现在执行第 143 条第 3 款、第 4 款和第 5 款规定时，某项修改影响到第 157 条、第 140 条和第 141 条所述行动和规定的执行，则景观规划的相关规定需在完成第 140 条第 3 款和第 4 款所述形式的宣传后方能生效。

5. 如果第 3 款所述协议没有达成或在联合审核和调整规划时没有执行，则第 143 条第 5 款、第 6 款、第 7 款和第 8 款所述规定不适用。

第 157 条　按以前法律要求的通知送达、清单编制、规定发布和措施确定

1. 在不妨碍第 143 条第 6 款、第 144 条第 2 款和第 156 条第 4 款落实的前提下，下列通知、清单和规定继续适用于所有意图和目的：

   a) 根据 1922 年 6 月 11 日第 778 号法律送达的因自然美或景色美而认定为具有重要公共价值的通知；

   b) 根据 1939 年 6 月 29 日第 1497 号法律编制的清单；

   c) 根据 1939 年 6 月 29 日第 1497 号法律公示显著公共价值的规定；

   d) 根据 1977 年 7 月 24 日共和国总统令第 616 号第 82 条第 5 款和经 1985 年 8 月 8 日第 431 号法律修改的 1985 年 6 月 27 日第 312 号法律第 1 条确认具有考古价值区域的规定。

   e) 根据 1999 年 10 月 29 日第 490 号立法令公示显著公共价值的规定；

f）根据 1999 年 10 月 29 日第 490 号立法令确认具有考古价值区域的规定；

2．本部分规定也适用于本法生效之日为公示显著公共价值或确认考古价值而提出建议或确定其地域范围的建筑物和区域。

第 158 条 大区的执行规定

1．在大区做出执行本法的专门规定之前，1940 年 6 月 3 日第 1357 号敕令批准的规章，只要适当仍然有效。

第 159 条 临时批准程序

1．在景观规划根据第 156 条或第 143 条获得批准或根据第 145 条对城市规划文件进行相应调整之前，负责第 146 条第 2 款所述审批事务的主管行政部门应将已经批准的事项立即通知监管部门，并向其提供当事方拟定的文件和审核结果。根据 1990 年 8月 7 日第 241 号法律，为了实现该法律的意图和目的，通知应同时送达当事方，对当事方来说，批准通知相当于相关程序的启动通知。

2．主管行政部门可以提出一份说明第 146 条第 5 款所述审核情况的报告。批准或拒绝批准的决定应在提出相关申请之后 6 天的强制性期限内做出。批准与否决定着以后采取何种截然不同的行动，意味着允许开建还是寻求别的开建资格。未经批准，不得开工。如果要求申请者提供附加文件或审核材料，上述期限可延长至收到要求提供的文件之日或完成审核之日。只能延长一次。1994 年 6 月 13 日第 495 号文化遗产部部长令第 6 条第 6 之 2 款所述规定适用于本款。

3．在任何情况下，文化遗产部都可以在收到完整的相关文件之后 60 天内做出合理的规定，使已经获得的批准无效。

4．如果第 2 款所述期限结束时没有做出批准与否的决定，有关当事人可向主管监管部门提出批准申请。主管监管部门应在收到申请后 60 天内做出决定。申请书应附上规定的文件提交给主管监管部门并通知主管行政部门。如要求附加文件或审核材料，则上述期限应延长至收到要求的文件或完成审核之日。期限只能延长一次。

5．如果景观资产在本法生效之日属于经 1985 年 8 月 8 日第 431 号法律修改并于 1985年 9 月 6 日前在《官方公报》上发布的 1985 年 6 月 27 日第 312 号法令第 1 之 5 条所述规定涉及的对象，则第 1 款及第 146 条和第 147 条所述的批准可以在景观规划获得批准之后获得。

第四部分　处　罚

第一编　行政处罚

第一章　与第二部分有关的处罚

第 160 条　责令将场所恢复原状

1. 如因违反第二部分第一编第三章有关保持和保存的规定而使文化财产受到损害，文化遗产部应责令当事者采取必要的措施将相关财产恢复到原来的状态。费用由当事者自己承担。
2. 如根据第 1 款之规定责令进行的恢复工程涉及重要的城市建设规划，有关程序的启动和最后做出的规定应通知相关都市区或自治市。
3. 如当事者不执行根据第 1 款规定下达的命令，文化遗产部得依职权执行该命令，费用由当事者承担。相关费用按强制性国家财产收费规定中确定的方式收取。
4. 如不能恢复到原来的状态，当事者必须赔付相当于损失物品或物品受损部分的价值。
5. 如果文化遗产部核定的受损金额不能被赔付方接受，最终金额应由一个三人委员会决定。三人委员会的成员分别由文化遗产部、赔付方和法院院长指定。相关费用由赔付方预支。

第 161 条　损坏被发现物品

1. 第 160 条所述处罚措施适用于违反第 89 条和第 90 条规定的义务，从而对第 91 条所述财产造成损坏者。

第 162 条　违规设置广告

1. 任何人违反第 49 条规定设置广告牌或其他广告媒体，都要根据 1992 年 4 月 30 日第 285 号立法令第 23 条及后续修改和补充的规定接受处罚。

第 163 条　丢失的文化财产

1. 不履行第四章第一节和第五章第一节规定的义务，导致文化财产失踪或流向国外者，得照价向国家赔偿。
2. 违法行为涉及一人以上者，共同或分别支付赔款。
3. 如文化遗产部核定的赔付金额不能被赔付者接受，最终金额应由一个三人委员会决定。三人委员会的成员分别由文化遗产部、赔付方和法院院长指定。相关费用由赔付方预支。
4. 若委员会的评估出现差错或明显不公平，可对其提出质疑。

第 164 条　违反有关权利和义务的法令

1. 违反第二部分第一编规定的禁令或不按该编规定的条件和方式实施的转让、协议和交易视为无效。
2. 文化遗产部应随时准备根据第 61 条第 2 款的规定行使优先购买权。

第 165 条　违反国际流转规定

1. 除第 174 条第 1 款所述犯罪行为之外，违反第二部分第一编第五章第一节和第二节规定，向国外转运第 10 条所述物品或财产者，处以 77.50 欧元至 465.00 欧元的罚款。

第 166 条　不提交出口文件

1. 根据"欧共体条例"向欧盟领土以外的地方出口文化财产但未向主管出口的办事机构提交一式三份 1993 年 3 月 30 日第 752/93 号欧共体条例规定的格式文件者，处 103.50 欧元至 620.00 欧元罚款。

第二章　与第三部分有关的处罚

第 167 条　责令恢复原状或支付赔偿金

1. 发生拒不履行或拒不执行第三部分第一编所述义务和命令，如负责景观环境保护的行政部门认为采取恢复措施对保护第 134 条所述文化财产较为有利，则当事人必须自费将该文化财产恢复到原来的状态，或赔付相当于财产损失或违法所得的款项，以数额高者为准。具体赔款金额根据官方的正式评估确定。
2. 责令当事者将文化财产恢复原状时要为其规定一个期限。
3. 如当事者拒不执行命令，负责景观保护的行政部门应通过地方行政长官行使职权，强制当事者支付赔款。
4. 采取第 1 款所述措施收取的款项用于受破坏区域的安全防护、景观价值恢复和改进工作。

第 168 条　违反设置广告的规定

1. 违反第 153 条规定设置广告牌或其他广告媒体者，按 1992 年 4 月 30 日第 285 号立法令第 23 条及后续修改的规定给予处罚。

第二编　刑事处罚

第一章　与第二部分有关的处罚

第 169 条　非法工程

1. 有下列违法行为者，处 6 个月至 1 年监禁，并处 775.00 欧元至 38734.50 欧元罚款：
   a) 未经批准拆除、移动、变更、重建或从事与第 10 条所述文化财产有关的任何工程；
   b) 未经监管人批准拆解壁画、铭牌、涂鸦、牌匾、碑文、壁龛和其他建筑装饰物，不管它们是否要向公众展示，也不管有没有按第 13 条规定进行了公示；
   c) 在确实紧急的情况下，为避免对第 10 条所述财产造成实质性损坏而采取必不可少的措施，但没有及时通知监管人，或没有在尽可能短的时间内将最后决定的工程项目报批。
2. 第 1 款所述刑罚措施适用于拒不执行监管人根据第 28 条下达的停工命令者。

第 170 条　非法使用

1. 将第 10 条所述文化财产用于与其历史或艺术性质不符或影响其保存或完整性之目的者，处 6 个月至 1 年监禁，并处 775.00 欧元至 38734.50 欧元罚款。

第 171 条　非法放置和移动

1. 未按监管人指定的方式将第 10 条第 1 款所述文化财产置于指定的位置者，处 6 个月至 1 年监禁，并处 775.00 欧元至 38734.50 欧元罚款。
2. 上述刑罚措施适用于因住所变动而将文化财产移放别处但未通知主管监管人的持有者，或未执行监管人为避免运输过程中发生损坏而做出的指示的文化财产持有者。

第 172 条　不执行间接保护决定

1. 拒不执行文化遗产部根据第 45 条第 1 款做出的指示者，处 6 个月至 1 年以下监禁，并处 775.00 欧元至 38734.50 欧元罚款。
2. 不采取第 46 条第 4 款所述防范措施者，按第 180 条规定惩处。

第 173 条　违反有关转让的规定

1. 有下列违法行为者，处 1 年以下监禁，并处 1549.50 欧元至 77469.00 欧元罚款：
   a) 未经必须的批准出让第 55 条和第 56 条所述的文化财产；
   b) 应在第 59 条规定的期限内公示文化财产转让或扣押文书而没有公示；
   c) 受优先购买权约束的文化财产转让人在第 61 条第 1 款规定的期限结束之前将财产交付。

第 174 条　非法出境和出口

1. 在没有获得自由流转证书或出口许可证的情况下，将具有艺术、历史、考古、人种－人类学、目录学、文献或档案价值的物品及第 11 条第 1 款 f) 项、g) 项和 h) 项所述物品输出境外者，处 1 年至 4 年监禁，并处 258 欧元至 5165.00 欧元罚款。
2. 第 1 款所述惩罚措施也适用于未能在规定期限内将经批准临时出境或出口的文化财产运回本国领土者。
3. 法官得下令没收相关文化物品，但与犯罪行为无关的个人物品除外。没收行动的采取要符合海关法有关禁止走私活动的规定。
4. 如犯罪人以出售具有文化价值的物品为目的从事公众推销或展示活动，在对其判刑之后还要根据《刑法典》第 30 条下达禁令。

第 175 条　违反考古研究的行为

1. 有下列违法行为者，处 1 年以下监禁，并处 310.00 欧元至 3099.00 欧元罚款：
   a) 未经许可从事第 10 条所述物品的考古探查或发现工作，或不执行行政管理部门做出的有关指示者；
   b) 未履行应尽的义务，在第 90 条第 1 款规定的期限内申报其偶然发现的第 10 条所述物品，或对其进行临时保存。

第 176 条　非法占有国家所有的文化财产

1. 占有按第 91 条规定属于国家的第 10 条所述文化财产者，处 3 年以下监禁，并处 31.00 欧元至 516.50 欧元罚款。
2. 获得第 89 条规定的探查特许者犯上述罪行，处 1 年至 6 年监禁，并处 103.00 欧元至 1033.00 欧元罚款。

第 177 条　为收回文化财产提供合作

1. 如犯罪人为收回被非法转移或输出国境的文化财产提供了决定性的、在一定程度上具有实质性重要意义的合作，按第 174 条和第 176 条规定对他们所犯罪行的惩罚可减轻三分之一到三分之二。

第 178 条　伪造艺术作品

1. 有以下违法行为者，处 3 个月至 4 年监禁，并处 103.00 欧元至 3099.00 欧元罚款：
   a）以获益为目的伪造、更改或复制绘画、雕塑和图形艺术作品或古董或具有历史或考古价值的物品；
   b）虽未参与伪造、更改或复制活动，但将绘画、雕塑和图形艺术作品或古董或具有历史或考古价值的物品的赝品、改制品或复制品作为真品销售，或以销售为目的持有或从国外引进，或使其流通；
   c）在知道真相的情况下仍出面证明 a）项和 b）项所述赝品、改制品或复制品为真品；
   d）在知道真相的情况下仍通过其他申明、评估、宣传、加盖印章或加贴标签等手段证明 a）项和 b）项所述赝品、改制品或复制品为真品，或为他们获得证明渠道。
2. 如犯罪行为发生在从事商业活动的过程之中，应加重惩罚，判刑之后还要根据刑法典第 30 条施行禁令。
3. 第 1 款所述惩罚应在法官指定的在全国范围内发行的并在 3 个不同地方出版的 3 家日报上公布。《刑法典》第 36 条第 3 款适用于本条。

第 179 条　不可惩罚的情形

1. 任何人复制、持有、销售或以其他方式经营绘画、雕塑或图形艺术品的复制品，或古董或具有历史或考古价值物品的复仿制品,如在展示或出售时以文字形式在物品上标明其为赝品,或由于复仿制品的特性或尺寸而不能用文字在物品上标明时,通过公示牌说明,则第 178 条规定对其不适用。第 178 条规定同样不适用于不从根本上改变原作的艺术品修复。

第 180 条 不服从行政管理措施

1. 除非构成更严重的犯罪,任何人不服从负责文化财产保护的行政部门根据本编规定下达的命令,按刑法典第 650 条规定的刑罚处罚。

第二章 与第三部分有关的处罚

第 181 条 未经批准或违反批准书规定的工程

1. 未经批准或违反批准书的规定在景观资产上从事工程施工活动者,按 1985 年 2 月 28 日第 47 号法律第 20 条规定处罚。
2. 对犯罪人的有罪判决应规定由犯罪人自己承担费用将景点恢复到原来状态。判决书副本应送达违法行为发生地的自治市。

第五部分　法律的暂行规定、废除和生效

第 182 条　过渡措施

1. 由 2001 年 10 月 24 日第 420 号部长令第 3 条取代的 2000 年 8 月 3 日第 294 号部长令第 7 条第 1 款对在本法生效之前进入国立大学接受有关景观修复的学位教育或学习者继续有约束力。

2. 由 2001 年第 420 号部长令第 3 条取代的 2000 年第 294 号部长令第 7 条第 2 款 a) 项、b) 项和 c) 项的规定继续有效。由 2001 年第 420 号部长令第 3 条取代的 2000 年第 294 号部长令第 7 条第 2 款 a) 项和 c) 项规定也适用于新法令生效之日前已进入国家或大区学校景观修复专业学习的 2002 – 2003 学年之前的学生，即使尚未拿到文凭。

3. 本法生效后 60 天内，大区和其他地方政府部门应制定实施本法第 103 条第 4 款指示的必要法规。若大区和其他地方政府部门未履行义务，文化遗产部将根据宪法第 117 条第 5 款规定代替他们采取行动。

第 183 条　最后条款

1. 第 13 条、第 45 条、第 141 条、第 143 条第 10 款和第 156 条第 3 款的规定不受 1994 年 1 月 14 日第 20 号法律第 3 条第 1 款规定的预防性管理措施约束。

2. 第 5 条和第 44 条的执行不得给国库带来新的更大负担。

3. 根据本法成立的各委员会的服务免费提供，在任何情况下都不得给国库带来新的更大负担。

4. 文化遗产部行使第 34 条、第 35 条和第 37 条规定的权力时发生的费用应限制在相关项目开支的预算拨款额度之内。

5. 国家为履行第 48 条第 5 款义务而提供的担保，根据 1978 年 8 月 5 日第 468 号法律第 13 条规定，列入经济和财政部预算附属项目。如国会要讨论担保费用，文化遗产部应提供相关报告。

6. 除明确表示对某些条款的修改之外，共和国各项法律不会以任何形式损害本立法令的各项原则。

7. 本法典定于 2004 年 5 月 1 日生效。

第 184 条　废除的法律条款

1. 废除下列法律条款：

——1939 年 6 月 1 日第 1089 号法律第 40 条，最终被 1999 年 7 月 12 日第 237 号法第 9 条取代的内容；

——1963 年 9 月 30 日第 1409 号共和国总统令，仅限于第 21 条第 1 款和第 3 款以及第 2 款分别被 1999 年 7 月 30 日第 281 号立法令修改和取代的内容，第 21 之 2 条和第 22 条第 1 款分别被 1999 年 7 月 30 日第 281 号立法令第 9 条合并和修改的内容；

——1972 年 1 月 14 日第 3 号共和国总统令，仅限于第 9 条；

——1992 年 4 月 30 日第 285 号立法令，仅限于被 1999 年 12 月 7 日第 472 号法律第 30 条合并的第 23 条第 3 款和第 13 款第 3 项第一句；

——1997 年 5 月 15 日第 127 号法律，仅限第 12 条第 5 款经 1998 年 12 月 23 日第 448 号法律第 19 条第 9 款修改的内容和第 6 款第一句；

——1997 年 10 月 8 日第 352 号法律，仅限 1999 年 7 月 12 日第 237 号法律第 3 条和第 4 条及 1999 年 12 月 21 日第 513 号法律第 4 条修改过的第 7 条；

——1998 年 3 月 31 日第 112 号立法令，仅限第 148 条、第 150 条、第 152 条和第 153 条；

——1999 年 7 月 12 日第 237 号法律，仅限第 9 条；

——1999 年 7 月 30 日第 281 号立法令，仅限第 8 条第 2 款和第 9 款；

——1999 年 10 月 29 日第 490 号立法令及后续修改与补充；

——2000 年 9 月 7 日第 283 号共和国总统令；

——2003 年 6 月 30 日第 196 号立法令，仅限第 179 条第 4 款；

——2003 年 7 月 8 日第 172 号法律，仅限第 7 条。

核准人：文化遗产和活动部部长　乌尔巴尼

附件 A

适用于第 63 条第 1 款、第 74 条第 1 款和第 3 款、第 75 条第 3 款 a）项

A. 文化财产的种类

1. 生成时间在 100 年以上的考古发现和下列物品：
   a）陆地和海上发掘和发现的物品；
   b）考古遗址发现的物品；
   c）考古收藏品。

2. 生成时间在 100 年以上的艺术、历史或宗教遗迹的重要组成成分以及解体的遗迹的组成成分。

3. 第 4 类和第 5 类之外在任何基质上用任何材料绘制的全手工绘画和图片（1）。

4. 在任何基质上绘制的水彩画、水粉画和蜡笔画。

5. 第 1 类和第 2 类之外用任何材料全手工制作的镶嵌图案（1）及在任何基质上全手工绘制的图画。

6. 原始雕版画、印刷品、丝网印花，原始石版印刷品及相关模板，原始海报（1）。

7. 除第 1 类之外的原始雕塑或雕刻艺术品及用原始工艺制作的复制品（1）。

8. 照片、影片及相关底片（1）。

9. 包括单件或系列收藏的地图和乐谱在内的古版本和手稿（1）。

10. 100 年以前的单件或系列收藏的书籍。

11. 200 年以前的印刷地图。

12. 档案及其载体，包括 50 年以前形成的任何要素。

13. a）动物学、植物学、矿物学和解剖学收藏品和样本。
    b）具有历史学、古生物学、人种学或钱币学价值的收藏品。

14. 75 年以前的运输工具。

15. 第 1 到 14 类中没有列入的生成时间 50 年以上的其他古董。
    列入第 1 到 15 类的文化财产只有其价值相当于或超过 B 项所述价值时方由本合并文本约束。

B．A 项所列文化财产的价值标准（欧元）

1）任何价值

　　1．考古发现

　　2．解体遗迹

　　9．古版本和手稿

　　12．档案

2）13,979.50

　　5．镶嵌图案和图画

　　6．雕版图

　　8．照片

　　11．印刷地图

3）27,959.00

　　4．水彩画、水粉画和蜡笔画

4）46,598.00

　　7．雕塑艺术

　　10．书籍

　　13．收藏品

　　14．运输工具

　　15．其他古董

5）139,794.00

　　3．油画

提出返还申请时必须确定符合价值条件。

（1）生成时间超过 50 年且不属作者所有。

核准人：文化遗产和活动部部长　乌尔巴尼

注 释

说明：

在此发布的注释是由各行政主管部门编写的，其依据是 1985 年 12 月 28 日第 1092 号共和国总统令批准的有关法律颁布、共和国总统令的发布、意大利共和国官方出版物的发布等规定的综合文本第 10 条第 3 款，目的是便于对所注法律条文的阅读。所引法律的价值和有效性不受注释影响。

关于欧共体指令的实质性内容见《欧共体官方公报》（OGEC）。

前言注释：

——2001 年 10 月 24 日第 248 号《官方公报》公布的 2001 年 10 月 18 日第 3 号宪法性法律修正的，1947 年 12 月 27 日第 298 号《意大利共和国官方公报》特刊公布的《意大利共和国宪法》第 76 条、第 87 条、第 117 条和第 118 条规定：

第 76 条　立法权，除非依据有指导性的原则和准则并在限定的时间和确定的内容范围内的决议，不得委托给政府行使。

第 87 条　共和国总统是国家元首并代表国家的统一。

他/她有权向国会提交咨文。

他/她有权宣布国会的选举并确定国会举行第一次会议的日期。

他/她有权授权政府向国会提交立法议案。

他/她有权颁布法律并发布具有法律效力的法令和规章。

他/她有权在宪法规定的情况下宣布举行全民公决。

他/她有权在法律规定的情况下任命国家公职人员。

他/她有权派遣和接受外交代表，批准国际条约，必要时须事先获得国会授权。

他/她统帅武装部队，依法主持最高国防委员会工作，根据国会的慎重考虑宣布国家战争状态。

他/她主持最高司法委员会工作。

他／她有权准予赦免和减刑。

他／她有权授予共和国荣誉。

第117条　立法权由国家和大区在宪法及欧盟条例和国际义务的制约下行使。

国家在下列事务上有垄断立法权：

a) 国家的对外政策和国际关系；国家与欧盟的关系；非属欧盟的本国公民的庇护权和合法地位；

b) 移民；

c) 共和国与宗教派别的关系；

d) 防务与武装部队；国家安全；武器、弹药与爆炸物；

e) 货币流通、储蓄与金融市场保护；竞争保护；货币制度；国家的税收与会计制度；资金来源平衡；

f) 国家机构和相关选举法律；国家公民投票；欧盟国会选举；

g) 国家行政规章与组织编制及国家政府机构；

h) 公共秩序与安全，地方行政警察除外；

i) 公民身份、婚姻状况和生卒登记机关；

j) 审判权限与规则；民事和刑事体系，行政司法；

k) 必须在全国范围内得到保障的公民与社会权利基本服务水平的确定；

l) 教育总则；

m) 社会保障；

n) 自治市、省和都市区的选举立法、政府机构和基本职能；

o) 海关、边防和跨国疾病预防；

p) 度量衡和时制；国家、大区和地方行政数据的统计与电子化协调；知识产权；

q) 环境、生态系统和文化财产保护。

共同立法事务涉及：国际关系和大区与欧盟的关系；对外贸易；职业保险与安全；对现存自治学校教育机构无歧视的教育，职业教育和培训除外；专业；科学技术研究与支持产业部门创新；维护健康；食品与营养；体育规则；公共安全；领土管理；民用港口与机场；主要的运输和航运网络；通讯规则；国民生产、运输与能源分配；补充性和辅助性社会保险；公共预算、公共资金与税收体系的和谐与协调；文化和环境遗产的强化及文化活动的促进与组织；储蓄银行；农村储蓄银行；地区性信贷机构；地区性土地与农业信贷机构。在共同立法事务中，除了基本原则的决定权属于国家立法机构之外，立法权属于大区。

除了明确规定属国家立法机构保留的权利之外，大区拥有对所有事物的立法权。

特伦托和博尔扎诺自治区在它们能力所及的事物上参与事关欧共体法规构成的决策活动，根据国家法律规定的程序执行欧盟的国际协定和协议。如不按国家法律行事，国家可代行其权力。

专属立法事物的立法权属于国家，除非国家将权利委托给大区。其他事物的立法权全属大区。自治市、省和都市区在组织规则和各自职能的行使方面拥有立法权。

大区法律要排除影响男女在社会、文化和经济生活中完全平等的任何障碍，促进选举中的男女机会平等。

大区法律应批准大区之间为促进职能的行使而达成的协定，也可以在得到共同机构认证的情况下批准协定。

大区可在自己的能力范围之内以国家法律允许的条件和形式与其他国家或其他国家的地方机构签订协定或协议。

第 118 条　行政管理职能交由自治市行使，但为确保统一行动，行政管理在某些情况下也可根据辅助性、差别性和适宜性原则交给省、都市区、大区和国家。

自治市、省和都市区是各自行政职能及国家和大区根据各自的能力赋予它们的行政职能的首要行使者。

国家和大区之间在第 117 条第 2 款 b）和 h）项所述事务上的协调方式由国家法律规定；国家和省之间在文化遗产保护方面的协议与协调方式也由国家法律规定。

国家、大区、都市区、省和自治市鼓励公民提出自治倡议，不管个人还是群体，以便根据辅助原则采取带有普遍意义的行动。

——1988 年 9 月 12 日第 214 号《官方公报》增刊公布的 1988 年 8 月 23 日第 400 号法律第 14 条——"政府活动条例和内阁任期规定"规定：

第 14 条（立法令）：

1. 政府根据《宪法》第 76 条通过的立法令应由共和国总统以"立法令"的名称发布，并在序言中说明授权发布法令的法律、内阁的决定及授权法所述程序的其他执行情况。

2. 立法令必须在授权法规定的期限内发布；政府通过的立法令文本应在期满之前至少 20 天内提交共和国总统公布。

3. 如授权法涉及需要分别处理的多项事务，政府可以就一项或多项事务采取相继措施履行。关于授权法规定的最后期限，政府应根据其行使立法权力的规则定期通知国会两院。

4. 行使立法权力的规定期限一旦超过 2 年，政府必须征求国会两院对授权发布法令的意见。两院主管各项事务的常设委员会应在 60 天内发表意见，明确指明其认为与授权法规定不一致的地方。在随后的 30 天内，政府应在对委员会的意见进行仔细审阅之后附上自己的观点和修改意见，返还委员会征求最后意见，后者必须在 30 天内拿出最后意见。

——关于"根据 1997 年 3 月 15 日第 59 号法律第 11 条成立文化遗产和活动部"的 1988 年 10 月 20 日第 368 号立法令在 1998 年 10 月 26 日第 250 号《官方公报》上公布。

——关于"根据 1997 年 10 月 8 日第 352 号法律第 1 条编辑文化遗产和文化活动立法条款合并文本"的 1999 年 10 月 29 日第 490 号立法令在 1999 年 12 月 27 日第 302 号《官方公报》增刊上公布。

——2002 年 7 月 8 日第 158 号《官方公报》公布的 2002 年 7 月 6 日第 137 号法律第 10 条关于"政府机构和内阁任期改革的授权法"，经 2003 年 2 月 18 日第 40 号《官方公报》公布的 2003 年 2 月 18 日第 24 号立法令第 1 之 2 条修改，后再经 2003 年 4 月 19 日第 92 号《官方公报》公布的 2003 年 4 月 17 日第 82 号法律修改，规定：

第 10 条（文化与环境资产、娱乐、体育、著作权与版权重新整理与编纂授权法）：

1. 根据第 1 条所述对文化遗产与活动部继续有效的授权，政府有权在当前法律生效之后 18 个月内通过一项或多项立法令重新整理和编纂〔仅限于 a）项〕涉及下列事务的法律条款：

a）文化与环境资产；

b）影像资料；

c）戏剧、音乐、舞蹈和其他娱乐；

d）体育；

e）著作权和版权。

2. 第 1 款所述立法令在不给国库增加新的或更多负担的情况下应坚持下列指导原则和标准：

a）遵守《宪法》第 117 条和第 118 条；

b）遵守欧洲共同体条例和国际协议；

c）提高文化遗产保护措施和相关文化活动的有效性，包括最大可能地利用已有资源并增加财政收入；明确文化遗产和文化活动领域的公共政策，以建立有效而透明的预算会计制度；理顺和简化程序；使各项工作程序适应新的计算机技术。

d）针对第 1 款 a）项所述：在对私有财产不做新的限制，不废除现有规章制度，并完全尊重国际协议，特别是有关文化财产流转的国际协议的基础上，更新文化和环境资产的鉴定、保存和保护措施。措施的更新还可通过建立向大区、地方部门、银行、民间团体和公共机构开放的基金得以实现；根据1998年10月2日第368号立法令第10条第1款b-2）项的规定，通过建立大区、地方部门、银行、民间团体和公共机构开放的基金，对可能会受到国家以外当事人特许的影响的服务项目进行重组；根据文化财产保存和保护的客观特征及需要，修改与文化财产有关的公开招标规定，调低使用不同程序确定承包商的门槛，以允许有专业技能和实践经验的工匠团体参与，重新审定授予合同所必需的规划层次，重新审定判定标准，并预测可能超出常规比例限制的程度；根据管理与政策分开的原则，同时特别注意其不兼容性，重新审定参与决定资助和扶持文化团体和机构相关活动的咨询机构的组织形式和职能，以明确界定技术部门的责任。在重新审定过程中，要明确文化遗产与文化活动管理和国家防务活动之间的合作关系，确保国防建设目标的实现；

e）针对第1款b）项和c）项所述：合理配置咨询机构及相关职能，包括精简机构数量和压缩机构规模；简化资助手续，重新审定参与确定可接受资助的机构和个人的咨询机构的组建及职能形式；改革这些咨询机构和部门的组织结构；修改对被分配资源的利用及相关措施效果的制约与平衡制度。

f）针对第1款d）项所述：协调立法，使本国立法与欧盟成员国激励措施的总原则保持一致；重建体育信贷机构的任务，确保大区和地方自治部门在体育信贷机构中的代表性；确保私人主体也能得到资助。

g）针对第1款e）项所述：根据1997年3月15日第59号法律第14条第1款b）项所述指导原则和标准，改组意大利作家与出版商协会。该协会的章程必须确保有足够数量的作家、出版商和有创作能力的个人参与其中，并确保有资格成员享受版权收入的最大透明度；根据欧盟在有关版权和相关权利事务上遵循的总原则，协调与数码、多媒体作品及软件生产和传播有关的立法。

3. 除关于《民法典》的一般性法律规定第15条外，第1款所述立法令应明确指出已经被取代或废除的条款。第1款所述立法令通过之前需与1997年8月28日第281号立法令第8条所述联合会议协商，并征求国会各主管委员会的意见。国会主管委员会应在收到相关请求之后60天内发表意见。60天的期限过后，立法令可自然通过。

4. 第1款所述立法令的相关规定可在生效后两年内根据本条所述的相同原则、标准和程序进行修改和补充。

第 1 条注释：

——1947 年 12 月 27 日第 298 号《官方公报》特刊公布的《意大利共和国宪法》第 9 条规定：

第 9 条：

共和国鼓励开展文化、科学和技术研究。

共和国保护国家的地理景观和历史、艺术遗产。

——《意大利共和国宪法》第 117 条内容见前言注释。

第 4 条注释：

——《意大利共和国宪法》第 118 条内容见前言注释。

第 9 条注释：

——1985 年 4 月 10 日第 85 号《官方公报》增刊公布的 1984 年 2 月 18 日在罗马签署并根据 1985 年 3 月 25 日第 121 号法律批准执行的关于修改意大利与罗马教廷 1929 年 2 月 11 日《拉特兰条约》的协议第 12 条规定：

第 12 条：

1. 罗马教廷和意大利共和国在各自的能力范围之内合作保护历史和艺术遗产。为使意大利法律适用于宗教事务，双方主管部门应为保护、强化和享用属于教会机构的具有宗教价值的文化财产共同制定适当的法律，并通过协议加强和促进属于教会机构的具有历史价值的档案和图书的保存与查阅工作。

2. 罗马教廷可继续根据自己的意愿将基督教墓地建于罗马土地或意大利领土其他地方，并负担后续看管、维护和保存费用，同时放弃其他墓地的使用权。根据国家的法律，不管第三方有什么权利，罗马教廷都可以从事必要的宗教圣物发掘和转移活动。"

——1947 年 12 月 27 日第 298 号《官方公报》特刊公布的《意大利共和国宪法》第 8 条规定：

第 8 条：

所有宗教派别在法律面前均享有同等的自由。

天主教以外的各种宗教派别，在不违反意大利法律的范围内，均有按其规章设立组织之权利。

它们同国家的关系，依其与相关政府部门之间的协议而制定的法律处理。

第 12 条注释：

——2003 年 10 月 2 日第 229 号《官方公报》增刊公布的 2003 年 9 月 30 日第 269 号法令"关于促进发展和完善公共账户的紧急规定"，后经 2003 年 11 月 24 日第 326 号法律修改，并在 2003 年 11 月 25 日第 274 号《官方公报》增刊上公布的第 27 条规定：

第 27 条（不可移动政府财产的文化价值鉴定）：

1. 1999 年 10 月 29 日第 490 号立法令第 2 条所述属于国家、大区、省、都市区、自治市和其他公共部门或机构的可移动和不可移动财产，在按第 2 款规定做出鉴定之前应按文化遗产保护规定的要求加以保护。

2. 鉴定第 1 款所述财产的艺术、历史、考古或人种－人类学价值由监管部门依职权或财产所有人提出的申请组织鉴定。鉴定工作要以文化遗产和活动部规定的总体原则为依据。

3. 如在接受鉴定的财产中没有发现第 2 款所述的价值，则这些财产无需按 1999 年第 490 号立法令的规定加以保护。

4. 如在对国家、大区和其他政府部门财产的鉴定中没有发现上述价值，应将这种鉴定结果通知主管机构，以便他们可在有关部委提不出别的理由对其公共价值进行评估的情况下下令放弃国家所有权。

5. ［本款在修订为法律时被删除］。

6. 根据第 2 款所述总指导原则被鉴定为具有艺术、历史、考古或人种－人类学价值的财产，应无限期按规定加以保护。确定具有上述价值将构成根据 1999 年第 490 号立法令所述合并文本第 6 条和第 7 条规定的公示。鉴定结果应按上述合并文本第 8 条规定进行登记。

7. 本条规定适用于第 1 款所述财产，即便它们所属的主体改变了它们的法律地位。

8. 首次执行本条规定时，国家财产局主管部门应在第 9 款所述法令发布后 30 天内向大区监管部门提交经过鉴定的国有或属于国家财产的建筑物清单，并附描述性说明，包括与具体建筑物有关的识别数据。

9. 清单的标准规格和描述性说明的行文方式及递送程序由文化遗产和活动部以法令形式规定，也可由其他相关行政部门代为规定。规定应在本法令生效后 30 天内发布，并与国家财产局和负责防务用不动产事务的国防部公共工程与国有财产总局的相关规定保持一致。

10. 大区监管部门应在收到申请后 30 天的期限内根据主管监管部门进行的调查和

发表的意见对建筑物是否存在文化价值做出鉴定，并在收到相关描述性说明材料之后 60 天内通知申请单位。从收到说明材料之后算起总期限 120 天内如没有通知，视同鉴定结论为没有上述价值。

11．如国家建筑物被鉴定为具有上述价值，其描述性说明材料应连同第 10 款所述调查材料和意见一起归入计算机档案，供国家财产局和国防部公共工程与国有财产总局查阅，以便它们对不动资产进行监控，并根据各自的能力和资格制定相关规则。

12．属于大区、其他地方政府部门及其他公共部门和机构的建筑物，应根据相关部门或机构的申请进行鉴定。申请鉴定时要同时提供各建筑物的描述性说明。第 10 款和第 11 款的规定适用于此条所述的鉴定过程。

13．在 2001 年 11 月 23 日第 410 号法律和 2002 年 12 月 27 日第 289 号法律第 80 条第 3 到第 5 款基础上修订形成的 2001 年 9 月 25 日第 351 号法令第 3 条第 15 款和 17 款规定的强化与强制过户程序适用于本条第 3 款所述不动产，也适用于根据 1996 年 12 月 23 日第 662 号法律第 3 条第 112 款及后续修订和 1998 年 12 月 23 日第 448 号法律第 44 条第 1 款认定的不动产。在 1998 年 12 月 23 日第 448 号法律第 44 条及后续修订中第 1 之 2 款和第 3 项被删除。

13 之 2．国家财产局应与国防部公共工程和国家财产总局配合，确定不再具有公共机构征用价值并准备列入 1996 年 12 月 23 日第 662 号法律第 3 条第 112 款及后续修改所述强制过户计划的国防部门现有不动产。

第 14 条注释：

——1990 年 8 月 18 日第 192 号《官方公报》公布的 1990 年 8 月 7 日第 241 号关于"行政程序与行政文件接触权的新规则和条例"的法律第 2 条规定：

第 2 条：

1．如果根据申请或其职责制定相关程序属于必须履行的法定义务，公共行政部门必须采取特别措施制定相关程序。

2．如果相关法规尚未直接确定出台各类程序的期限，公共行政部门应予确定。如果相关程序由其他方面制定，出台期限从着手制定或收到申请之日开始算起。

3．如果公共行政部门不按第 2 款所述规定确定期限，则上述期限为 30 天。

4．按第 2 款规定做出的决定应根据条例予以公布。

第 16 条注释：

——1972 年 1 月 17 日第 13 号《官方公报》公布的 1971 年 11 月 24 日关于"简化行政

申诉程序"的第 1199 号共和国总统令。

第 29 条注释：

——1988 年 9 月 12 日第 214 号《官方公报》增刊公布的 1988 年 8 月 23 日第 400 号法律"政府活动条例和内阁任期规则"第 17 条，经 1993 年 2 月 6 日第 30 号《官方公报》增刊公布的 1993 年 2 月 3 日第 29 号立法令第 74 条和 1999 年 2 月 12 日第 35 号《官方公报》增刊公布的 1999 年 2 月 5 日第 25 号法律第 11 条修订，及 1997 年 3 月《官方公报》第 63 号增刊公布的 1997 年 3 月 15 日第 59 号法律第 13 条补充规定：

第 17 条（条例）：

1. 根据内阁会议的决定和国务会议的咨询意见（国务会议必须在接收申请后 90 天内拿出咨询意见），共和国总统可通过命令发布规范下列事务的条例：

    a) 法律、立法令和欧共体条例的生效；

    b) 包含原则性规则和条例的法律与立法令的实施和执行，保留给大区处理的事务除外；

    c) 尚无依照法律或依照具有法律效力的法令制定的条例存在的事务，涉及保留给立法性条例的事务除外；

    d) 根据法律规定公共行政部门的组织和职能；

    e) ［已被删除］。

2. 共和国总统应根据内阁的决定和国务会议的咨询意见以总统令的形式发布条例，以规范《宪法》未保留给法律处理的专门事务。这些专门事务是由共和国法律授权政府行使条例制定权、决定规范这些事务的一般规则和现行法律的废除，具有授权法的效力。

3. 一旦获得法律的明确授权，政府的部或其下属当局通过部长令对其主管事务发布条例。由一个以上部共管的事务，相关条例可通过部际部长令制定，但要以相应的法律授权为条件。部颁条例和部际条例不得规定与政府条例相违的规则，发布之前必须通知内阁总理。

4. 第 1 款所述条例及部颁条例或部际条例必须以"条例"的名称颁布，事先征求国务会议的意见，获得审计法院的批准和登记，并在《官方公报》上公布。

4 之 2. 根据第 2 款发布的条例，部属办事机构的组织编制和规章需由主管部的部长经与内阁总理和财政部部长协商后提出建议，方可确定。所定组织编制和规章制度应符合 1993 年 2 月 3 日第 29 号立法令及后续修改确定的原则，并体现和遵循下列标准：

    a) 重组部长和副部长直属办事机构，体现它们对决策指导机关及决策部门与行

政管理部门之间沟通纽带的支持具有专属管辖权;

b) 根据取消重复性职能的灵活度标准对最终职能和辅助职能的多样性安排及其相似职能的组织调整,确定处于全面管理、中心管理和边缘管理等不同层次上的办事机构;

c) 制定相应措施,对机构的效率和效果进行定期检查;

d) 对编制方案的执行情况进行定期说明并根据实践情况进行定期修改;

e) 发布非强制性部长指令,界定综合管理机关内部管理人员的任务。

——1998 年 10 月 26 日第 250 号《官方公报》公布的关于"根据 1997 年 3 月 15 日第 59 号法律第 11 条设立文化遗产和活动部"的 1998 年 10 月 20 日第 368 号立法令第 9 条规定:

第 9 条(培训和研究学校):

1. 专业培训和研究学校在下列机构开办:中央文化遗产修复研究院、准宝石工作室和中央受损图书研究院。

2. 第 1 款所述机构组织培训并开设专业课程,既可与大学和其他机构以及意大利境内外团体合作,也可参与这些机构和团体的创意活动并为之做出贡献。

3. 有关培训和研究学校的课程设置、入学要求和教师选拔标准,根据 1988 年 8 月 23 日第 400 号法律第 17 条第 3 款的规定,经内阁总理办公厅内政服务局局长和财政、预算与经济规划部部长同意后,由文化遗产和活动部部长通过部长令制定部颁条例加以规定。以前建立的学校经部长令批准也可设立分校。

4. 1963 年 9 月 30 日第 1409 号共和国总统令第 14 条所述的学校重组工作按根据第 3 款所述方式通过的条例执行。

——1997 年 8 月 30 日第 202 号《官方公报》公布的 1997 年 8 月 28 日第 281 号立法令第 4 条关于"国家、大区和特伦托、博尔扎诺两自治省常设会议的职能和任务的界定与扩展以及大区、省和自治市与国家 – 城市会议和地方自治实体在共同关心的事务与任务上的联合行动"规定:

第 4 条(中央政府、大区与特伦托、博尔扎诺两自治省之间的协调一致):

1. 中央政府、大区与特伦托、博尔扎诺两自治省在贯彻公平合作、实现行政管理工作有效性和经济目标方面可通过国家 – 大区会议达成一致意见,统筹各方力量,做好共同关心的事情。

3. 协调一致的决定必须在中央政府、大区及特伦托、博尔扎诺两自治省省长的明确同意下做出。

第 41 条注释：

——1988 年 8 月 23 日第 400 号法律第 17 条内容见第 29 条注释。

第 46 条注释：

——1990 年 8 月 7 日第 241 号法律第 2 条见第 14 条注释。

第 53 条注释：

——1942 年 4 月 4 日第 79 号《官方公报》特刊公布的，经 1942 年 3 月 16 日第 262 号敕令批准的《民法典》第 822 条规定：

第 822 条（政府财产）：

属于国家或国家某一地区的财产包括根据法律属于公有的海岸、海滩、港口、码头、江河、溪流、湖泊和其他水域及指定用于国防的工程设施。

下列财产属于国家所有时也是政府财产：道路、高速公路、铁路、机场、高架水渠，及根据相关法律被认定为具有历史、考古和艺术价值的建筑物、博物馆、画廊、档案馆、图书馆及根据有关法律被视为公共财产的其他财产。

第 69 条注释：

——1971 年 11 月 24 日第 1199 号共和国总统令见第 16 条注释。

第 73 条注释：

——关于文化财产出口的 1992 年 12 月 9 日第 3911/92 号欧共体条例在 1993 年 3 月 1 日第 17 号《官方公报》第 2 号特刊上公布，后经发布于 1996 年 12 月 27 日第 16 号《官方公报》第 2 号特刊上的 1996 年 12 月 16 日第 2469/96 号欧盟条例和发布于 2001 年 7 月 23 日第 57 号《官方公报》第 2 号特刊上的 2001 年 5 月 14 日第 974/01 号欧盟条例修改。

——关于"从成员国领土非法转移之文物的返还"的 1993 年 3 月 15 日第 93/7 号欧共体指令公布于 1993 年 7 月 12 日第 54 号《官方公报》第 2 号特刊上，后经发布于 1997 年 6 月 16 日第 45 号《官方公报》第 2 号特刊的 1997 年 2 月 17 日第 96/100 号欧洲议会和欧盟委员会指令和公布于 2001 年 9 月 10 日第 71 号《官方公报》第 2 号特刊的 2001 年 6 月 5 日第 2001/38 欧洲议会和欧盟委员会指令修改。

第 74 条注释:

——1992 年 12 月 9 日第 3911/92 号欧共体条例见第 73 条注释。

第 75 条注释:

——公布于 1957 年 12 月 23 日第 317 号《官方公报》上的 1957 年 10 月 14 日第 1203 号法律批准生效的关于成立欧洲经济共同体的条约第 30 条,由 1998 年 7 月 6 日公布于第 155 号《官方公报》增刊上的 1998 年 6 月 16 日第 209 号法律批准生效的《阿姆斯特丹条约》第 6 条取代并重新编号,规定:

    第 30 条 [修改后的第 36 条]:
    第 28 条 [修改后的第 30 条] 和第 29 条 [修改后的第 34 条] 规定不得妨碍基于公共道德、公共政策或公共安全,人类及动植物健康与生存保护,具有艺术、历史或考古价值的国家珍宝的保护,或工商财产保护等方面的考虑而对进口、出口或货物运输活动采取禁止或限制措施,但这些禁止或限制措施并不意味着对成员国间贸易的随意歧视或变相限制。
——1993 年 12 月 9 日第 3911/92 号欧共体条例见第 73 条注释。

第 76 条注释:

——1993 年 3 月 15 日第 93/7 号欧共体指令见第 73 条注释。

第 77 条注释:

——1940 年 10 月 28 日第 253 号《官方公报》增刊公布的 1940 年 10 月 28 日第 1443 号敕令批准的《民事诉讼程序法典》第 163 条,后经 1950 年 8 月 16 日第 186 号《官方公报》增刊公布的 1950 年 7 月 14 日 581 号法律第 7 条和 1990 年 12 月 1 日第 281 号《官方公报》增刊公布的 1990 年 11 月 26 日第 353 号法律第 7 条修订,规定:

    第 163 条 (传票内容):
    诉状应通过传票要求出庭定期的听审办理。

法院院长应在每个诉讼年度开始的时候发布由上诉法院院长批准的命令，确定每周专为当事人首次出庭听审的天数和次数。

传票内容必须包括：

1）诉状提交的法院；

2）原告姓名、住址；被告姓名、住址；原告和被告代理人或助手的姓名、住址。如果原告或被告属于法人实体、未取得法人地位的社团或委员会，则传票内容必须包括其名称及代表他们出庭的机构或办事处；

3）诉讼请求对象的确定；

4）依法构成诉讼理由的事实和要素及相关结论；

5）具体指明原告欲出示的有利证据，特别是其希望提供的文件；

6）代理律师的姓名和及其权限说明；

7）听审日期的确定：根据第 166 条的要求及规定形式进行的听审，提前 20 天向被告发出出庭的传票；根据第 168 之 2 条确定的审判，提前 10 天向被告发出传票要求被告至指定的法官面前听审。传票还要警告当事人：根据第 167 条规定，上述时间内不到庭将被罚款。

根据第 125 条签署的传票由当事人或其代理人送交法院官员，并根据第 137 条规定履行通知义务。

第 84 条注释：

——1992 年 12 月 9 日第 3911/92 号欧共体条例见第 73 条注释。

——1993 年 3 月 15 日第 93/7 号欧共体指令见第 73 条注释。

第 87 条注释：

——1995 年 6 月 24 日在罗马外交大会通过的国际统一私法协会《关于被盗或非法出口文物公约》最后文件及附件由 1999 年 6 月 7 日第 213 号法律批准生效，并公布于 1999 年 7 月 2 日第 153 号《官方公报》。

第 91 条注释：

——《民法典》第 822 条的内容见第 53 条注释。

——1942 年 4 月 4 日第 79 号《官方公报》特刊公布的 1942 年 3 月 16 日第 262 号敕令批准的《民法典》第 826 条规定：

第 826 条（国家、省和自治市财产）：

　　以上各条所述范围之外属于国家、省和自治市的物品构成国家财产或分别构成省或自治市财产。

　　不可让与的国家财产包括：根据相关法律属于国家森林财产的森林；土地所有人不得免费使用的矿山、采石厂和泥炭沼；具有历史、考古、古人类学、古生物学价值和艺术价值的物品，不管它们是由什么人以什么方式发现的；构成共和国总统办公设备及兵营、军备、军用飞机和战舰设备的物品。

　　不可让与的国家财产或省、自治市财产包括用于办公的建筑物及其设备和其他用于公共服务目的的财产。

第 92 条注释：

——1988 年 8 月 23 日第 400 号法律第 17 条内容见第 29 条注释。

第 128 条注释：

——1909 年 6 月 20 日第 364 号法律"关于制定不可让与的古玩和美术品管理条例"由 1909 年 6 月 28 日第 150 号《官方公报》公布。

——1922 年 6 月 11 日第 778 号法律关于"自然美境与具有特殊历史价值建筑物保护措施"由 1922 年 6 月 24 日第 148 号《官方公报》公布。

——1939 年 8 月 8 日第 184 号《官方公报》公布的 1939 年 6 月 1 日第 1089 号法律第 2 条、第 3 条、第 5 条和第 21 条关于"具有艺术和历史价值之物品的保护"规定：

第 2 条：

　　同样受本法保护的还有鉴于它们总体上与政治、历史、文学、艺术和文化相关而被认定为具有特别重要价值并构成国民教育部部长行政通报对象的不可移动物品。

　　根据部长的要求，通报应在土地登记簿上登记，并对每个无论享有何种合法权利的所有人、占有人或持有人皆有效力。

第 3 条：

　　国民教育部部长应以行政通报的形式通知具有第 1 条所述特别重要价值之物品的所有人、占有人或持有人。

　　涉及建筑物处于原始状态还是添加了新元素的确定，根据前条第 2 款的规定执行。

已通报具有特别重要价值的可移动物品的清单由国家教育部保存，副本交王国地方政府存档。

相关人员可以查阅清单。

第 5 条：

国民教育部部长经与全国教育、科学和艺术委员会协商，可从传承、知名度和特殊环境价值考虑，通报总体上具有特殊艺术与历史价值的收藏品或收藏系列。

未经国民教育部部长批准，已通报的收藏品或收藏系列不得流散，不管有什么合法的权利。

第 21 条：

为保护本法所述不可移动物品的完整性、透视或自然采光不受损害，防止改变其安放或装饰条件，国民教育部部长有权规定它们的距离、保护措施及其他条款。

这种权力的行使不受建筑条例或城市规划的制约。

根据本条做出的指示必须按照部部长的要求在土地登记簿上登记，并对上述指示所涉物品的每个无论享有何种合法权利的所有人、占有人或持有人皆有效力。

——1963 年 10 月 31 日第 285 号《官方公报》公布的 1963 年 9 月 30 日第 1409 号共和国总统令关于"国家档案馆组织与人事安排规定"第 36 条规定：

第 36 条（明显历史价值的公示）：

根据符合行政程序的合法命令公示档案或个人合法所有、占有或持有的单份文件的明显历史价值是档案监管人的任务。

个人如对档案监管人的命令不服，可以在 60 天内向内务部部长提出申诉。内务部部长应在与档案高级理事会协商之后对申诉做出裁决。

——1999 年 12 月 27 日第 302 号《官方公报》增刊公布的，关于"根据 1997 年 10 月 8 日第 352 号法律第 1 条对涉及文化和环境财产事务的法律规定进行汇编"的 1999 年 10 月 29 日第 490 号立法令第 6、7、8 和 49 条规定：

第 6 条（公示）：

1. 在不违背第 2 条第 4 款规定的情况下，部长应就第 2 条第 1 款 a）项所列具有特别重要价值的不属于第 5 条第 1 款所述主体的物品进行公示。

2. 部长还应对第 2 条第 1 款 b）项所述具有特别重要价值的物品、第 2 条第 1 款 c）项所述具有杰出价值的收藏品或系列收藏物品和第 2 条第 4 款 c）项所述具有著名历史价值的物品进行公示。

3. 公示的效力由第 10 条予以规定。

4. 第 2 条第 2 款 c) 项所述私人所有物品的特别重要价值应由所在地大区进行公示。如大区不作为，由部根据 1972 年 1 月 14 日第 3 号共和国总统令第 9 条第 3 款的规定进行公示。

第 7 条（公示程序）：

1. 部长应依据第 6 条的规定直接启动公示程序，或根据监管人的建议启动程序，该建议也可在大区、省或自治市的要求下做出，同时应通知所有人、占有人或持有人。

2. 通知的内容应包括：财产的鉴定因素、自行估价或推荐估价、第 4 款有关预期效力的说明以及不少于 30 天的反馈意见期限。

3. 凡涉及建筑群的公示程序，应通知所在地市政当局。

4. 作为预防性措施，通知应确定本编第 2 章第 1 节和第 3 章第 1 节规定的适用。

5. 当主管部根据 1990 年 8 月 7 日第 241 号法律第 2 条第 2 款规定所确定的公示期限结束后，第 4 款所述的效力随即终止。

6. 大区在行使第 6 条第 4 款所赋予的职权时，应依照上述各条款的规定办理。

第 8 条（公示的通知）：

1. 根据第 6 条规定进行的公示应告知相关财产的所有权人、占有人或持有人。

2. 凡公示涉及做广告宣传的不动产，应按主管部要求在土地登记簿登记，并对每个所有权人、占有人或持有人均有效力。

3. 大区根据第 6 条第 4 款规定所进行的公示应通报主管部。

第 49 条（间接保护的指令）：

1. 为防止本编所规定的不动产文物受损，避免透视或自然采光受影响，避免周围环境或外观的改变，主管部有权自行规定距离、措施和其他规章制度，也可在监管人的建议下做出指令。

2. 该权力的行使可不受有关建筑条例和城市规划规定的约束。

3. 有关启动公示程序的通知应依据第 2 条第 2 款规定的方式进行。如因被通知人数过多或工作量过大而无法逐一通知，可采取适当的广告方式周知。行政部门有权采取预防性措施通知本人。

4. 依据本条所制定的指令应在土地登记簿登记，并对前述每个相关所有权人、占有人和持有人均具有法律效力。

5. 第 7 条第 3 款规定也适用于有关建筑群的通告。

第 129 条注释：

——1871 年 6 月 28 日关于 "将《民法典》实施的暂行规定第 24 和 25 条适用范围延伸

至罗马省”的第 286 号法律，当天公布于第 174 期《官方公报》。

——1883 年 7 月 8 日关于“保护画廊、图书馆和其他艺术和古物收藏品”的第 1461 号法律，于 1883 年 7 月 12 日公布于第 162 期《官方公报》。

——1891 年 11 月 23 日关于“批准 1871 年 6 月 28 日第 286 号（第 2 系列）法律第 4 条和 1883 年 7 月 8 日第 1461 号法律的实施细则”的第 653 号敕令　1891 年 12 月 5 日公布于第 285 期《官方公报》。

——1892 年 2 月 7 日关于“保护画廊、图书馆和其他艺术和古物收藏的品”的第 31 号法律，2 月 8 日公布于第 32 期《官方公报》。

第 130 条注释：

——1911 年 10 月 2 日第 1163 号关于“国家档案馆”的敕令，1911 年 11 月 8 日公布于第 260 期《官方公报》。

——1913 年 1 月 30 日第 363 号关于“1909 年 6 月 20 日第 363 号法律和 1912 年 6 月 23 日第 688 号法律关于古物和艺术品法令实施细则”的敕令，1913 年 6 月 5 日公布于第 130 期《官方公报》。

第 139 条注释：

——1986 年 7 月 8 日关于“建立环境部和环境破坏事项的规定”的第 349 号法律第 6 条，1986 年 7 月 15 日公布于第 162 期《官方公报》。

第 13 条：

1. 环境部应颁布法令对全国性的环境保护协会或那些活动范围不少于 5 个大区的环保组织予以认定。该认定应依据这些组织章程确定的计划目标、内部条例，及其活动延续性和对外关系等，在事先征求全国环境委员会意见的基础上进行。该委员会应在环境部提出要求后的 3 个月内予以答复，如逾期不表态，环境部得自行决定。

2. 为获得按第 12 条第 1 款 c）项要求的三名全国环境委员会初步组成人员候选名单，部长应在本法生效 30 天内，根据第一款所确定的标准对全国性环保协会或那些活动范围不少于 5 个大区的环保组织进行初步认定，并将有关情况通知议会。

第 142 条注释：

——1933 年 12 月 11 日关于“供水和电力系统法规汇编”的第 1775 号敕令，1934 年 1

月 8 日公布于第 5 期《官方公报》。

——2001 年 3 月 18 日关于"根据 2001 年 3 月 5 日第 57 号法律第 7 条的规定确立林业部门的方针和现代化"的第 227 号立法令，2001 年 6 月 15 日公布于第 137 期《官方公报》。该法第 2 条规定如下：

第 2 条（树木和树木栽培的定义）：

1. 就本立法令和其他在共和国领土范围内施行法规的效力而言，树木、森林和林地的地位是相同的。

2. 在本立法令生效 12 个月内，各大区应确定其辖区内树木的定义以及下列内容：
   a）作为树木应有的起码长度、宽度和覆盖面积；
   b）树与树中间的隔离带和空地面积；
   c）因特殊自然条件不能视为树林的情况。

3. 下列情况被视为树林：
   a）以水土保持、空气净化和保护水资源、生物多样性、景观和总体环境保护等任务为目的必须植树造林之土地；
   b）由于林业生产、生物和非生物的灾难，或由于意外事故、火灾等原因而暂时失去树木和灌木覆盖的林区；
   c）面积不超过 2000 平方米的林中隔离带和其他空地。

4. 第 2 款、第 6 款所述之定义可适用于根据 1999 年 10 月 20 日第 490 号立法令第 146 条第 1 款 g）项所述有树木覆盖土地的认定。

5. 所谓树木栽培的意思是指，仅以生产树木和培育生物量为目的的非林地植树造林。该种植生长期结束后是可逆转的。

6. 如果大区不能颁布与第 2 款相关的规定或自身无法确定不同定义，那么树木应被视为覆盖木本植物的土地，而不论这些地方是否存在自然或人工种植的灌木植物如：栗树林、软木林和地中海灌木丛等，也不论这些植物生长处于何阶段，但不包括公共和私人的园林、沿街道旁的林带、正在培育的成片栗子树、果树林和第 5 款涉及的树木栽培。这里所指的植物形态及其种植土地需具备以下条件：即沿树干底部外侧测量，面积不得超过 2000 平方米，平均宽度不得超过 20 米，覆盖率不得超过 20%。1956 年 7 月 18 日第 759 号法律关于软木林定义的规定仍然有效。此外，以水土保持、空气净化和保护水资源、生物多样性、景观及总体环境保护为目的的必须植树造林的土地，以及树木间的隔离带和其他面积不超过 2000 平方米的空地亦应视作树林。

——1976 年 3 月 13 日关于"1971 年 2 月 2 日在腊姆萨尔签订的有国际意义的水鸟栖息湿地公约的实施"的第 448 号共和国总统令，1976 年 7 月 3 日公布于第 173 期《官方公报》。

——1968 年 4 月 2 日第 1444 号部长令关于"根据 1967 年 8 月 6 日第 765 号法律第 17 条规定，在制定新的城市规划法规或修改现行法规时，须遵守有关建筑物的密度、高度和建筑结构之间的距离的强制性限制，以及住宅用地、企业用地和公共空间或集体活动、公共绿地或停车场等空间相互之间的最大比例等强制性限制"，1968 年 4 月 16 日公布于第 97 期《官方公报》。

——1971 年 10 月 22 日第 865 号法律第 18 条关于"公共住宅建筑规划与协调；公用征地条例；对 1942 年 8 月 17 日第 1150 号法律、1962 年 4 月 18 日第 167 号法律和 1964 年 9 月 29 日第 847 号法律的修订和附加条款；从简化和协议中获益的住宅建筑区的杰出工程项目支出的核准"，1971 年 10 月 30 日公布于第 276 期《官方公报》，规定：

第 18 条：

为实施上述第 16 条的规定，自本法生效 6 个月内，市政当局应根据市议会的决议，划定建筑群中心占地的范围。如果市议会未形成决议，为使征地程序获得良好效果，市政当局在征得市议会同意后，应说明该地区是否用于建筑群中心。

就每个建筑群中心或居住区而言，其界限应沿着所有建筑群中心区和围墙内的部分土地，从其外延连贯的周长线起予以划界。分散的居住小区和外部地区即使受到城市进程的影响，也不必划入建筑群中心的范围。

假如本条第 1 款所确定的期限已满而无任何作为，应由大区为建筑群中心划界。

第 144 条注释：

——有关 1986 年 7 月 8 日第 349 号法律第 13 号条规定见第 139 条注释。

第 145 条注释：

——1998 年 3 月 31 日第 112 号关于"1997 年 3 月 15 日第 59 号法律第 1 章关于将国家的行政管理职能和任务授予大区和地方部门的实施细则"的立法令，1998 年 4 月 21 日公布于第 92 期《官方公报》，该法第 52 条规定如下：

第 52 条（有全国性意义的任务）：

1. 根据 1997 年 3 月 15 日第 59 号法律第 1 条第 4 款 c）项的规定，所谓具有全国性意义的任务是指：为负责具有重要自然、环境价值的国土地区和土地保护机构，以及负责属于国家的基础设施网络和其他工程的国土机构、城镇地区系统确立工作方针，以及确立开发国家的"南方"区和经济贫困地区的方针。

2. 就城市政策和土地规划事务与 1997 年 3 月 15 日第 59 号法律第 1 条第 4 款 e）

项所述国际组织和欧盟进行联系和协调工作属于国家的职权范围。

3. 本条第1款所涉及的任务应以联席会议制定协议的方式予以实施。

4. 1977年7月24日第616号共和国总统令第81条第1款正式废止。

第146条注释：

——1990年8月7日关于"行政程序和获取行政管理文件权利的新规定"的第241号法律，1990年8月18日公布于第192期《官方公报》。

——1986年7月8日第349号法律第13条见第139条注释。

第147条注释：

——1990年8月7日第241号关于"行政管理程序和获取行政管理文件权利之新规定"的法律第14条、第14之2条、第14之3条、第14之4条，1990年8月18日公布于第192期《官方公报》，规定如下：

第14条：

1. 当需要对行政程序涉及的不同公共利益同时进行审查时，作为惯例，主办行政部门应召集业务协调会。

2. 如果主办部门需取得协议、协调行动、获得或放弃许可，或在程序启动15天内征求其他部门的意见而未获批准，就必须召开业务协调会。

3. 当需要同时审查具有相同活动和结果的若干个行政程序所涉及的利益时，亦可召开业务协调会。因此，协调会应由主办行政部门召集，或者根据事先所达成的协议，由一个与普遍公共利益相关的行政部门召集。就公共工程而言，1994年2月11日第109号法律第7条及其此后的修订条款继续沿用。业务协调会还可应其他任何有关行政部门的要求召开。

4. 如果私人领域的活动需得到涉及多个行政管理部门的批准，业务协调会将根据相关行政部门的请求，由具有最终决定权的行政部门召集。

5. 如果公共工程需要得到特许，特许机关应在不违反大区关于环境影响评估法律规定的前提下，15天内召集部门协调会。

第14之2条：

1. 涉及复杂工程项目的业务协调会应依据有关方面理由充分的书面请求召集，该请求应在提交最终申请或设计之前提出，以便验证申请人是否具备获得许可所需资格。在此情况下，协调会须在提出请求后30天内做出裁定，相应的费用由申请人承担。

2. 当行政程序涉及公共工程的实施和公共利益时，业务协调会应就初步设计方案提出看法，其目的是根据现行法律的要求，确定最终设计方案所需的协议、意见、特许、批准、获得或放弃许可等条件。与此同时，负责环境和国土景观保护、历史和艺术遗产保护和健康保护的各行政部门，应针对各自主管的利益，就设计方案所采取的解决办法提出看法。如果有关方面提交的文件中不含有妨碍设计实施的内容，上述行政部门应在45天期限内提出最终设计方案获得特许证书所应具备的条件和要素。

3. 如果需要对环境影响进行评估，业务协调会应根据有关环境影响评估的法律规定，在完成对环境影响进行初步评估后30天内提出看法。如不能按第1款规定的90天期限内完成初步评估，协调会务必要在此后的30天内提出看法。在协调会上，负责对环境进行评估的部门应就项目开发和环境影响分析提出要求。在此过程中，作为环境评估程序的一个组成部分，上述部门应对各主要替代方案进行审查，包括零方案，并在已有文件的基础上，审查是否存在不符合有关规定的情况，比如说计划中的工程选址等。如无此类问题，该部门应在业务协调会上提出获得最终设计特许证书应具备的条件和要素。

4. 在出现第1、2、3款所涉及的情况时，业务协调会应依据已掌握的文件提出看法。此后只有在发生重要情况，包括基于私人对最终设计方案提出的评论，方可对当初的意见进行更改或补充。

5. 如果发生第2款所涉及的情况，主导程序的主管部门应将依据业务协调会对根据草案意见拟定的最终方案提交各相关行政部门，并在最终方案提交后第30天到第60天之间召集协调会。如果是政府采购商品和服务合同或特许授予公共工程，颁发合同和授予公共工程的行政部门应依据1994年2月11日第109号法律及其后续修改的规定，以初步设计方案为基础召集部门协调会。

第14之3条：

1. 业务协调会就其工作组织问题的决定以出席成员的多数票表决通过。

2. 第一次举行业务协调会应在会议召开10天前通知到各有关部门，可以采取电子邮件形式通知。有关部门如不能按期与会，应在收到通知后5天内提出改变会期的要求。因此，主办部门应协调商定新会期，会议应自原订会期起10天之内举行。

3. 与会行政部门应在业务协调会举行的第一次会上，或者依据第14之2条规定在提交申请或最终设计方案后举行的第一次会上，确定通过最终决议的期限。除非出现第4条规定涉及的情况，否则，协调会工作时间不会超过90天。如果90天期限届满时未采取行动，有关部门应依据第14之4条第2款及以下的规定办理。

4. 当需要对环境影响进行评估时，业务协调会一旦收到评估意见就应提出看法。如在规定期限内不能完成环境影响的评估工作，有关责任部门应在期限过后30天内召集协调会并提出看法。不过，如确有进一步研究的必要，并经多数与会者同意，该30天期限可向后顺延30天。

5. 关于环境影响评估已做出决定的办事程序，有关第14之4条第3款、第16条第3款和第17条第2款的各项规定只适用于负责公共卫生保障的部门。

6. 每个受邀与会的行政部门应指派一名授权代表参加协调会，并就其职权范围内的所有决定发表具有约束力的意见。

7. 在业务协调会上凡不明确表态者，或在收到最终决议后30天内未将符合情理的不同意见告知主办部门者，以及在同样期限内未对协调会做出的最终决议提出异议的与会者，其所代表的部门将被视为同意协调会的决议。

8. 在举行业务协调会期间，将要求项目申请人或设计者进行说明或提供补充文件。如无法在会上提供所需文件，应在此后30天内对所提交的文件重新审查。

9. 最终规定只要符合业务协调会所通过的最终决议，即可代替与会行政部门或收到与会邀请的部门在其权限内所给予的批准、特许、许可、放弃或许可证等。

10. 最终规定若涉及需要进行环境影响评估的工程项目，应与该评估意见概要一起公布于《官方公报》和全国性日报。如大区需进行环境评估，还应刊登于大区新闻公告上。自《官方公报》公布之日起，利益相关方进行司法控告的时限即行终止。

第14之4条：

1. 经常参加业务协调会的一个或若干部门代表，如有不同意见，须在协调会期间明确提出，否则将不予受理。所提意见应有充分依据和理由，并应包括为获得批准而对设计进行的修改做出详细说明，但不得涉及与业务协调会无关的问题。

2. 如果一个或若干部门代表在业务协调会上对主办部门的建议提出不同看法，该主办部门应根据多数与会者意见，在第14之3条第3款所规定的强制性期限内做出决议。决议一经产生即具有法律效力。

3. 如果负责国土环境和景观保护、历史和文化遗产保护或公共卫生保健等部门明确提出了不同意见，在提意见的部门或主办部门属国家行政部门的情况下，有关决议须提交内阁审议。在其他情况下，应提交国土管理职权部门审议。内阁或国土管理部门应在30天内做出决定。如对初步调查进行评估比较困难，内阁总理或大区会议主席以及省长、市长可将此期限延长，但不得超过60天。

4. 如果大区有不同意见，内阁根据第3款规定的权限做出决定应有大区会议主席的参与。为此，应向其发出与会邀请。大区主席可出席审议，但无表决权。

5. 如工程需进行环境影响评估，或会议做出否定性评估决议，得适用1999年7月

30 日第 303 号立法令第 12 条第 2 款采用的 1988 年 8 月 23 日第 400 号法律第 5 条第 2 款 c）之 2 项的规定。

——1986 年 7 月 8 日关于"环境部和环境损害法规"的第 349 号法律第 6 条，1986 年 7 月 15 日公布于第 162 期《官方公报》，规定如下：

第 6 条：

1. 在本法生效后 6 个月内，政府应向议会提交关于实施欧共体环境影响指令的法律草案。

2. 该欧共体指令一旦成为国家法律，内阁就应依据 1985 年 6 月 27 日颁布的第 85/337 号欧共体指令，根据环境部部长建议并征求科学委员会的意见，就适用于本条第 3、4、5 款规定的、可能对环境产生较大影响的工程项目的技术规范和类别做出决议。内阁总理将据此颁布命令加以确认。

3. 上述第 2 款所涉及的工程设计在获得批准前，为进行环境影响评估，应上报环境部和文化和环境遗产部，地方一级应上报大区。报告的内容应包括对工程地点、关于液体和固体废料以及环境污染和噪音排放等情况的详细说明，还应包括用于消除环境损害和对环境实施监测的装置的说明。报告的内容应公布在与工程有关的大区发行量最大的日报和全国性日报上。

4. 环境部经咨询相关大区的意见并与文化和环境遗产部取得一致意见后，应在 90 天期限内就环境状况提出评估意见。期满后工程设计的审批程序可恢复正常，除非内阁因特殊情况决定延长期限。对于那些涉及文化和景观保护方面的工程，环境部部长应与文化和环境遗产部部长取得一致意见后再做决定。

5. 如果负责工程实施的主管部不同意环境部所做的评估，问题应提交内阁决定。

6. 关于第 3 款规定所涉及的工程的实施，如环境部部长发现与第 4 款所述的环境兼容性意见有较大出入，或存在任何破坏生态和环境平衡基本要求的情况，应下令中止工程，并将问题提交内阁决定。

7. 文化和环境遗产部部长得就其职权内的事务行使权力。

8. 如发生 1985 年 6 月 27 日第 312 号法令第 1 之 2 条第 2 款规定以及经修改并入同年 8 月 8 日第 431 号法律规定所涉及的情况，文化和环境遗产部部长在与环境部部长取得一致意见后，应依据 1977 年 7 月 24 日颁布的第 616 号共和国总统令第 4 条和第 82 条规定行使权力。

9. 只要符合现行法律规定，任何公民都可以在环境影响评估报告公布后 30 天内，就涉及环境影响评估的工程问题，向环境部、文化和环境遗产部以及相关的大区提交书面的请愿书、评论或意见。

第 153 条注释：

——1992 年 4 月 30 日第 285 号立法令第 23 条第 4 款关于"高速路新法规"于同年 5 月 18 日公布于第 114 期《官方公报》。该法后经 1993 年 9 月 10 日第 360 号立法令第 13 条修订，同年 9 月 15 日公布于第 217 期《官方公报》增刊；经 1999 年 12 月 7 日第 472 号法律第 30 条再次修订，同年 12 月 16 日公布于 294 期《官方公报》增刊；后经 2003 年 6 月 27 日第 151 号立法令第 1 条再次修订，同年 6 月 30 日公布于第 149 期《官方公报》。该法经再次修订后，与 2003 年 8 月 1 日第 214 号法律合并，同年 8 月 12 日公布于 186 期《官方公报》。该款规定如下：

4．在道路旁或附近竖立大型广告牌或其他方式的广告装置，须得到依法拥有道路的部门的批准。在建筑群中心区内，如果道路属于国家、大区或省所有，在不损害所有权主体的技术性弃权情况下，其管辖权属于自治市。

第 156 条注释：

——1999 年 10 月 29 日第 490 号立法令关于"依照 1997 年 10 月 8 日第 352 号法律第 1 条对文化和环境财产立法规定进行汇编"的法律，同年 12 月 27 日公布于第 302 期《官方公报》增刊，第 149 条规定如下：

第 149 条（景观规划）：

1．为确保护景观和环境价值，大区应制定景观规划或城市土地规划，就与辖区内土地以及 146 条所述环境资产有关的环境利用和强化做出具体规定。

2．在第 140 条所列名单中的第 139 条 c）、d）两部分和 144 条所涉及的广袤土地而言，第 1 款所规定的景观规划是非强制性的。

3．如果大区未能贯彻第 1 款的规定，应依照 1977 年 7 月 24 日第 616 号共和国总统令第 4 条规定以及 1997 年 3 月 15 日修订的第 59 号法律第 8 条办理。

4．如果危及受本法保护的资产的价值，主管部长在与环境部部长和大区取得一致意见后，并在不违反第 164 条规定的前提下，可采取矫正或改进的措施。

第 157 条注释：

——关于 1922 年 6 月 11 日 778 号法律，参见第 128 条注释。

——1939 年 6 月 29 日第 1497 号关于"保护自然风光"的法律，同年 10 月 14 日公布于 241 期《官方公报》。

——1977 年 7 月 24 日第 616 号共和国总统令第 86 条关于"1975 年 7 月 22 日第 382 号法律第 1 条所述的授权条款的实施规定"，同年 8 月 29 日公布于第 234 期《官方公报》增刊。该条经 1985 年 6 月 27 日第 312 号法令第 1 条加以补充，同年 6 月 29 日公布于第 152 期《官方公报》。经再次修订后并入 1985 年 8 月 8 日第 431 号法律，同年 8 月 22 日公布于第 197 期《官方公报》。该条规定：

第 82 条（环境资产）：

中央政府及其下属机构应将自然风光的认定、保护及采取惩罚措施的行政职能授权给大区。

授权条款所涉及的行政职能有：

a) 对自然风光予以认定。但不得妨碍文化和环境部部长在咨询全国文化和环境遗产委员会意见后，将其列入经过大区批准的自然风光名录；

b) 批准和修改的职权；

c) 开发道路和采矿；

d) 安装大型广告牌和其他形式的广告设施；

e) 采取预防性措施，即便这些资产未列入相关名录；

f) 采取拆除和惩罚的措施；

g) 根据 1939 年 6 月 29 日第 1497 号法律第 2 条和 1975 年 12 月 3 日第 805 号共和国总统令第 31 条的规定，中央政府及其分支机构在各省设立的委员会的职权；

h) 1971 年 11 月 29 日第 1097 号法律规定的关于保护欧加内丘陵的授权。

依据 1939 年 6 月 29 日第 1497 号法律所发布的具有显著公共利益的自然与全景风光的公告，未经全国环境遗产委员会同意，不得撤销和中止。

当工程项目损害了可能被确定为自然风光的环境资产时，即使这些资产未列入保护名录，文化和自然遗产部部长仍有权禁止工程实施或下令暂停实施。

根据 1939 年 6 月 29 日第 1497 号法律规定，以下景区被列入限制开发范畴：

a) 拥有伸入水面 300 米的狭长地带的沿海地区，包括海面上的岛屿；

b) 拥有伸入水面 300 米的狭长地带的沿湖地区，包括湖面上的岛屿；

c) 根据 1933 年 12 月 11 日第 1775 号敕令批准的合并法规定列为自来水和发电厂用地的河流、溪流和水道及其两岸 150 米宽的堤岸或坝基；

d) 阿尔卑斯山脉海拔 1600 米以上地区，或亚平宁山脉海拔 1200 米以上地区及其岛屿；

e) 冰川和冰川谷地；

f) 属于国家和大区的公园和自然保护区，以及公园外围的保护区；

g) 森林和树木覆盖的地区，即使是受到火灾的破坏，以及限制植树造林的地区；

h）属于农业大学的地区和指定为民事用途的地区；

i）包括在 1976 年 3 月 13 日第 448 号共和国总统令所涉及名录中的湿地；

j）火山；

k）具有考古价值的地区。

前款所述限制令不适用于根据 1968 年 4 月 2 日第 1444 号部长令所制定的城市规划法确定的 A 类和 B 类地区以及仅为多年实施规划之一部分的其他地区。如市政当局无相应规定，限制令同样不适用于 1971 年 10 月 22 日第 865 号法律第 18 条确定的建筑群中心及其周边地区。

1939 年 6 月 29 日第 1497 号法律第 1 条 2）项所述的资产，即使处于前款所述地区，仍受到景观规定限制。

在本条第 5 款 g）项所述森林和树木地带允许进行下述活动：栽培植物的砍伐，造林和再造林，进行改造、防火和保护等符合相关现行法规规定并经批准的工作。

根据 1939 年 6 月 29 日第 1497 号法令第 7 条所做的授权须在 60 天的期限内决定是否批准。大区做出批准决定后，应立即通知文化和环境遗产部部长，并报送相关文件。如逾期不决，相关当事人可在 30 天内要求文化和环境遗产部部长予以批准，部长应在收到请求之日起 60 天内做出决定。在任何情况下，文化和环境遗产部部长可在接到通知之日起 60 天内，根据合理的条件，撤销大区做出的批准决定。

凡需要获得批准的工程涉及由国家行政部门负责实施的项目，文化和环境遗产部部长必须在 60 天内，根据 1939 年 6 月 29 日第 1497 号法律第 7 条的规定做出准予或不准的决定，即便该决定有悖于大区的决定。

关于 1927 年 7 月 29 日第 1443 号敕令所述的搜寻和挖掘活动，文化和环境遗产部部长可根据上述第 9 款的规定，在咨询工业、商业和工艺部部长后予以批准。

那些不改变遗址状况或建筑外观的普通或特殊的维护、加固和保护性修复工程，不必按 1939 年 6 月 29 日第 1497 号法律第 7 条的规定得到批准。那些不改变建筑结构条件的农业、林业和畜牧业活动或其他民用工程，只要这些活动和工程不改变国土的水文地质系统，也不必得到批准。

对本条第 5 款所述限制开发活动的监督工作，应由文化和环境遗产部所属机构负责进行。

——关于 1999 年 10 月 29 日第 490 号立法令，请参见前言注释。

第 158 条注释：

——1940 年 6 月 3 日第 1357 号敕令关于"1939 年 6 月 29 日第 1497 号法律实施条例"，

同年 10 月 5 日公布于第 234 期《官方公报》。

第 159 条注释：

——关于 1990 年 8 月 7 日第 241 号法律，请参见第 146 条注释。

——1994 年 6 月 13 日第 495 号部长令关于"1990 年 8 月 7 日第 241 号法律第 2 条和第 4 条关于程序的时限和官方报告的实施条例"，同年 8 月 11 日公布于第 187 期《官方公报》增刊。经 2002 年 6 月 19 日第 165 号部长令第 3 条修订，同年 8 月 2 日公布于第 180 期《官方公报》。该条例规定如下：

第 6 条（程序性时限）：

1. 程序结束的时限是指条款的采纳日期，如果条款必须在相关人士申明收到后才能生效，该时限是指接受者接到通知的日期。

2. 在程序进行中的某些阶段涉及文化和环境遗产部以外的行政部门的权限，但不属于 1990 年 8 月 7 日第 241 号法律第 16 和 17 条规定的情况，此时的程序性时限应将这些部门办结所需时间计算在内。为此目的，上述各部门应在本条例生效后 60 天内，共同核实各自所确定的时限在整个程序的最后期限内是否与其阶段的完成一致。如发现有差异，文化和环境遗产部应根据条例规定的形式进行调整，除非法律对此另有规定。

3. 第 1 款和第 2 款规定之期限为最长时限，即使该期限已过，行政部门仍有义务及时迅速办理，除非不守时限带来了其他后果。

4. 当需要对主办部门的办理情况进行预防性检查时，完成办理程序的期限不包括条款实施的整合所需时间。作为对接受检查的行为的补充，主办部门应指定某个机构负责进行检查，并确定检查的时限。该机构应在确定的时限内行使职权。

5. 除非另行确定时限，为主要程序所确定的时间期限同样适用于更改先前发布的命令。

6. 如果法律规定有关当事人提交的申请从其提交后一段期间届满就被视为批准或不批准，那么法律或条例所确定的时限就构成了"缄默即批准"或"缄默即拒绝"，也应成为行政部门做决定时应遵守的时限。如果法律规定了新情况，或者为"缄默即批准"或"缄默及拒绝"规定了新时限，那么列在附表中的时限就应视情况加以合并或修改。

6 之 2. 在初步调查阶段，如需澄清问题和补充材料，或技术性核实，主管部门应立即通知第 4 条第 1 款所涉及的部门，以及提供补充材料的行政部门。因此，办案时限应予中止，只能中止一次，时间自通知之日起不超过 30 天。同时，在收到有关文件或获得技术性核实结果后，时限重新起算。

——1985 年 6 月 27 日第 312 号法令第 1 之 5 条关于"补充 1977 年 7 月 24 日第 616 号共和国总统令第 82 条的保护具有特殊环境价值地区的紧急规定"，6 月 29 日公布于第 152 期《官方公报》。后经修订并入 1985 年 8 月 8 日第 431 号法律，8 月 22 日公布于第 197 期《官方公报》。该条规定：

第 1 之 5 条：

1. 1984 年 9 月 26 日公布于的第 265 期《官方公报》的 1984 年 9 月 21 日部长令第 2 条所述地区和财产，在大区采纳前述第 1 之 2 条所指规划之前，属于禁止改变土地组织和进行建筑工程的范畴，除非是那些不改变遗址条件和建筑外观的普通或特别的维护、加固和保护性修缮工程。

第 162 条注释：

——关于 1992 年 4 月 30 日第 285 号立法令第 23 条，参见第 153 条注释。

第 166 条注释：

——关于 1992 年 12 月 9 日第 3911/92 号欧共体理事会条例，参见第 71 条注释。

——1993 年 3 月 30 日第 752/93 号欧共体委员会条例关于"文化财产出口的第 3911/92 号欧共体理事会条例的实施条例"，同年 5 月 20 日公布于第 39 期《官方公报》第 2 系列。经 1998 年 7 月 16 日第 1526/98 号欧共体委员会条例修订，同年 11 月 5 日公布于第 87 期《官方公报》第 2 系列。

第 168 条注释：

——关于 1992 年 4 月 30 日第 285 号立法令第 23 条的内容，参见第 153 条注释。

第 180 条注释：

——1930 年 10 月 19 日第 1398 号敕令批准的《刑法典》，10 月 26 日公布于第 251 期《官方公报》。该法第 650 条规定如下：

第 650 条（违反法律规定）：

任何人如果违反了基于正义和公共安全、秩序和卫生而制定的法律规定，如果不构成更严重的罪行，应处以 3 个月以上的监禁和不超过 40 万里拉的罚款。

第 181 条注释：

——1985 年 2 月 28 日第 47 号法律"关于控制城市规划和建筑及对建筑工程的惩处、抢救和矫正的规定"，同年 3 月 2 日公布于第 53 期《官方公报》。经 1985 年 4 月 23 日第 146 号法令第 7 之 2 条修订，4 月 24 日公布于第 97 期《官方公报》。后经再次修订合并成为 1985 年 6 月 21 日第 298 号法令，同年 6 月 22 日公布于第 146 期《官方公报》。该法第 20 条规定如下：

第 20 条（刑罚）：

在违法行为不构成更严重的罪行并保留行政处罚权的前提下，可适用下列刑罚：

　a）凡违反本法和 1942 年 8 月 17 日第 1150 号法律及其后的修订和补充规定的可适用部分，以及违反建筑条例、城市规划和特许授权规定的指示和实施方案，处以最高达 2000 万里拉的罚款；

　b）对于完全不符合特许授权的工程实施，或未经特许授权擅自施工，或者在收到停工令后仍继续施工等行为，将处以最高达两年的监禁，并处 1000 万到 1 亿里拉的罚款；

　c）凡违反第 18 条第 1 款的规定出于建筑目的非法分配土地的行为，处以最高达两年的监禁和 3000 万至 1 亿里拉的罚款。在受施工限制的历史、艺术、考古景观或环保区域实施工程建筑，基本或完全不符合特许规定或根本没有特许授权擅自施工的行为，也适用同样的刑罚。

前款规定取代了 1977 年 1 月 28 日第 10 号法律第 17 条的规定。

第 182 条注释：

——2000 年 8 月 3 日第 294 号部长令"关于实施可移动文化财产的修复、维修和建筑财产外观装饰的专业资质认定条例"，同年 10 月 20 日公布于第 246 期《官方公报》。后被 2001 年 10 月 24 日第 420 号部长令取代，同年 12 月 1 日公布于第 280 期《官方公报》。其第 7 条规定如下：

第 7 条（文化财产的修复者）：

1. 依据本条例以及 1999 年 12 月 21 日第 554 号共和国总统令第 224 条的规定，文化财产的修复者是指，拥有 1998 年 10 月 20 日第 367 号立法令第 9 条所规定的国家修复专科学校毕业证书，该校学习课程不少于 4 年，或拥有历史艺术遗产保护和修复专业的大学学位的人。

2. 自本条例生效之日起，文化财产的修复者也指如下人员：

　　a) 拥有属于国家或大区的修复专科学校两年以上学习文凭，并亲自参与个人财产修复工程的人。或哪些直接参与修复工程管理的长期雇员或有长期合同关系的人，这些人应经常参与实施经由负责财产保护和外观装饰的权威部门认证的工程施工，参与施工的时间应为在校学习时间的两倍以上，或者最低不得少于两年；

　　b) 亲自参与上述财产修复工程实施的人，或那些直接参与修复工程管理的长期雇员或有长期合同关系的人，他们参与实施经由负责财产保护和外观装饰的权威部门认证的工程施工的时间应不少于 8 年时间；

　　c) 拥有国家或大区的修复专科学校两年以上学习文凭的人，或那些亲自参与动产修复或外观装饰工程的时间不少于 4 年的人，或那些直接参与修复工程管理的长期雇员或有长期合同关系的人。这些人应经常参与实施经由负责财产保护的权威部门认证的工程施工，并获得资质认证，或完成了根据 2001 年 12 月 31 日颁布的文化遗产和活动部部长令所规定的课程培训者。

——关于《意大利共和国宪法》第 117 条的内容，参见前言注释。

第 183 条注释：

——1994 年 1 月 14 日第 29 号法律第 3 条"关于审计法院的司法管辖和审计的规定"，同日公布于第 10 期《官方公报》。经 1996 年 10 月 23 日第 543 号立法第 2 条修订，同日公布于第 249 期《官方公报》。后经再次修订并入 1996 年 12 月 20 日第 639 号法律，同年 12 月 21 日公布于第 299 期《官方公报》。后又经 1998 年 3 月 31 日通过、同年 4 月 8 日公布的第 80 号立法令第 43 条的修改，经 2000 年 11 月 24 日通过、当日公布的第 340 号法律第 27 条的修改，经 2000 年 12 月 23 日通过、12 月 29 日公布的第 388 号法律第 49 条的修改，以及 2001 年 3 月 30 日通过、5 月 9 日公布的第 165 号立法令第 72 条的修改。第 3 条规定如下：

第 3 条（审计法院的审计条例）：

1. 审计法院专门针对以下尚未产生法律效力的措施依法进行合法性的预先审查：

　　a) 内阁经慎重考虑所采取的措施；

　　b) 内阁总理的决定，以及涉及确定机构编制计划、行政管理职务的任命、政策指导和行政行为的实施的部委决定；

　　c) 有对外影响的条例措施，涉及实施欧共体条例所需的开支和行动的规划决定；

　　d) 部际委员会的决定，或资金的分配，或就 b)、c) 项所述事项所作的决定。

e）[已废除];

f）处置国家财产和不动产的措施;

g）下列合同的批准令:不包括公共公司在内的国家行政部门所签合同;与 1923 年 11 月 18 日第 2440 号敕令第 19 条第 1 款所假设情况无关的任何价值 的资产;合同金额以欧洲货币单位计算超过欧共体关于合同判定程序实施条 例所确定的价值的政府商品采购和服务合同;价格超过上述条款所述价值十 分之一的其他债务合同;

h）关于国家预算变更、预算平衡的评估和财政部关于将当年支出列入下年度的 先期意见的命令;

i）根据部长书面命令启动的行为;

j）内阁总理认为需要临时预先检查的行为,或在一段确定时间内,依据事后发 现的违规行为的影响和性质,由审计法院决定进行预先审查的行为。

2．如果主管审查的机构在收到后 30 天内未将有关规定转交审查部门,那么待审查 的规定将生效。但如果主管机构要求进行澄清或提供补充材料以便做出判断, 则应中止上述时限。如果收到行政部门的反对意见 30 天后,主管机构未将有关 规定转交审查部门,待审查的规定将生效。审查部门应自规定转交之日起或自 收到司法令要求提供的材料之日起 30 天内,依法做出裁定。期限一到,待审查 的规定即产生效力。

3．审计法院的审查部门应依据基本原则,在各部门全体会上做出决定,分门别类 确定或由国家行政部门认定的、非常重要的财政措施,逐一提交法院,以便在 一定期限内进行审查。审计法院可在收到措施后 15 天内要求重审,在此期间措 施仍有效。行政部门应将重新审查后所采取的措施提交审计法院,法院如发现 有违规情况,应通报行政部门。

4．即使仍在财政年度当年,审计法院仍应对公共管理部门的预算和资产、预算外 活动和欧共体所提供资金等方面的管理情况做进一步审查,以便查清管理的合 法性和正当性,以及每个行政部门内部审查的有效性。同时,在其他审查的基 础上,通过对实施行政行为的成本、手段和时间所进行的评估、核实行政作为 的结果是否符合法律确定的目标。审计法院每年都应确定审查计划和参照标准。

5．就大区的行政管理而言,审查的内容包括是否与涉及基本原则和规划的法律所 确定的目标一致。

6．审计法院每年至少应向议会和大区委员会报告一次审计的结果。法院的审计报 告也要送交相关行政部门,并在适当场合就这些部门的情况发表意见。行政部 门应向法院和选举机构通报其所采取的改进措施。

7．就地方部门而言,经 1982 年 2 月 26 日第 51 号法律修订合并的 1981 年 12 月 22

日第 786 号法令，以及随后的修订和增补规定依然有效。1958 年 3 月 21 日第 259 号法律中有关那些通常由国家赞助的部门的规定亦然。审计法院的报告应包括内部审查之有效性评估。

8. 审计法院在行使本条规定所赋予的权力时，可要求行政部门或内部审查机构提供任何文件或信息，也可直接或下令进行审查和评估。1993 年 11 月 15 日第 453 号法令第 2 条第 4 款的规定适用于此问题。审计法院可要求管辖区以外的公共行政部门对认为是违规的行为重审。行政部门应向审计法院提交其在重新审查后所采取的措施，法院则应告知综合管理机构所查出的违规情况。1993 年 2 月 3 日第 29 号立法令及其后续修订、1993 年 2 月 13 日第 39 号立法令和 1980 年 7 月 11 日第 312 号法律第 166 条均有额外增加审查的规定，这些法律规定只要与本法规定不相抵触即可适用。

9. 关于审计法院的法律汇编是根据 1934 年 7 月 12 日第 1214 号敕令及此后的多次修订而颁布实施的，在行使审查权过程中，该汇编有关程序规则只要与本法规定不抵触，即可适用。

10. 审查机关的人员组成：作为该机构的负责人的审计法院院长、负责协调工作的部门负责人和所有被赋予审查任务的法官。该机构下设 4 个委员会，审计法院院长和部门领导是当然委员。各委员会按不同审查类型或具体事件划分权限，至少要有 11 名成员参加表决才能作决定。全体会议由审计法院院长主持，组成人员包括各协调部门负责人和 35 名负责审查工作的法官。法官人选每年由主席团确定，所依据的原则是：每个委员会至少出 3 名法官，每一个大区以及特伦托、博尔扎诺自治省负责行政审计的部门至少出 1 名法官。全会须由 21 名成员表决方能做出决定。

10 之 2. 审查机构每年举行全会时，应确定行动计划、各委员会的工作和责任，以及包括审计法院院长在内的各委员会的人员组成标准。

11. 关于审计法院的法律汇编第 24 条已被 1953 年 3 月 21 日第 161 号法律第 1 条所代替，根据该法所提供的可能性，如果主审法官之间对行为的合法性看法出现分歧，审查部门应做出裁决。提出仲裁要求的法官应参与有关裁决的会议。

12. 被要求根据第 4 款规定进行额外审查的法官，应依据年度工作计划开展工作。但如需进行及时评估或核查有关情况和措施，法官可依据充分理由暂不考虑年度计划，但要报告审查部门。

13. 上述第 1 款有关规定不适用于与货币、信贷、动产和现金有关的行为和措施。

——1978 年 8 月 5 日第 468 号法令"关于对国家预算公共会计的部分条例进行改革"，8 月 22 日公布于第 233 期《官方公报》，其第 13 条规定如下：

第 13 条（政府担保）：

　　国家给予政府机构和其他主体的基本担保和辅助担保的名单列入财政部预算附录。

第 184 条注释：

——1939 年 6 月 1 日第 1089 号法律关于"保护具有艺术和历史价值的文物"，同年 8 月 8 日公布于第 184 期《官方公报》。

——1963 年 9 月 30 日第 1409 号共和国总统令关于"国家档案馆的组织和职员的条例"，同年 10 月 31 日公布于第 285 期《官方公报》。

——1972 年 1 月 14 日第 3 号共和国总统令关于"将支持学校、地方博物馆和图书馆及其职员和办事机构的政府行政职能转让给大区"，同年 1 月 19 日公布于第 15 期《官方公报》。

——1997 年 5 月 15 日第 127 号法律关于"提高行政管理、决策和审查程序效率的紧急措施"，同年 5 月 17 日公布于第 113 号《官方公报》增刊。

——1997 年 10 月 8 日第 352 号法律关于"文化财产条例"，同年 10 月 17 日公布于第 243 期《官方公报》增刊。

——1998 年 3 月 31 日第 112 号立法令关于"为实施 1997 年 3 月 15 日第 59 号法律第 1 章的规定，将国家行政职能和任务转让给大区和地方部门"，同年 4 月 21 日公布于第 92 期《官方公报》增刊。

——1999 年 7 月 12 日第 237 号法关于"建立当代艺术文献资料和强化中心、建立新博物馆、修订文化财产立法和文化活动措施"，同年 7 月 26 日公布于第 173 号《官方公报》。

——1999 年 7 月 30 日第 281 号立法关于"以历史、统计和科学研究为目的的个人数据的处理规定"，同年 8 月 16 日公布于第 191 期《官方公报》。

——关于 1999 年 10 月 29 日第 490 号立法令，参见前言注释。

——2000 年 9 月 7 日第 283 号共和国总统令关于"转让国家历史和艺术财产的不动产法律的条例"，同年 10 月 13 日公布于第 240 期《官方公报》。

——2003 年 6 月 30 日 196 号立法令关于"个人数据保护法典"，同年 7 月 29 日公布于第 174 期《官方公报》增刊。

——2003 年 7 月 8 日第 172 号法律关于"重新组织和重新推广娱乐性航海和海上旅游的规定"，7 月 14 日公布于第 161 期《官方公报》。

编 后 记

2006 年 1 月，国家文物局和意大利文化遗产与艺术活动部签署《关于文化遗产保护合作的谅解备忘录》，进一步加强中意两国在文化遗产保护领域的合作与交流。2008 年 1 月，意大利文化遗产与艺术活动部向我局提供了《意大利文化与景观遗产法典》英文版资料。意大利作为文化遗产保护管理具有代表性的国家之一，其法律法规对我国文化遗产保护管理有着重要的借鉴意义。为更好地介绍意大利文化遗产法律实践成果，国家文物局组织专业机构、法律专家进行翻译和审校，由文物出版社出版《意大利文化与景观遗产法典》中英文版。希望此书能为我国文化遗产法制建设提供有益的经验和启示。

此书翻译和审校过程中，北京信达雅翻译有限责任公司、中国人民大学法学院文化遗产法研究所的专家付出了辛勤的劳动，意大利驻华大使馆对译稿校核也提供了有益的帮助，在此一并表示真诚的感谢。

国家文物局

2009 年 8 月

LEGISLATIVE DECREE no. 42 of 22 January 2004

CODE OF THE CULTURAL AND LANDSCAPE HERITAGE

Ministero per i beni e le attività culturali

Roma , Giugno 2004

LAWS AND OTHER REGULATORY ACTS

LEGISLATIVE DECREE no. 42 of 22 January 2002

Code of the Cultural and Landscape Heritage, pursuant to article 10 of law no. 137 of 6 July 2002

THE PRESIDENT OF THE REPUBLIC

Having regard to articles 76, 87, 117 and 118 of the Constitution;

Having regard to article 14 of law no. 400 of 23 August 1988;

Having regard to legislative decree no. 368 of 20 October 1998, establishing the Ministry for Cultural Heritage and Activities, in accordance with article 11 of law no. 59 of 15 March 1997, and subsequent modifications and additions;

Having regard to legislative decree no. 490 of 29 October 1999, containing the consolidated text of the legislative provisions pertaining to the cultural and environmental heritage, in accordance with article 1 of law no. 352 of 8 October 1997;

Having regard to article 10 of law no. 137 of 6 July 2002;

Having regard to the preliminary resolution of the Council of Ministers adopted in the meeting of 29 September 2003;

Having obtained the opinion of the Unified Conference, established under legislative decree no. 281 of 28 August 1997;

Having obtained the opinion of the competent Commissions of the Senate of the Republic and of the Chamber of Deputies;

Having regard to the resolution of the Council of Ministers, adopted in the meeting of 16 January 2004;

On the recommendation of the Minister for Cultural Heritage and Activities, in accord with the Minister for Regional Affairs;

EMANATES

the following legislative decree:

Art. 1

1. The consolidated code of the cultural and landscape heritage, composed of 184 articles and annex A is approved, with the endorsement of the recommending Minister.
This decree, affixed with the State Seal, will be included in the Official Collection of the regulatory acts of the Italian Republic. All persons who are obliged to do so, must abide by it and ensure that it is complied with.

Dated at Rome, 22 January 2004

CIAMPI

BERLUSCONI, *President of the Council of Ministers*
URBANI, *Minister for Cultural Heritage and Activities*
LA LOGGIA, *Minister for Regional Affairs*

APPROVED, Minister of Justice: CASTELLI

FIRST PART
GENERAL PROVISIONS

Article 1
Principles

1. In implementation of article 9 of the Constitution, the Republic shall protect and enhance the cultural heritage in accordance with the powers set out in article 117 of the Constitution and according to the provisions of this Code.

2. The protection and enhancement of the cultural heritage shall concur to preserve the memory of the national community and its territory and to promote the development of culture.

3. The State, the Regions, the Metropolitan Areas, the Provinces and Municipalities shall ensure and sustain the conservation of the cultural heritage and foster its public enjoyment and enhancement.

4. Other public bodies shall, in carrying out their activities, ensure the conservation and the public enjoyment of their cultural heritage.

5. Private owners, possessors or holders of property belonging to the cultural heritage must ensure its conservation.

6. The activities concerning the conservation, public enjoyment and enhancement of the cultural heritage indicated in paragraphs 3, 4 and 5 shall be carried out in accordance with the laws on protection.

Article 2
Cultural Heritage

1. The cultural heritage consists of cultural property and landscape assets.

2. Cultural property consists of immovable and movable things which, pursuant to articles 10 and 11, present artistic, historical, archaeological, ethno-anthropological, archival and bibliographical interest, and of any other thing identified by law or in accordance with the law as testifying to the values of civilisation.

3. Landscape assets consist of the buildings and areas indicated in article 134, which are the expression of historical, cultural, natural, morphological and aesthetic values of the land, and any other assets identified by law or in accordance with the law.

4. Cultural heritage property belonging to the government shall be designated for public enjoyment, compatibly with the needs of government use and on condition that no

protection reasons to the contrary persist.

Article 3
Protection of the Cultural Heritage

1. Protection consists in the exercise of the functions and in the regulation of the activities aimed at identifying, on the basis of adequate investigative procedures, the properties constituting the cultural heritage and at ensuring the protection and conservation of the aforesaid heritage for purposes of public enjoyment.

2. Protection functions are also carried out by means of provisions aimed at conforming or regulating rights and behaviour inherent to the cultural heritage.

Article 4
Functions of the State in the Protection of the Cultural Heritage

1. In order to ensure the unified exercise of the functions of protection, under article 118 of the Constitution, the same functions are attributed to the Ministry for Cultural Heritage and Activities, hereinafter referred to as "Ministry", which shall exercise the aforesaid functions directly. It may also confer their exercise on the Regions, through forms of agreement and co-ordination pursuant to article 5, paragraphs 3 and 4. Functions which have already been conferred on the Regions under paragraphs 2 and 6 of the same article 5 shall not be affected.

2. The Ministry shall exercise the functions of protection on cultural property belonging to the State even when such property has been placed under the care of or granted in use to administrations or subjects other than the Ministry.

Article 5
Co-operation of the Regions and of Other Territorial Government Bodies in the Protection of the Cultural Heritage

1. The Regions as well as Municipalities, Metropolitan Areas and Provinces, hereinafter referred to as "other territorial government bodies", shall co-operate with the Ministry in the exercise of its protection functions in accordance with the provisions of Title I of the Second Part of this Code.

2. The protection functions provided for by this Code concerning manuscripts, autographs, papers, documents, incunabula, and book collections not belonging to the State and not subject to State protection, as well as books, prints and engravings not belonging to the State, shall be exercised by the Regions.

3. On the basis of specific agreements or arrangements and subject to the prior opinion of the Permanent Conference for Relations between the State, the Regions and the autonomous provinces of Trento and Bolzano, hereinafter referred to as "State-Regions Conference", the Regions may also exercise the functions of protection on private book collections, as well as geographical maps, musical scores, photographs, films or other audio-visual material, with the relative negatives and matrixes, not belonging to the State.

4. In the forms provided for in paragraph 3 and on the basis of the principles of differentiation and suitability, additional forms of co-ordination with the Regions which request it with regard to protection may be identified.

5. Agreements or arrangements may provide for particular forms of co-operation with other local government bodies.

6. The administrative functions for the protection of landscape assets shall be conferred on the Regions according to the provisions set out in the Third Part of this Code.

7. With regard to the functions referred to in paragraphs 2, 3, 4, 5 and 6, the Ministry shall have the power to direct and supervise, and shall have substitutive power in cases of persistent inaction and non-fulfilment of tasks and responsibilities.

Article 6
Enhancement of the Cultural Heritage

1. Enhancement consists in the exercise of the functions and in the regulation of the activities aimed at promoting knowledge of the cultural heritage and at ensuring the best conditions for the utilization and public enjoyment of the same heritage. Enhancement also includes the promotion and the support of conservation work on the cultural heritage.

2. Enhancement is carried out in forms which are compatible with protection and which are such as not to prejudice its exigencies.

3. The Republic shall foster and sustain the participation of private subjects, be they single individuals or associations, in the enhancement of the cultural heritage.

Article 7

Functions and Tasks relating to the Enhancement of the Cultural Heritage

1. This Code establishes the fundamental principles concerning the enhancement of the cultural heritage. The Regions shall exercise their legislative powers in compliance with these principles.

2. The Ministry, the Regions and the other local government bodies shall pursue the co-ordination, harmonisation, and integration of the activities for the enhancement of public property.

Article 8

Regions and Provinces with Special Autonomy

1. In the matters regulated by this Code, the powers attributed to the special statute Regions and the autonomous provinces of Trento and Bolzano by statute law and by the relevant implementation regulations, shall remain in effect.

Article 9

Cultural Property of Religious Interest

1. The Ministry and, where applicable, the Regions shall attend to the exigencies of cultural property of religious interest belonging to bodies and institutions of the Catholic Church and of other religious denominations, according to the needs of worship, and in agreement with the respective authorities.

2. Likewise, the provisions established in the agreements concluded under article 12 of the Agreement for the Modification of the Lateran Agreement signed on February 18, 1984, ratified and made enforceable with law no. 121 of 25 March 1985, or by the laws issued on the basis of agreements underwritten with religious denominations other than the Catholic Church, under article 8, paragraph 3 of the Constitution, shall also be complied with.

SECOND PART
CULTURAL PROPERTY

TITLE I
PROTECTION

Chapter I
Object of Protection

Article 10
Cultural Property

1. Cultural property consists in immovable and movable things belonging to the State, the Regions, other territorial government bodies, as well as any other public body and institution, and to private non-profit associations, which possess artistic, historical, archaeological or ethno-anthropological interest.

2. Cultural property also includes:

   a) the collections of museums, picture galleries, art galleries and other exhibition venues of the State, the Regions, other territorial government bodies, as well as any other government body and institute;

   b) the archives and single documents of the State, the Regions, other territorial government bodies, as well as of any other government body and institute;

   c) the book collections of libraries of the State, Regions, other territorial government bodies, as well as any other government body and institute.

3. Cultural property shall also include the following, when the declaration provided for in article 13 has been made:

   a) immovable and movable things of particularly important artistic, historical, archaeological or ethno-anthropological interest, which belong to subjects other than those indicated in paragraph 1;

   b) archives and single documents, belonging to private individuals, which are of particularly important historical interest;

   c) book collections, belonging to private individuals, of exceptional cultural interest;

   d) immovable and movable things, to whomsoever they may belong, which are of particularly important interest because of their reference to political or military history, to the history of literature, art and culture in general, or as testimony to the identity and history of public, collective or religious institutions;

e) collections or series of objects, to whomsoever they may belong, which through tradition, renown and particular environmental characteristics are as a whole of exceptional artistic or historical interest.

4. The things indicated in paragraph 1 and paragraph 3, letter *a*) include:

   a) the things which pertain to palaeontology, prehistory and primitive civilisations;

   b) things of numismatic interest;

   c) manuscripts, autographs, papers, incunabula, as well as books, prints and engravings with their relative matrixes, of a rare or precious nature;

   d) geographical maps and musical scores of a rare and precious nature;

   e) photographs, with their relative negatives and matrixes, cinematographic films and audio-visual supports in general, of a rare and precious nature;

   f) villas, parks and gardens possessing artistic or historical interest;

   g) public squares, streets, roads and other outdoor urban spaces of artistic or historical interest;

   h) mineral sites of historical or ethno-anthropological interest;

   i) ships and floats possessing artistic, historical or ethno-anthropological interest;

   j) types of rural architecture possessing historical or ethno-anthropological interest as testimony to the rural economy tradition.

5. Without prejudice to the provisions of articles 64 and 178, the things indicated in paragraph 1 and paragraph 3, letters *a*) and *e*), which are the work of living authors or which were not produced more than fifty years ago, are not subject to this Title.

Article 11

Property Subject to Specific Protection Provisions

1. Without prejudice to the application of article 10, the following shall, whenever the premises and conditions occur, be considered cultural property, insofar as they are the object of specific provisions of this Title:

   a) frescoes, escutcheons, graffiti, plaques, inscriptions, tabernacles and other building ornaments, whether or not they be exhibited to public view, referred to in article 50, paragraph 1;

b) artists' studios, referred to in article 51;

c) public areas referred to in article 52;

d) works of painting, sculpture, graphic art and any art created by a living author or which was not produced more than fifty years ago, referred to in articles 64 and 65;

e) the works of contemporary architecture of particular artistic value, referred to in article 37;

f) photographs, with their relative negatives and matrixes, samples of cinematographic works, audio-visual material or sequences of images in movement, the documentation of events, oral or verbal, produced by any means, more than twenty-five years ago, referred to in article 65;

g) means of transport which are more than seventy-five years old, referred to in articles 65 and 67, paragraph 2;

h) property and instruments of interest for the history of science and technology which are more than fifty years old, referred to in article 65;

i) the vestiges identified by the laws in force pertaining to the protection of the historical heritage of World War I, referred to in article 50, paragraph 2.

Article 12
Verification of Cultural Interest

1. Immovable and movable things indicated in article 10, paragraph 1, which are the work of artists who are no longer living and which were produced more than fifty years ago, shall be subject to the provisions of this Title until such time as the verification referred to in paragraph 2 has been carried out.

2. The competent organs of the Ministry shall, ex officio or upon request accompanied by the relative identifying information made by the parties to whom the things belong, verify the presence of artistic, historical, archaeological and ethno-anthropological interest in the things indicated in paragraph 1, on the basis of guidelines of a general nature established by the Ministry itself in order to ensure uniformity of assessment.

3. For immovable property belonging to the State, the request referred to in paragraph 2 shall include lists of the properties and the relative descriptive information sheets. The criteria for the preparation of the lists, the modalities for drawing up the descriptive information sheets and the transmission of lists and information sheets shall be established by means of a ministerial decree adopted in accord with the State Property Agency and,

for buildings granted in use to the Defence administration, also in agreement with the competent directorates general for works and State property. The Ministry shall, with its own decrees, fix the criteria and the procedures for the preparation and submission of the request for verification and of the relative identifying documentation, on the part of the other parties referred to in paragraph 1.

4. Should the interest mentioned in paragraph 2 not be found in the things subjected to verification, the same things shall be excluded from the application of the provisions of this Title.

5. In the case of a negative assessment for things belonging to the State, the Regions and other territorial government bodies, the file containing the relative information shall be forwarded to the competent offices so that they may order the release of the property from State ownership, should, according to the assessment of the administration concerned, no other reasons persist to the contrary in the public interest.

6. The things referred to in paragraph 3 and those referred to in paragraph 4 for which release from public ownership has been ordered may, for the purposes of this Code, be freely alienated.

7. The ascertainment of artistic, historical, archaeological or ethno-anthropological interest, carried out in accordance with the general guidelines referred to in paragraph 2, shall constitute declaration under article 13, and the relative measure shall be registered in the manner provided for by article 15, paragraph 2. The properties shall remain definitively subject to the provisions of this Title.

8. The descriptive information sheets for immovable properties belonging to the State which have been assessed positively, along with the measure referred to in paragraph 7, shall be stored in a computerised archive accessible to the Ministry and the State Property Agency, for the purposes of monitoring immovable property assets and planning work according to their respective institutional competences.

9. The provisions of this article shall apply to the things referred to in paragraph 1 even when the subjects to whom they belong in any way change their legal status.

10. The provisions of article 27, paragraphs 8, 10, 12, 13 and 13-*bis*, of decree law no. 269 of 30 September 2003, converted, with modifications into law no. 326 of 24 November 2003, shall remain in force.

Article 13
Declaration of Cultural Interest

1. The declaration shall ascertain the existence, in the thing in question, of the interest required under article 10, paragraph 3.
2. The declaration is not required for properties referred to in article 10, paragraph 2. Such properties remain subject to protection even when the subjects to whom they belong in any way change their legal status.

Article 14
Declaration Procedure

1. The superintendent shall initiate the procedure for the declaration of cultural interest, and may also do so in response to a motivated request from the Region or any other interested territorial government body, notifying the proprietor, possessor or holder, by whatever legal right, of the thing in question.
2. The notification shall contain the elements for the identification and assessment of the thing resulting from preliminary investigations, the indication of the effects referred to in paragraph 4, as well as the indication of the time limit, which in any case may be no less than thirty days, for the presentation of any observations.
3. If the procedure concerns building complexes, the notification shall also be forwarded to the Municipality or Metropolitan Area.
4. Notification shall, as a preventive measure, entail the application of the provisions set out in Chapter II, in Section I of Chapter III, and in Section I of Chapter IV of this Title.
5. The effects indicated in paragraph 4 shall cease upon expiry of the time limit for the declaration procedure, which the Ministry shall establish in accordance with article 2, paragraph 2 of law no. 241 of 7 August 1990.
6. The declaration of cultural interest shall be adopted by the Ministry.

Article 15
Notification of Declaration

1. The declaration provided for under article 13 shall be notified to the owner, possessor or

holder, by whatever legal right, of the thing in question, by a process server or by means of registered letter with receipt of delivery notification.

2. Where things subject to public notice with regard to immovable or movable property are concerned, the declaration measure shall, at the request of the superintendent, be recorded in the relative registers and shall have efficacy for any subsequent owner, possessor or holder by whatever legal right.

Article 16
Administrative Appeal against Declaration

1. Appeal against the declaration referred to in article 13 may be made to the Ministry, on grounds concerning legitimacy or the merits, within thirty days of the declaration notification.

2. The proposition of appeal shall entail the suspension of the effects of the measure contested. As a precautionary measure, the application of the provisions established under Chapter II, under Section I of Chapter III and under Section I of Chapter IV of this Title shall remain in force.

3. After consulting the competent advisory body, the Ministry shall rule on the appeal within the time limit of ninety days from receipt of the same.

4. Should the appeal be granted, the Ministry shall annul or modify the contested measure.

5. The provisions of decree no. 1199 of the President of the Republic of 24 November 1971 shall apply.

Article 17
Cataloguing

1. With the participation of the Regions and other territorial government bodies, the Ministry shall ensure the cataloguing of cultural property and shall co-ordinate related activities.

2. The procedures and modalities for cataloguing shall be established by ministerial decree. To this end, the Ministry shall, with the collaboration of the Regions, identify and define common methodologies for gathering, exchanging, accessing and processing data at the national level and for the computerised integration of the same into the databanks of the State, the Regions and other territorial government bodies.

3. The Ministry and the Regions, which may also avail themselves of the collaboration of universities, shall work together for the definition of programmes concerning studies, research and scientific initiatives regarding cataloguing and inventory methodologies.

4. Following the modalities set out in the Ministerial decree referred to in paragraph 2, the Ministry, the Regions and other territorial government bodies shall be responsible for cataloguing the cultural property in their possession and, in agreement with the proprietors, other cultural property as well.

5. The data referred to in this article shall be gathered into the national catalogue of cultural properties.

6. The consultation of the information concerning the declarations issued in accordance with article 13 shall be regulated so as to guarantee the safety of the property and the safeguarding of confidentiality.

Chapter II
Supervision and Inspection

Article 18
Supervision

1. The supervision of cultural property is the task of the Ministry.

2. The supervision of the things indicated in article 12, paragraph 1, belonging to the State, irrespective of the party holding them in use or having them in their care, shall be carried out directly by the Ministry. For the exercise of supervisory powers over the things indicated in article 12, paragraph 1, belonging to the Regions and to other territorial public bodies, the Ministry shall also proceed by availing itself of forms of agreement and co-ordination with the regions.

Article 19
Inspection

1. The superintendents may at any time proceed to carry out inspections for the purpose of

ascertaining the existence and the state of conservation and conditions of custody of the cultural properties, with prior notification of no less than five days, with the exception of cases of extreme urgency.

Chapter III
Protection and Conservation

Section I
Protection Measures

Article 20
Forbidden Actions

1. Cultural properties may not be destroyed, damaged or adapted to uses not compatible with their historic or artistic character or of such kind as to prejudice their conservation.
2. The archives cannot be dismembered.

Article 21
Actions subject to authorisation

1. The following actions are subject to the authorisation of the Ministry:
    a) the demolition of things constituting cultural property, even with subsequent reconstitution;
    b) the removal of cultural properties, even when temporary, without prejudice to the provisions of paragraphs 2 and 3;
    c) the dismemberment of collections and series;
    d) the discarding of documents in the public archives and in private archives for which a declaration under article 13 has been issued;
    e) the transfer to other corporate entities of organised sets of documentation belonging to public archives, as well as of archives belonging to private persons.
2. The removal of cultural properties, as a result of a change in the holder's residence or

place of business, shall be declared in advance to the superintendent, who may, within thirty days of receipt of notification, prescribe the measures necessary to prevent damage to the properties during transportation.

3. The removal of current archives of the State and of government bodies and institutions shall not be subject to authorisation.

4. In cases other than those set out in the above paragraphs, the execution of work of any kind on cultural properties is subject to authorisation by the superintendent.

5. The authorisation shall be granted on the basis of the project drawing or, when sufficient, on the basis of the technical description of the work presented by the applicant, and may contain prescriptions.

Article 22
Authorisation Procedure for Construction

1. In cases other than those set out in articles 25 and 26, the authorisation provided for in article 21, paragraph 4, relating to public and private construction shall be issued within the time limit of one hundred and twenty days of receipt of application on the part of the Superintendency.

2. Whenever the Superintendency requests clarification or additional elements for assessment, the time limit indicated in paragraph 1 shall be suspended until the requested documentation is received.

3. In cases where the Superintendency proceeds to carry out verifications of a technical nature, having notified the applicant in advance, the time limit indicated in paragraph 1 shall be suspended until the results of the official verification are acquired and in any case for not more than thirty days.

4. When the time limit established in paragraphs 2 and 3 has elapsed with no response, the applicant may enjoin the administration to take action. The request for authorisation shall be deemed granted should the administration fail to take action within thirty days following receipt of the enjoinment.

Article 23
Simplified Building Permit Procedures

1. When works authorised under article 21 also require a building permit, it is possible to

resort to declaration of the start of works, in the cases provided for by the law. To this end, the interested party shall forward the acquired authorisation, along with the related project design, to the Municipality when the declaration is made.

Article 24
Work on Public Property

1. For work on public cultural properties to be carried out on the part of administrations of the State, Regions, other territorial government bodies, as well as any other government body and institution, the authorisation necessary under article 21 may be expressed within agreements between the Ministry and the government body concerned.

Article 25
Conference of Services

1. In procedures related to projects and works affecting cultural properties, in which a conference of services is used, the authorisation necessary under article 21 shall be issued during the conference session by the competent organ of the Ministry with a reasoned declaration, shall be recorded in the minutes of the conference and shall include any prescriptions established for the realisation of the project.
2. Should the Ministerial organ express justified dissent, the acting administration may request the President of the Council of Ministers to rule on the conclusion of the proceeding, following deliberation of the Council of Ministers.
3. The recipient of the favourable conclusive decision adopted in the services conference shall inform the Ministry of the fulfilment of the prescriptions established by the conference.

Article 26
Assessment of Environmental Impact

1. For work projects to be subjected to environmental impact assessment, the authorisation provided for in article 21 shall be expressed by the Ministry in a joint session of the government bodies concerned for the decision on environmental compatibility, on the basis of the final project plan to be submitted for the purpose of the aforesaid assessment.
2. When an examination of the plan effected in accordance with paragraph 1 shows that the

project is not in any way compatible with the protection exigencies of the cultural properties which would be affected, the Ministry shall take a negative decision, notifying the Ministry of the Environment and Land Protection. In such case, the environmental impact assessment procedure shall be deemed to have been concluded negatively.

3. If, while the work is being carried out, actions occur which conflict with the authorisation expressed in the forms set out in paragraph 1, and are such as to put at risk the integrity of the cultural properties subject to protection, the superintendent shall order suspension of the work.

Article 27
Emergency Situations

1. In cases of absolute urgency, temporary work which is indispensable to avoiding damage to the protected property may be carried out, on condition that the Superintendency be immediately notified. The project design of the definitive work must be forwarded to the Superintendency in due time for the necessary authorisation.

Article 28
Precautionary and Preventive measures

1. The superintendent may order the suspension of works begun contrary to the provisions of articles 20, 21, 25, 26 and 27 or of those carried out in a manner that fails to conform with the authorisation.

2. The superintendent shall also have the power to order the interdiction or suspension of work relative to the things indicated in article 10, even when the assessment referred to in article 12, paragraph 2 has not yet been carried out, or the declaration referred to in article 13 has not yet been issued.

3. The order referred to in paragraph 2 shall be deemed to be revoked if, within thirty days of receipt of the same, notification of the start of the assessment or declaration procedure has not been communicated by the superintendent.

4. In cases of public works carried out in areas of archaeological interest, even when assessment referred to in article 12, paragraph 2 has not been carried out, or the declaration referred to in article 13 has not been issued, the superintendent may request that preventive archaeological sample analysis be carried out on the aforesaid areas at the expense of

the principal commissioning the public work.

Section II
Conservation Measures

Article 29
Conservation

1. The conservation of the cultural heritage is ensured by means of a consistent, co-ordinated and programmed activity of study, prevention, maintenance and restoration.

2. Prevention is defined as the set of activities capable of limiting situations of risk connected to the cultural property within its context.

3. Maintenance is defined as all the activities and work carried out for the purpose of controlling the conditions of the cultural property and maintaining the integrity, functional efficiency and identity of the property and its parts.

4. Restoration is defined as direct intervention on a property by means of a set of operations aimed at the material integrity and the recovery of the aforesaid property, the protection and the transmission of its cultural values. In the case of immovable property situated in areas declared to be at risk of earthquake on the basis of the laws and regulations in effect, restoration shall include work for structural upgrading.

5. The Ministry shall define guidelines, technical regulations, criteria and models for the conservation of cultural properties, and in doing so may avail itself of the participation of the Regions and the collaboration of universities and competent research institutes.

6. With the provisions of existing laws and regulations regarding the design and execution of works to be carried out on architectonic property remaining in effect, the work of maintenance and restoration of movable cultural properties and the decorated surfaces of architectonic properties shall be carried out exclusively by those who are qualified restorers of cultural property in accordance with the regulations in this regard.

7. The job descriptions of restorers and other workers who carry out activities which are complementary to restoration or to other activities of conservation of movable cultural property and of decorated surfaces of architectonic properties are defined by the Minister's decree adopted under article 17, paragraph 3, of law no. 400 of 23 August 1988, in agreement with the State-Regions Conference.

8. The criteria and quality control levels to be met by the teaching of restoration are defined by the Minister's decree pursuant to article 17, paragraph 3, of law no. 400 of 1988 in accord with the Minister of Education, Universities and Research, and with prior consultation of the State-Regions Conference.

9. Instruction in restoration is provided by schools of higher education and training established under article 9 of legislative decree no. 368 of 20 October 1998, as well as by the centres referred to in paragraph 11 and other public and private bodies accredited by the State. The Minister's decree adopted in accordance with article 17, paragraph 3 of law no. 400 of 1988 in accord with the Ministry of Education, Universities and Research, and with prior consultation of the State-Regions Conference, identifies the procedures for accreditation, the minimum requirements for the organisation and functioning of the educational bodies referred to in the present paragraph, the procedures for the supervision of teaching activities and of the final examination, which must include the participation of at least one Ministry representative, as well as the characteristics of the teaching staff.

10. The training of professional figures who carry out activities which are complementary to restoration or other activities of conservation is ensured by public and private entities in accordance with Regional regulations. The relative courses shall meet the criteria and quality control levels defined by agreement in the State-Regions Conference, pursuant to article 4 of legislative decree no. 281 of 28 August 1997.

11. By means of special arrangements or agreements, the Ministry and the Regions, with the participation of universities and other public and private entities as well, may together establish centres, which may also be of an inter-regional nature, and which are endowed with corporate personality and entrusted with activities in research, experimentation, study, documentation and execution of conservation and restoration work on cultural property, of particular complexity. Schools of superior training for the teaching of restoration may likewise be established within these centres, under paragraph 9.

Article 30
Conservational Obligations

1. The State, the Regions, and other territorial government bodies as well as any other government body and institution must ensure the safety and conservation of the cultural property in their possession.

2. The bodies indicated in paragraph 1 and private non-profit associations shall, with the ex-

ception of current archives, collocate the cultural properties in their possession in the place of their destination and in the manner indicated by the superintendent.

3. Private proprietors, possessors or holders of cultural properties must ensure the conservation of the aforesaid properties.

4. The bodies indicated in paragraph 1 must conserve and organise their archives in their entirety, and compile an inventory of their historical archives, consisting of documents relating to matters concluded over forty years ago. Proprietors, possessors or holders by whatever legal right, of private archives for which a declaration has been issued under article 13 are subject to the same obligation.

Article 31
Voluntary Conservation Work

1. Restoration and other conservation work carried out on cultural property on the initiative of the proprietor, possessor or holder by whatever legal right shall be authorised under article 21.

2. In issuing the authorisation, the superintendent shall, at the request of the interested party, give his opinion as to the eligibility of the work for State funding provided for under articles 35 and 37 and may certify the necessary nature of the aforesaid work for the purpose of eligibility for the tax deductions provided for by law.

Article 32
Obligatory Conservation Work

1. The Ministry may oblige the proprietor, possessor or holder by whatever legal right, to carry out work necessary to ensure the conservation of cultural property, or it may take direct action.

2. The provisions in paragraph 1 shall also apply to the obligations set out in article 30, paragraph 4.

Article 33
Procedures for the Execution of Obligatory Conservation Work

1. For the purposes of article 32, the superintendent shall compile a technical report and

declare the necessary nature of the measures to be carried out.

2. The technical report shall be sent, along with notification of start of procedure, to the proprietor, possessor or holder of the property, who may submit his/her observations within thirty days of receipt of the documents.

3. If the superintendent does not deem direct execution of the measures to be necessary, he/she shall assign the proprietor, possessor or holder a time limit for the presentation of the plans for the work to be carried out, in execution and pursuance of the technical report.

4. The plan presented shall be approved by the superintendent with any prescriptions that may be deemed necessary and a time limit shall be fixed for the start of work. For immovable property, the plan presented shall be forwarded by the superintendent to the Municipality or to the Metropolitan Area, which may express a reasoned opinion within thirty days of receipt of notification.

5. If the proprietor, possessor or holder of the property fails to fulfil the obligation to present the plan, or fails to take action to modify it according to the indications of the superintendent within the time limit fixed by the latter, or if the project is rejected, the Ministry shall proceed to direct execution.

6. In cases of urgency, the superintendent may immediately adopt the necessary conservation measures.

Article 34
Charges for Obligatory Conservation Work

1. The expenses incurred for measures carried out on cultural properties, whether they have been imposed or directly executed by the Ministry under article 32, shall be paid by the proprietor, possessor or holder. Nevertheless, if the measures are of particular significance or if they are carried out on properties granted in use to, or for enjoyment by, the public, the Ministry may participate in the expenses in whole or in part. In this case, it shall determine the amount of the expenses it intends to sustain and shall notify the party concerned.

2. If the expenses of the measures have been sustained by the proprietor, possessor or holder, the Ministry shall proceed to their reimbursement, and may also do so by part payments on account under article 36, paragraphs 2 and 3, keeping within the amount determined under paragraph 1.

3. With regard to expenses incurred in direct action measures, the Ministry shall determine

the amount to be charged to the proprietor, possessor or holder and shall pursue recovery of the expenses in the forms provided for by the laws in force regarding the compulsory collection of government property revenues.

Article 35

Financial Contribution by the Ministry

1. The Ministry may contribute to the expenses borne by the proprietor, possessor or holder of the cultural property for the execution of measures provided for in article 31, paragraph 1, for a sum not exceeding half of the same. If the measures are of particular significance or if they concern property used or enjoyed by the public, the Ministry may contribute to the expenses for up to the entire amount.

2. The provision in paragraph 1 shall also apply to measures taken with regard to historical archives provided for in article 30, paragraph 4.

3. In determining the percentage of the funding contributions referred to in paragraph 1, other public funding and any private funding for which taxation benefits have been obtained shall be taken into account.

Article 36

Disbursement of Funding

1. Funding shall be granted by the Ministry after the work has been completed and the costs effectively borne by the beneficiary have been verified.

2. Payments on account may be disbursed on the basis of the regularly certified progress of the work.

3. The beneficiary must return amounts received if the work has not been-completely or in part-properly carried out. The recovery of the relative sums shall be achieved following the procedures provided for by the laws in force regarding the compulsory collection of government property revenues.

Article 37

Interest Subsidies

1. The Ministry may grant interest subsidies for mortgages granted by credit institutions to

proprietors, possessors or holders by whatever legal right of immovable cultural properties, for carrying out authorised conservation works.

2. The funding is granted in the maximum amount corresponding to the interest calculated at an annual rate of six percentage points on the capital disbursed as mortgage.

3. The funding is disbursed directly to the credit institution following procedures to be established by agreement.

4. Funding under paragraph 1 may also be granted for conservation work on works of contemporary architecture for which the superintendent has, at the request of the owner, acknowledged particular artistic value.

Article 38

Opening to the Public of Buildings that Have Undergone Conservation Work

1. Buildings that have been restored or on which other conservation measures have been carried out with the State participating in the expenses in whole or in part, or for which interest subsidies have been granted, shall be made accessible to the public according to procedures established, for each individual case, by special arrangements or agreements to be stipulated between the Ministry and the individual proprietors upon the assumption of the burden of expenses under article 34 or upon granting of funding under article 35.

2. The arrangements and agreements shall establish the time limits for the obligation to open to the public, taking into consideration the type of work done, the artistic and historical value of the buildings and of the cultural property contained therein. Arrangements and agreements shall be forwarded, by the superintendent, to the Municipality or the Metropolitan Area in which the buildings are located.

Article 39

Conservation Work on State Property

1. The Ministry shall provide for the conservation exigencies of cultural properties belonging to the State, even when these are committed to the care of—or granted in use to—other administrations or other entities, following consultation with the aforesaid administrations or entities.

2. Except in cases where a different agreement has been stipulated, the planning and execu-

tion of the measures referred to in paragraph 1, relative to immovable property, shall be taken on by the aforesaid administration or entity, with the Ministry retaining competence for issuing the authorisation for the project and for supervising the work.

3. For the execution of work referred to in paragraph 1, relative to immovable property, the Ministry shall forward the plan and notify start of work to the Municipality or Metropolitan Area.

Article 40

Conservation Work on Property Belonging to the Regions and Other Territorial Government Bodies

1. For cultural properties belonging to the Regions and to other territorial government bodies, the measures provided for under article 32 shall be established, except in cases of absolute urgency, on the basis of agreements with the interested body.

2. The agreements may also pertain to the contents of the prescriptions referred to in article 30, paragraph 2.

3. Conservation measures on cultural property involving the State, the Regions and other territorial government bodies, as well as other public and private entities, are ordinarily the object of preventive planning agreements.

Article 41

Obligation to Deposit Documents Kept by State Administrations with the State Archives

1. The judicial and administrative organs of the State shall deposit with the Central Archive of the State and with the State Archives the documents concerning matters concluded more than forty years ago, along with the instruments which ensure their consultation. Military service and extraction rolls shall be deposited seventy years after the birth year to which they refer. Notary archives shall deposit notary deeds received by notaries who retired from the exercise of the profession prior to the last one hundred-year period.

2. The superintendent of the Central Archive of the State and the directors of the State Archives may accept the deposits of more recent documents when there is danger of dispersal or damage.

3. No deposit may be received unless discarding operations have been carried out. Deposit

expenses are charged to the depositing administrations.

4. The archives of government offices which have been abolished or of public bodies which have been extinguished shall be deposited with the Central State Archive and with the State Archives, unless their transferral, in whole or in part, to other bodies becomes necessary.

5. Commissions, which are to include representatives of the Ministry and the Ministry of Internal Affairs as members, shall be established within the organs indicated in paragraph 1, with the tasks of supervising the proper keeping of current and deposited archives, of collaborating in the definition of criteria for the organisation, management and conservation of documents, of proposing the discarding of documents referred to in paragraph 3, of managing the deposits provided for in paragraph 1, and of identifying documents of a confidential nature. The composition and functioning of the Commissions shall be regulated by a decree adopted by the Minister for Cultural Heritage and Activities in agreement with the Minister of Internal Affairs, under article 17, paragraph 3 of law no. 400 of 23 August 1988. Discarding shall be authorised by the Ministry.

6. The provisions of the present article shall not apply to the Ministry for Foreign Affairs, nor shall they apply to the General Staff of the Army, the Navy and the Air Force as concerns documentation of a military and operational nature.

Article 42
Conservation of the Historical Archives of Constitutional Organs

1. The Presidency of the Republic shall conserve its documents in its own historical archives, according to the rules and regulations adopted by the President of the Republic by his own decree, on the recommendation of the General Secretary of the Presidency of the Republic. The procedures for consultation and access to the documents preserved in the historical archives of the Presidency of the Republic shall be established by the same decree.

2. The Chamber of Deputies and the Senate of the Republic shall conserve their documents in their own historical archives, in accordance with the rules and regulations of their respective presidential offices.

3. The Constitutional Court shall conserve its documents in its own historical archives, in accordance with the provisions established by the regulation adopted under the laws in force pertaining to the constitution and functioning of the same Court.

Article 43
Obligatory Custody

1. The Ministry shall have the power to have movable cultural property transferred and temporarily conserved in public institutions, in order to guarantee its safety and ensure its conservation pursuant to article 29.

Article 44
Gratuitous Loan and Deposit of Cultural Property

1. The directors of archives and of institutions which administer or have on deposit artistic, archaeological, bibliographical and scientific collections may, with the prior consent of the competent Ministerial organ, receive movable cultural property from private owners on gratuitous loan for the purpose of permitting its enjoyment by the public, when property of particular importance or which represents a significant addition to public collections is concerned, and on condition that the conservation of the aforesaid property in public institutions does not prove to be particularly onerous.

2. The term of the gratuitous loan cannot last less than five years and shall be deemed to be tacitly extended for a period equal to the agreed term whenever one of the contracting partners has not communicated notification of cancellation to the other at least two months prior to the expiry of the term. The parties may consensually dissolve the gratuitous loan before expiry as well.

3. The directors shall adopt any measure necessary for the conservation of the property received on gratuitous loan, notifying the lender. The related expenses shall be borne by the Ministry.

4. The properties shall be protected by suitable insurance coverage at the expense of the Ministry.

5. The directors may, with the prior consent of the competent Ministerial organ, also receive on deposit cultural properties belonging to government bodies. The costs of conservation and custody referred specifically to the deposited properties are borne by the depositing body.

6. With regard to what is not expressly provided for by the present article, the provisions regarding gratuitous loans and deposits shall apply.

Section III

Other Forms of Protection

Article 45

Prescriptions for Indirect Protection

1. The Ministry shall have the power to prescribe the distances, measures and other regulations aimed at preventing that the integrity of immovable cultural property be put at risk, that their perspective or natural light be damaged or that conditions of the setting or decorous aspect of the buildings be altered.

2. The prescriptions referred to in paragraph 1, adopted and notified under articles 46 and 47, shall be immediately enforceable. The territorial government bodies concerned shall incorporate the same prescriptions into building regulations and urban planning instruments.

Article 46

Indirect Protection Proceeding

1. The superintendent shall initiate the proceeding for indirect protection, which he may also do at the request of the Region or other interested territorial government bodies, and shall notify the proprietor, possessor or holder by whatever legal right of the building to which the prescriptions refer. If the number of recipients is such that personal notification is not possible or proves particularly burdensome, the superintendent shall communicate the start of proceeding by means of suitable forms of advertising.

2. The notification of start of proceeding for indirect protection shall identify the building for which there is intent to adopt prescriptions for indirect protection and shall indicate the essential contents of such prescriptions.

3. In the case of complexes of buildings, notification shall also be sent to the Municipality or the Metropolitan Area.

4. As a precautionary measure, notification shall entail the temporary prohibition to modify the building with regard to the aspects referred to in the prescriptions contained in the aforesaid notification.

5. The effects indicated in paragraph 4 shall cease upon expiry of the term of the relative

proceeding, established by the Ministry under article 2, paragraph 2 of law no. 241 of 7 August 1990.

Article 47

Notification of Prescriptions for Indirect Protection and Administrative Appeal

1. The provision containing the prescriptions for indirect protection shall be notified to the proprietor, possessor or holder by whatever legal right of the buildings concerned, by a process-server or by means of registered letter with notification of receipt of delivery.

2. The provision shall be recorded in the building registers and shall have efficacy for any successive proprietor, possessor or holder by whatever legal right of the buildings to which the same prescriptions refer.

3. Administrative appeal against the provision containing the prescriptions for indirect protection shall be admissible under article 16. The intent to appeal, however, shall not entail the suspension of the effects of the provision contested.

Article 48

Authorisation for Exhibits and Expositions

1. The loan of the following for exhibits and expositions is subject to authorisation:
    a) movable things indicated in article 12, paragraph 1;
    b) movable properties indicated in article 10, paragraph 1;
    c) movable properties indicated in article 10, paragraph 3, letters *a*) and *e*);
    d) collections and individual items pertaining to them, referred to in article 10, paragraph 2, letter *a*); book collections indicated in article 10, paragraph 2, letter *c*) and paragraph 3, letter *c*); as well as archives and single documents indicated in article 10, paragraph 2, letter *b*), and paragraph 3, letter *b*).

2. When authorisation concerns properties belonging to the State or which have been placed under State protection, the request shall be presented to the Ministry at least four months prior to the start of the event and shall indicate the party responsible for the safekeeping of the works on loan.

3. The authorisation shall be issued taking into consideration the conservation exigencies of the properties and also, for those belonging to the State, the exigencies of public enjoyment; it shall be subject to the adoption of measures necessary to ensure the integrity of

the properties. The criteria, procedures and modalities for issuing the authorisation shall be established by ministerial decree.

4. The granting of authorisation is moreover subject to the insurance of the things and properties on the part of the applicant, for the value indicated in the application, with prior verification of its adequacy by the Ministry.

5. For exhibits and events within the national territory promoted by the Ministry, or with the participation of the State, or government bodies or institutions, the insurance provided for in paragraph 4 may be substituted by the assumption of the relative risks on the part of the State. Government guaranty is issued according to the procedures, modalities and conditions established by ministerial decree, in consultation with the Ministry for the Economy and Finance. The relevant costs will be provided for through the utilisation of the resources available in the reserve fund for obligatory and routine expenses established in the statement of expenditure estimates of the Ministry for the Economy and Finance.

6. The Ministry shall, at the request of the party concerned, have the power to declare the important cultural or scientific interest of exhibits or expositions of cultural properties and of any other initiative of a cultural nature, for purposes of the application of tax relief measures provided for under tax law.

Article 49
Advertising Bills and Hoardings

1. It is forbidden to place or affix hoardings or other means of advertising on buildings or in areas protected as cultural property. The superintendent may nevertheless authorise placement or posting when no harm ensues to the appearance, decorous aspect or public enjoyment of the said buildings or areas. The authorisation shall be forwarded to the Municipality for the purposes of any authorising provision to be granted under its competence.

2. It shall be forbidden to place hoardings or other means of advertising along roads located within or near the properties indicated in paragraph 1, unless authorisation is granted in accordance with the laws and regulations regarding road traffic and advertising in the streets and on vehicles, with the prior favourable decision of the superintendent with regard to the compatibility of collocation and type of means of advertising with the appearance, decorous aspect and public enjoyment of the properties under protection.

3. In relation to the properties indicated in paragraph 1, the superintendent may, after

assessing compatibility with their artistic or historical nature, authorise or permit the use for advertising purposes of the coverings of the scaffoldings mounted for the execution of conservation or restoration work for a period of time that does not exceed the duration of the work. For this purpose, the tender contract for the aforesaid works must be attached to the application for the permit or assent.

Article 50
Detachment of Cultural Properties

1. It is forbidden to order and carry out, without the authorisation of the superintendent, the detachment of frescoes, escutcheons, graffiti, tablets, inscriptions, tabernacles and other ornaments, whether or not they be displayed to public view.

2. It is forbidden to order and carry out, without the authorisation of the superintendent, the detachment of escutcheons, graffiti, tablets, inscriptions, and tabernacles, and to remove memorial stones and monuments, constituting vestiges of World War I under the laws and regulations in this regard.

Article 51
Artists' Studios

1. It is forbidden to change the designated use of artists' studios, or to remove their contents, consisting of works, documents, relics and the like, when such contents, considered as a whole and in relation to the context within which they are contained, are declared to be of particularly important interest for their historical value, under article 13.

2. It is moreover forbidden to change the designated use of artists' studios which fall within the traditional studio with skylight typology and which have been adapted to this use for at least twenty years.

Article 52
Commercial Activity in Areas of Cultural Value

1. With the resolutions provided for in the laws on the reform of the regulations pertaining to the commercial sector, the Municipalities shall, with prior consultation of the super-

intendent, identify the public areas having archaeological, historical, artistic and environmental value in which commercial activity is to be forbidden or subject to particular conditions.

Chapter IV
Circulation Within the National Territory

Section I
Alienation and Other Means of Transferral

Article 53
State Cultural Property

1. Cultural properties belonging to the State, the Regions and other territorial government bodies which correspond to the characteristics of the typologies indicated in article 822 of the civil code constitute the cultural property of the State.

2. The properties of the State cultural heritage may not be transferred, nor may they be the object of rights in favour of third parties, except in the ways set out in this Code.

Article 54
Non-alienable Properties

1. The following cultural properties belonging to the State cannot be alienated:
    a) buildings and areas of archaeological interest;
    b) buildings recognised as national monuments by measures having the force of law;
    c) the collections of museums, picture galleries, art galleries and libraries;
    d) archives.

2. The following cannot equally be alienated:
    a) immovable and movable things belonging to subjects indicated in article 10, paragraph 1, which are the work of non-living artists and whose production goes back more than fifty years, until release from State ownership occurred, if necessary, following the

verification procedures set out in article 12;

b) movable things which are the work of living artists or whose production does not go back more than fifty years, if these are included in collections belonging to the bodies indicated in article 53;

c) single documents belonging to the bodies referred to in article 53, as well as the archives and single documents of government bodies and institutions other than those indicated in the aforesaid article 53;

d) immovable things belonging to the bodies indicated in article 53 which have been declared to be of particularly important interest, testifying to the identity and history of public, collective or religious institutions as set out in article 10, paragraph 3, letter *d*).

3. The properties and things referred to in paragraphs 1 and 2 may be transferred between the State, the Regions and other territorial government bodies.

4. The properties and things indicated in paragraphs 1 and 2 may be used exclusively according to the modalities and for the purposes provided for in Title I of this Part.

Article 55
Alienability of Buildings Belonging to State Cultural Property

1. Immovable cultural properties which are part of the State's cultural property and which are not included among those listed in article 54, paragraphs 1 and 2, cannot be alienated without the authorisation of the Ministry.

2. The authorisation referred to in paragraph 1 may be granted under the following conditions:

a) alienation must ensure the protection and enhancement of the properties, and in any case must not hinder public enjoyment;

b) the authorisation provision must indicate designated uses that are compatible with the historical and artistic nature of the buildings and must be such that no harm is done to their conservation.

3. The authorisation to alienate entails the release from State ownership of the cultural properties to which it refers. These properties remain subject to protection under article 12, paragraph 7.

Article 56
Other Types of Alienation Subject to Authorisation

1. The following are also subject to authorisation by the Ministry:

    a) the alienation of cultural properties belonging to the State, the Regions and other territorial government bodies, other than those indicated in article 54, paragraphs 1 and 2, and article 55, paragraph 1.

    b) the alienation of cultural properties belonging to government bodies other than those indicated in letter *a*) or to private non-profit associations, with the exception of the things and properties indicated in article 54, paragraph 2, letters *a*) and *c*).

2. Authorisation is also required in cases of partial sale of collections or series of objects and of book collections by bodies and associations indicated in in paragraph 1, letter *b*).

3. The provisions of the preceding paragraphs shall also apply to the constitution of mortgages and pledges and to legal transactions which may entail the transfer of the cultural properties indicated therein.

4. The deeds which entail the transfer of cultural properties to the State, including transfers in payment of taxes owed, shall not be subject to authorisation.

Article 57
Regulations for Authorisation to Alienate

1. The application for authorisation to alienate shall be submitted by the body to which the properties belong and shall be accompanied by the indication of the current designated use and the programme of necessary conservation measures.

2. With regard to the properties indicated in article 55, paragraph 1, the authorisation may be issued by the Ministry at the recommendation of the Superintendency, after consultation with the Region and, through the Region, with other interested territorial government bodies, under the conditions established in paragraph 2 of the aforesaid article 55. The prescriptions and the conditions contained in the authorisation provision shall be included in the deed of transfer.

3. The alienated property may not undergo work of any kind unless the relative project has had prior authorisation under article 21, paragraph 4.

4. With regard to the properties indicated in article 56, paragraph 1, letter a), and the prop-

erties of the government bodies and institutions indicated in article 56, paragraph 1, letter b) and paragraph 2, authorisation may be granted when the same properties bear no interest for public collections and alienation does not seriously harm their conservation or impair public enjoyment.

5. With regard to the properties indicated in article 56, paragraph 1, letter b)and paragraph 2, belonging to private non-profit organisations, authorisation may be granted when no serious harm ensues from the transfer to the conservation or the public enjoyment of the aforesaid properties.

Article 58
Authorisation to Exchange

1. The Ministry may authorise the exchange of properties indicated in articles 55 and 56, and of single properties belonging to government collections, with others belonging to bodies, institutions and private individuals, including foreign bodies, institutions and individuals, when an increase in the national cultural patrimony or an enrichment of public collections ensues from the exchange.

Article 59
Declaration of Transfer

1. Deeds which transfer, in whole or in part, by whatever legal right, property or the possession of cultural properties shall be reported to the Ministry.

2. The declaration shall be made within 30 days:

   a) by the alienor or the transferor of possession of the property, in the case of alienation made for a money consideration or not for value, or of transferral of possession;

   b) by the purchaser, in the case of transferral occurring in procedures of forced or bankruptcy sale or by force of an adjudication which produces the effect of a transfer contract which is not concluded;

   c) by the heir or the legatee, in the case of succession because of death. For the heir, the time limit begins with the acceptance of the inheritance or with the presentation of the declaration to the competent tax offices; for the legatee the time limit begins with the opening of the will, except in the case of renunciation under the provisions of the civil code.

3. The declaration shall be presented to the competent superintendent in the place where the properties are located.

4. The declaration shall contain:

   a) identification of the parties and the signature of the same or of their legal representatives;

   b) the information identifying the properties;

   c) the indication of the place where the properties are located;

   d) the indication of the nature and conditions of the deed of transfer;

   e) the indication of the habitual residence in Italy of the parties concerned for the purposes of any communications provided for by the present Title.

5. A declaration lacking any of the indications provided for in paragraph 4 or with incomplete or imprecise indications shall be deemed not to have been submitted.

Section II
Pre-emption

Article 60
Purchase by Pre-emption

1. The Ministry or, in the case provided for in article 62, paragraph 3, the Region or another interested territorial government body, shall have the power to purchase by pre-emption cultural properties alienated for a money consideration at the price established in the deed of transfer.

2. When the property is alienated with other properties for a single money consideration or is transferred without a money consideration or is exchanged, its monetary value shall be officially determined by the party which proceeds to pre-emption under paragraph 1.

3. When the alienor does not wish to accept the assessment established under paragraph 2, the monetary value of the thing shall be determined by a third party, designated by agreement between the alienor and the party exercising pre-emption. If the parties do not agree on the appointment of the third party, or on a replacement should the nominee not wish or not be able to accept the appointment, the designation shall, at the request of one of the parties, be made by the president of the court in the area in which the contract was concluded. The relative costs shall be advanced by the alienor.

4. The assessment of the third party may be contested in the case of error or manifest inequity.

5. Pre-emption may be also exercised when the property is by any legal right given in payment.

Article 61
Conditions of Pre-emption

1. Pre-emption shall be exercised within sixty days of the date of receipt of the declaration provided for in article 59.

2. In the case in which the declaration is omitted or presented late or proves incomplete, pre-emption shall be exercised within one hundred and eighty days from the time that the Ministry receives the late declaration or in any case acquires all the elements constituting the same under article 59, paragraph 4.

3. The pre-emption provision shall be notified to the alienor and the purchaser within the time limits indicated in paragraphs 1 and 2. The property shall pass to the State from the last notification date.

4. When the time limit prescribed in paragraph 1 is still pending, the effects of the deed of transfer are suspended until the exercise of pre-emption occurs and the alienor is forbidden to carry out delivery of the thing.

5. The State is not bound by the clauses of the contract of alienation.

6. In the case in which the Ministry exercises its right of pre-emption on part of the things alienated, the buyer is entitled to rescind the contract.

Article 62
Pre-emption Procedure

1. Upon receipt of declaration of a deed subject to pre-emption, the superintendent shall give immediate notification to the Region and the other territorial government bodies in whose territory the property is located. Where a movable property is concerned, the Region shall inform the public through its own Official Bulletin and, if necessary, through any other suitable means of advertising at the national level, with the description of the work and the indication of its price.

2. The Region and other territorial government bodies shall, within thirty days of the decla-

ration, present a recommendation for pre-emption to the Ministry, accompanied by the resolution of the competent organ which shall order the necessary financial coverage for the costs, to be provided for in the budget of the body concerned.

3. When the Ministry does not wish to exercise its right of pre-emption, it shall notify the interested body within forty days of receipt of declaration. The aforesaid body shall take on the relative expenses, adopt the pre-emption provision and notify the alienor and the purchaser within and not beyond seventy days of the aforesaid declaration. Ownership of the property shall be transferred to the body which has exercised right of pre-emption, from the last notification date.

4. In the cases referred to in article 61, paragraph 2, the time limits indicated in paragraph 2 and in the first and second sentences of paragraph 3 are respectively, ninety, one hundred and twenty, and eighty days from the late declaration or from the date of the acquisition of the elements constituting the same declaration.

Section III
Commercial Activity

Article 63
Obligation to Report Commercial Activity and Keep a Register.
Obligation to Declare Sale or Purchase of Documents

1. The local authority for public safety authorised, under the laws pertaining to the matter, to receive preventive declaration of commercial trade in antique or used objects, shall forward to the superintendent and to the Region a copy of the aforesaid declaration, presented by the dealer in the things included in the categories indicated in letter A of Annex A of the present legislative decree.

2. Those who deal in the things indicated in paragraph 1 shall make daily entries of the operations carried out in the register prescribed by the regulations pertaining to public safety, and shall describe the characteristics of the aforesaid things. The value limits above which a detailed description of the things commercially traded becomes obligatory shall be defined by decree adopted by the Ministry in agreement with the Ministry of Internal Affairs.

3. The superintendent shall verify the fulfilment of the obligation indicated in the second

sentence of paragraph 2 by means of periodical inspections, which may also be carried out by officers delegated for the purpose by him/her. The verification shall be carried out by officers of the Region in cases where protection under article 5, paragraphs 2, 3 and 4 is exercised. The inspection report shall be notified to the concerned party and to the local public safety authorities.

4. Dealers in documents, the owners of auction houses, as well as public officials charged with the sale of real estate must forward to the superintendent the list of documents of historical interest offered for sale. Private owners, possessors or holders by whatever legal right of archives who purchase documents having the aforementioned interest, shall be subject to the same obligation within ninety days of acquisition. The superintendent may start the procedure referred to in article 13 within ninety days of notification.

5. The superintendent may in any case ascertain ex officio the existence of archives or single documents of which private individuals are proprietors, possessors or holders by whatever legal right, or for which a particularly important historical interest may be presumed.

Article 64
Certificates of Authenticity and Provenance

1. Whosoever conducts activities of sale to the public, of exposition for commercial purposes or of mediation for the purpose of selling works of painting, sculpture, graphic art or of antique objects or objects of historical or archaeological interest, or whosoever in any case habitually sells the aforesaid works or objects, must provide the buyer with documentation certifying authenticity, or at least probable attribution, and provenance; or, lacking such, declaration must be provided containing all the information available with regard to the authenticity of the work or object or to its probable attribution and provenance, according to the procedures provided for by the legislative and regulatory provisions pertaining to administrative documentation. Such a declaration, where the nature of the work or the object permits, shall be affixed upon a photographic copy of the same.

Chapter V

Circulation Within International Territory

Section I

Exit from National Territory and Entry into National Territory

Article 65
Definitive Exit

1. The definitive exit of movable cultural property indicated in article 10, paragraphs 1, 2 and 3 from within the territory of the Republic is forbidden.

2. The exit of the following is also forbidden:

   a) movable things belonging to the subjects indicated in article 10, paragraph 1, which are the work of no longer living artists and whose production goes back more than fifty years, until the verification provided for by article 12 is carried out.

   b) properties, to whomsoever they may belong, which are included in the categories indicated in article 10, paragraph 3, and which the Ministry, after consultation with the competent advisory body, has preventively identified and for which it has excluded exit, for defined periods of time, because it would be harmful for the cultural heritage in relation to the objective characteristics and the provenance of the aforesaid properties and to the milieu to which they belong.

3. Apart from the cases provided for in paragraphs 1 and 2, the definitive exit of the following from the territory of the Republic are subject to authorisation according to the procedures established in the present Section and in Section II of this Chapter:

   a) things, to whomsoever they may belong, which present cultural interest and which are the work of no longer living artists and whose production goes back more than fifty years;

   b) archives and single documents, belonging to private individuals, which present cultural interest;

   c) properties included in the categories indicated in article 11, paragraph 1, letters *f*), *g*) and *h*), to whomsoever they may belong:

4. The exit of the things referred to in article 11, paragraph 1, letter *d*) is not subject to

authorisation. The interested party must nevertheless demonstrate to the competent export office that the things to be transferred abroad are the work of a living artist or that their production does not go back more than fifty years, according to the procedures and modalities established by Ministerial decree.

Article 66
Temporary Exit for Events

1. The temporary exit from the territory of the Republic of the things and cultural properties indicated in article 65, paragraphs 1, 2, letter *a*), and paragraph 3, may be authorised for art events, exhibits or expositions of great cultural interest, on condition that the integrity and safety of the aforesaid things are ensured.

2. The following may not, in any case, be removed from national territory:

   a) properties which are susceptible to damage during transportation or in unfavourable environmental conditions;

   b) properties which constitute the principal collection of a determined and integral section of a museum, picture gallery, art gallery, archive or library or of an artistic or bibliographical collection.

Article 67
Other Cases of Temporary Exit

1. The things and cultural properties indicated in article 65, paragraphs 1, 2, letter *a*), and 3 may also be authorised to exit temporarily when:

   a) these constitute the private furniture of Italian citizens who, in diplomatic and consular seats, European Union institutions or international organisations, fill offices which require the persons concerned to move abroad, for a period of time which is not to exceed the duration of their mandate;

   b) they constitute the interior décor of diplomatic and consular seats abroad;

   c) they must undergo analysis, investigations or conservation work which must necessarily be carried out abroad;

   d) their exit is requested in the implementation of cultural accords with foreign museum institutions under reciprocity agreements, for the duration established in the same accords, which may nevertheless not exceed four years.

2. The temporary exit from the territory of the Republic of means of transportation over seventy-five years old for participation in international exhibits and meetings is not subject to authorisation except when a declaration has been made for them under article 13.

Article 68
Certificate of Free Circulation

1. Whosoever wishes to definitively remove the things and properties indicated in article 65, paragraph 3, from the territory of the Republic, must make a declaration to that effect and present them to the competent export office, indicating at the same time the market value for each item, in order to obtain the certificate of free circulation.

2. Within three days of presentation of the things or properties, the export office shall notify the competent offices of the Ministry, which within the following ten days shall furnish it with any useful cognitive element with regard to the objects presented for definitive exit.

3. Having ascertained the fairness of the indicated value, the export office shall, with a reasoned decision, which may also be based on information received, issue or deny the certificate of free circulation, notifying the party concerned within forty days of the presentation of the thing or property.

4. In assessing granting or denial of the certificate of free circulation the export offices shall abide by the general guidelines established by Ministry, after consultation with the competent advisory body.

5. The certificate of free circulation is valid for a three-year period and shall be issued in three original copies, one of which shall be filed in the official documents archive; the second shall be consigned to the party concerned and must accompany the circulation of the object; the third shall be forwarded to the Ministry for the formation of the official certificates register.

6. Denial shall entail the start of declaration proceedings, under article 14. To this purpose, contemporaneously with denial, the elements indicated in article 14, paragraph 2, shall be communicated to the party concerned and the things or properties shall be subject to the provisions of paragraph 4 of the aforesaid article.

7. For the things or properties belonging to bodies subject to Regional supervision, the export office shall consult the Region, whose opinion shall be delivered within the peremptory term of thirty days from the date of receipt of the request and, when the aforesaid opinion is negative, it shall be binding.

Article 69

Administrative Appeal Against Denial of Certificate

1. Appeal to the Ministry against a denial of certificate is admissible, within the thirty days following, on grounds of legitimacy or merits.

2. After consulting the competent advisory body, the Ministry shall rule on the appeal within the term of ninety days from the presentation of the same.

3. The declaration proceedings shall be suspended from the date of presentation of administrative appeal and until the expiry of the term indicated in paragraph 2, but the properties shall remain subject to the provisions indicated in article 14, paragraph 4.

4. When the Ministry acknowledges the appeal as valid, it shall return the relative documents to the export office, which shall take action accordingly within the following twenty days.

5. The provisions of decree no. 1199 of the President of the Republic of 24 November 1971 shall apply.

Article 70

Compulsory Purchase

1. Within the time limit indicated in article 68, paragraph 3, the export office may recommend to the Ministry the compulsory purchase of the thing or the property for which the certificate of free circulation has been requested, contemporaneously notifying the Region and the party concerned, to whom it shall moreover declare that the object subject to the purchase recommendation shall remain in the custody of the aforesaid office until the conclusion of the relative procedure. In such case, the time limit for issuing the certificate is extended to sixty days.

2. The Ministry shall have the option to purchase the thing or property for the value indicated in the declaration. The purchase provision shall be notified to the party concerned within the peremptory term of ninety days from the declaration. Until such time as notification of the purchase provision occurs, the party concerned may decide against the exit of the object and take action to withdraw the same.

3. Should the Ministry not wish to proceed to purchase, it shall, within sixty days of the declaration, notify the Region in whose territory the recommending export office is locat-

ed. The Region shall have the option to purchase the thing or the property in accordance with the provisions of article 62, paragraphs 2 and 3, pertaining to the financial coverage of the costs and the assumption of the relative promise to purchase. The relative provision shall be notified to the party concerned within the peremptory term of ninety days from the declaration.

Article 71
Certificate of Temporary Circulation

1. Whosoever intends, under articles 66 and 67, to temporarily remove from the territory of the Republic the things and properties indicated therein, must declare such intention and present the items to the competent export office, indicating at the same time the market value for each item and the party responsible for its safekeeping abroad, in order to obtain the certificate of temporary circulation.

2. Having ascertained the fairness of the value indicated, the export office shall, with a reasoned decision, issue or deny the certificate of temporary circulation, dictating the prescriptions necessary and notifying the party concerned within forty days of the presentation of the thing or property. Administrative appeal against denial of temporary circulation shall be admissible following the procedures set out in article 69.

3. When the thing or property presented for temporary exit possesses the interest required under article 10, the elements indicated in article 14, paragraph 2 shall be communicated to the party concerned, contemporaneously with the positive or negative decision, for the purposes of the start of declaration proceedings, and the object shall be subject to the measures set out in article 14, paragraph 4.

4. In assessing the granting or denial of the certificate, the export offices shall abide by the general guidelines established by the Ministry, after consulting the competent advisory body. For cases of temporary exit regulated by article 66 and article 67, paragraph 1, letters *b*) and *c*), the granting of the certificate shall be subject to authorisation under article 48.

5. The certificate shall also indicate the time limit for the return of the things or properties, which may be extended at the request of the party concerned, but may not in any case exceed eighteen months from the time of their removal from the national territory, with the exception of the provisions of paragraph 8.

6. The granting of the certificate shall always be conditional to the insurance of the proper-

ties on the part of the party concerned for the value indicated in the application. For exhibits and events promoted abroad by the Ministry or, with State participation, by government bodies, by Italian Cultural Institutes abroad or by supra-national organisations, the insurance may be substituted by the assumption of the relative risks by the State, under article 48, paragraph 5.

7. For cultural properties indicated in article 65, paragraph 1, as well as for the things or properties indicated in paragraph 3, temporary exit shall be guaranteed by means of a security bond, which may consist of a surety policy, issued by a banking institution or an insurance company, for a sum exceeding by ten per cent the value of the property or thing as assessed when the certificate was issued. The surety shall be seized by the administration when the objects admitted for temporary exportation do not return to the national territory within the time limit established. Surety is not required for properties belonging to the State and to public administrations. The Ministry may exonerate institutions of particular cultural importance from the obligation to provide surety.

8. The provisions of paragraphs 5 to 7 do not apply to the cases of temporary exit provided for in article 67, paragraph 1.

Article 72
Entry into National Territory

1. The shipment to Italy by a Member State of the European Union or the importation from a third country of the things or properties indicated in article 65, paragraph 3, shall, upon application, be certified by the export office.

2. Certificates declaring that shipment and importation have occurred shall be issued on the basis of documentation suitable for identifying the thing or the property and for proving provenance from the territory of the Member State or third Country from which the thing or property has been respectively shipped or imported.

3. The certificates declaring that shipment and importation have occurred shall be valid for five years and may be extended upon request by the party concerned.

4. Conditions, modalities and procedures for granting and extending certificates may be established by ministerial decree, with particular regard for the ascertainment of the provenance of the thing or property shipped or imported.

Section II

Exportation from European Union Territory

Article 73

Denominations

1. In the present Section and in section III of this Chapter the following denominations shall be used:

   a) "EEC Regulation" shall mean Council Regulation (EEC) no. 3911/92 of 9 December 1992, as modified by Council Regulation (EC) no. 2469/96 of 16 December 1996 and by Council Regulation (EC) no. 974/01 of 14 March 2001.

   b) "EEC Directive" shall mean Council Directive 93/7/EEC of 15 March 1993, as modified by Directive 96/100/EC of the European Parliament and of the Council, of 17 February 1997, and by Directive 200/38/EC of the European Parliament and of the Council, of 5 June 2001;

   c) "requesting State" shall mean the Member State of the European Union which initiates the action for restitution under Section III.

Article 74

Exportation of Cultural Properties from the European Union

1. The exportation outside European Union territory of the cultural properties indicated in Annex A of this Code is governed by the EEC Regulation and the present article.

2. The export licence provided for in article 2 of the EEC Regulation shall be issued by the export office contemporaneously with the certificate of free circulation, or not more than thirty months from the granting of the latter on the part of the same office. The licence shall be valid for six months.

3. In the case of temporary exportation of a property listed in Annex A of this Code, the export office shall issue the temporary export licence under the conditions and according to the modalities established in articles 66, 67 and 71.

4. The provisions of Section I of this Chapter shall not apply to cultural properties which have entered State territory with an export licence which has been issued by another European Union Member State in accordance with article 2 of the EEC Regulation, for

the duration of the validity of the same licence.

5. For the purposes of the EEC Regulation, the Ministry's export offices shall be the authority responsible for granting export licences for cultural properties. The Ministry shall compile and keep the list of export licences granted, notifying the Commission of the European Communities of any changes within two months of their occurrence.

Section III

Restitution of Cultural Properties Illegally Taken out of the Territory of a Member State of the European Union

Article 75
Restitution

1. Cultural properties illegally taken out of the territory of a European Union Member State after 31 December 1992 shall be returned in accordance with the provisions of the present section.

2. Cultural properties are deemed to be those properties which, even after their exit from the territory of the requesting State, are defined, on the basis of the laws in force therein, as belonging to the national cultural heritage, in accordance with article 30 of the Treaty Establishing the European Economic Community, substituted by article 6 of the Treaty of Amsterdam, and by the relative laws and regulations of ratification and execution.

3. Restitution is admissible for the properties included in one of the following categories:

    a) properties indicated in Annex A;

    b) properties which are part of public collections inventoried in museums, archives and collections of books for conservation. Public collections are defined as the collections owned by the State, the Regions, other territorial government bodies and any other public body and institution, as well as collections which are significantly financed by the State, the Regions or the other territorial government bodies;

    c) properties included in ecclesiastical inventories.

4. The exit of cultural properties shall be deemed illegal when aforesaid exit occurs in violation of the EEC Regulation or of the legislation of the requesting State on the protection of the national cultural heritage, or when the property has not been returned upon expiry of the temporary exit or export term.

5. The exit of properties for which temporary exit or export has been authorised shall be deemed illegal when the prescriptions established under the provision set out in article 71, paragraph 2 have been violated.

6. Restitution shall be admissible if the conditions indicated in paragraphs 4 and 5 subsist when the application is brought forward.

Article 76

Assistance and Collaboration for European Union Member States

1. For Italy, the central authority established under article 3 of the EEC Directive is the Ministry. In carrying out the various tasks indicated in the Directive, the Ministry shall avail itself of its central and branch organs, as well as of the co-operation of other Ministries, other organs of the State, the Regions and other territorial government bodies.

2. For the discovery and restitution of cultural properties belonging to the heritage of another European Union Member State, the Ministry shall:

   a) ensure its collaboration with the competent authorities of the other Member States;

   b) arrange for investigations within its national territory with the aim of localising the cultural property and identifying the possessor or holder. The investigations shall be ordered upon request of the requesting State, which is to be accompanied by any useful information or documents for facilitating the investigation, with particular attention paid to the location of the property;

   c) notify the Member States concerned of the discovery on national territory of a cultural property whose illegal exit from a Member State may be presumed on the basis of precise and concordant evidence;

   d) facilitate the operations which the Member State concerned carries out, with regard to the property which is the object of the notification referred to in letter c), to verify the existence of the premises and conditions indicated in article 75, on condition that such operations be carried out within two months of aforesaid notification. When the verification fails to be carried out within the established term, the provisions contained in letter *e*) shall not apply;

   e) order, where necessary, the removal of the property and its temporary safekeeping in public institutions, as well as any other measure necessary to ensure its conservation and prevent its removal from the restitution process;

   f) promote the amicable settlement of any dispute concerning restitution between the requesting State and the possessor or holder by whatever legal right of the cultural property. To this purpose, and taking into consideration the character of the parties concerned and the nature of the property, the Ministry may recommend to the requesting State and the possessing or holding parties the settlement of the dispute by means of arbitration, to be carried out according to Italian law, and it shall to this end acquire the formal agreement of both parties.

Article 77
Action for Restitution

1. For cultural properties illegally taken out of their territory, European Union Member States may bring an action for restitution before the ordinary courts of law, in accordance with article 75.
2. The action shall be brought before the court which has jurisdiction over the area in which the property is located.
3. In addition to the prerequisites established in article 163 of the civil procedures code, the summons must contain:
    a) a document describing the item claimed which certifies it as cultural property;
    b) the declaration by the competent authorities of the requesting State regarding the illegal exit of the property from national territory.
4. The summons shall, in addition to the possessor or the holder by whatever legal right of the property, be notified to the Ministry in order to be filed in the special register for recording judicial claims for restitution.
5. The Ministry shall immediately notify the central authorities of the other Member States that the summons has been filed in the register.

Article 78
Lapse of Time-limit for Action

1. The action for restitution shall be brought within the peremptory term of one year, starting from the day when the requesting State knew that the property illegally taken out of its national territory is to be found in a determined place and identified the possessor or holder of the property by whatever legal right.
2. The action for restitution is limited in any case within the term of thirty years from the

day of the illegal exit of the property from the territory of the claimant State.

3. There is no time limit for action for restitution for the properties indicated in article 75, paragraph 3, letters *b*) and *c*).

Article 79
Compensation

1. In ordering the restitution of the property, the court may, upon request of the party concerned, award compensation determined on the basis of equitable criteria.

2. In order to obtain the compensation provided for in paragraph 1, the party concerned must demonstrate that, in the act of purchasing he/she exercised due diligence under the circumstances.

3. The possessor of the property through donation, inheritance or bequest may not enjoy a more favourable position than that of the person from whom he/she acquired the object.

4. The requesting State which is obliged to pay compensation may recoup its losses from the party responsible for illegal circulation residing in Italy.

Article 80
Payment of Compensation

1. Compensation is paid by the requesting State contemporaneously with the restitution of the property.

2. Payment and delivery of the property shall be transcribed in a procès verbal by a notary public, a court official or a public officer designated for the purpose by the Ministry which shall receive a copy of the aforesaid procès verbal.

3. The procès verbal shall constitute title for the cancellation of the registration of the claim.

Article 81
Charges for Assistance and Collaboration

1. The expenses related to the search for, removal and temporary custody of the property to be returned, as well as other expenses ensuing from the application of article 76, and those inherent to the implementation of the ruling which orders restitution, shall be borne by the requesting State.

Article 82

Action for Restitution on Behalf of Italy

1. The action for restitution of cultural property which has been illegally taken from Italian soil shall be brought by the Ministry, in accord with the Ministry for Foreign Affairs, before the judge of the European Union Member State in which the cultural property is found.

2. The Ministry shall avail itself of the law officers of the State.

Article 83

Destination of the Returned Property

1. In cases where the returned cultural property does not belong to the State, the Ministry shall provide for its custody until it is delivered to the person having legal right to it.

2. The delivery of the property is subject to reimbursement to the State of the expenses incurred for the action for restitution process and custody of the property.

3. When it is not known who has the right to delivery of the property, the Ministry shall inform the public of the action for restitution through notice published in the *Official Gazette* of the Republic of Italy and through other forms of advertising.

4. In cases where the person having a right to the property fails to request its delivery within five years of the date of publication in the *Official Gazette* of the notice provided for in paragraph 3, the item shall become government property. After consulting the competent advisory body and the Regions concerned, the Ministry shall order that the property be assigned to a museum, library or archive of the State, a Region or another territorial government body, in order to best ensure protection for it and public enjoyment within the most suitable cultural context.

Article 84

Information to the European Commission and the National Parliament

1. The Ministry shall inform the Commission of the European Community of the measures adopted by Italy to ensure implementation of the EEC Regulation and shall receive the corresponding information forwarded to the Commission by other Member States.

2. On an annual basis, the Ministry shall, in an annex to the budgetary expenditure estimates of the Ministry, forward to Parliament a report on the implementation of this Chapter as well as the implementation of the EEC Directive and EEC regulation in Italy and in the other Member States.

3. Every three years, after consultation with the competent advisory body, the Ministry shall prepare a report for the Commission on the application of the EEC regulation and the EEC directive indicated in paragraph 1. The report shall be forwarded to Parliament.

Article 85
Databank of Stolen Cultural Property

1. A databank of stolen cultural property is established within the Ministry, according to modalities established by ministerial decree.

Article 86
Agreements with other European Union Member States

1. For the purpose of encouraging and fostering greater reciprocal knowledge of the cultural heritage, as well as of the legislation and the way in which protection is organised in the other European Union Member States, the Ministry shall promote suitable agreements with the corresponding authorities of the other Member States.

Section IV
UNIDROIT Convention

Article 87
Stolen or Illegally Exported Cultural Properties

1. The restitution of cultural properties indicated in the annex to the UNIDROIT Convention on the international return of stolen or illegally exported cultural properties is governed by the provisions of the aforesaid Convention and the related laws of ratification and enforcement.

Chapter VI
Findings and Discoveries

Section I
Searches and Fortuitous Discoveries within the National Territory

Article 88
Search Activities

1. Archaeological searches and, in general, activities for finding the things indicated in article 10 in any part of the national territory shall be reserved to the Ministry.

2. The Ministry may order the temporary occupation of the buildings where the searches and activities indicated in paragraph 1 are to be carried out.

3. The proprietor of the building shall be entitled to compensation for the occupation, which shall be determined in accordance with the modalities established by the general provisions for expropriation for public use. The compensation may be paid in money, or, upon request of the proprietor, by releasing the things found or part of them when these are not of interest to the collections of the State.

Article 89
Search Concession

1. The Ministry may grant concession to public or private subjects to carry out the search activities and work indicated in articles 88, and may on behalf of the concessionaire issue the order for occupation of the buildings where the work is to be carried out.

2. In addition to the prescriptions set out when concession is granted, the concessionaire must comply with all other prescriptions which the Minister shall deem necessary. If the concessionaire fails to comply with the prescriptions, the concession shall be revoked.

3. The concession may also be revoked when the Ministry wishes to take over the execution or continuation of the works. In such case, the expenses incurred by the concessionaire for work hitherto carried out shall be reimbursed to the aforesaid concessionaire and the amount shall be established by the Ministry.

4. When the concessionaire decides not to accept the assessment of the Ministry, the amount shall be established by a qualified assessor appointed by the president of the tribunal. The related costs shall be advanced by the concessionaire.

5. The concession provided for in paragraph 1, may also be granted to the proprietor of the buildings in which the works are to be carried out.

6. The Ministry may, upon request, consent that the things found remain, in whole or in part, within the Region or other territorial government body for exhibition purposes, on condition that the body should possess a suitable venue and can ensure the conservation and custody of the aforesaid things.

Article 90
Fortuitous Discoveries

1. Whosoever fortuitously discovers immovable or movable things indicated in article 10 shall report the discovery to the superintendent or mayor or to the public security authorities within twenty-four hours and shall provide for the temporary conservation of the things, leaving them in the condition and place in which they were found.

2. When movable things are concerned for which it is not possible to ensure custody otherwise, the discoverer shall have the power to remove them in order to better ensure their safety and conservation until such time as the visit of the competent authorities occurs and, if need be, the discoverer may ask for the assistance of public authorities.

3. Every holder of things discovered fortuitously must abide by the provisions for conservation and custody set out in paragraphs 1 and 2.

4. Costs incurred for custody and removal shall be reimbursed by the Ministry.

Article 91
Ownership and Qualification of the Things Found

1. The things indicated in article 10, found underground or in sea beds by whomsoever and howsoever, shall belong to the State and, depending on whether they be immovable or movable, shall become part of government property or of its inalienable assets, pursuant to articles 822 and 826 of the civil code.

2. Whenever demolition of a building is carried out on behalf of the State, the Regions, other territorial government bodies or other public bodies or institutions, the by-product

material which by contract has been reserved for the demolition firm shall not include the things found as a result of the demolition which possess the interest indicated in article 10, paragraph 3, letter *a*). Any agreement to the contrary shall be null and void.

Article 92
Finding Reward

1. The Ministry shall offer a reward not exceeding one quarter of the value of the things found to:

    a) the proprietor of the building in which the finding occurred;

    b) the concessionaire of the search activities, pursuant to article 89;

    c) the accidental discoverer who has fulfilled the obligations set out in article 90.

2. The proprietor of the building who has obtained the concession provided for in article 89 or is the discoverer of the thing in question, shall be entitled to a reward which may not exceed half of the value of the things found.

3. A discoverer who has entered and searched the property of another person without the consent of the proprietor or holder shall not be entitled to a reward.

4. The reward may be paid in money or with the release of a part of the things found. In lieu of the reward, the interested party may obtain, upon request, a tax credit for the same sum, in accordance with the modalities and with the limits established by decree adopted by the Ministry of the Economy and Finance in accord with the Ministry, pursuant to article 17, paragraph 3 of law no. 400 of 23 August 1988.

Article 93
Assessment of Reward

1. The Ministry shall provide for the assessment of the reward for the persons or parties entitled pursuant to article 96, following assessment of the value of the things found.

2. During the assessment process, each of the persons or parties entitled shall receive partial payment of the reward in an amount not exceeding one fifth of the value, assessed on a provisional basis, of the things found.

3. If the persons or parties entitled do not accept the definitive assessment of the Ministry, the value of the things found shall be determined by a third party, appointed by agreement of the parties concerned. If they do not reach agreement for the appointment of a

third party or for its replacement, whenever the third party appointed does not wish to or cannot accept the appointment, the appointment shall be made, upon request of one of the parties, by the president of the court having jurisdiction over the area in which the things were found. The costs of the assessment shall be advanced by the person or party entitled to the reward.

4. The assessment of the third party may be contested in case of error or manifest inequity.

Section II
Searches and Fortuitous Findings in Areas Adjacent to National Waters

Article 94
UNESCO Convention

1. Archaeological and historical objects found in the seabed of areas of seawaters extending for twelve marine miles from the external boundary of national waters are protected under the "Rules pertaining to measures for underwater cultural heritage" annexed to the UNESCO Convention on the protection of the underwater cultural heritage, adopted in Paris on November 2, 2001.

Chapter VII
Expropriation

Article 95
Expropriation of Cultural Property

1. Immovable and movable cultural property may be expropriated by the Ministry for reasons of public use, when the expropriation responds to an important need to improve the conditions of protection for the purposes of public enjoyment of the aforesaid properties.

2. The Ministry may, upon request, authorise the Regions and other territorial government

bodies, as well as other public bodies and institutions, to carry out the expropriation referred to in paragraph 1. In such case it shall declare public use for the purposes of expropriation and shall transfer the deeds to the interested body for the prosecution of the procedure.

3. The Ministry may also order expropriation on behalf of a public non-profit association, taking direct responsibility for the relative procedure.

Article 96
Expropriation for Instrumental Purposes

1. Buildings and areas may be expropriated for reasons of public use when this is necessary for insulating or restoring monuments, for ensuring natural light or perspective, for protecting or improving their decorous aspect or increasing public enjoyment, or for facilitating access to them.

Article 97
Expropriation for Archaeological Interest

1. The Ministry may proceed to the expropriation of buildings for the purpose of carrying out work of archaeological interest or search activities for the discovery of the things indicated in article 10.

Article 98
Declaration of Public Use

1. Public use shall be declared by ministerial decree or, in the case of article 96, by a provision adopted by the Region and communicated to the Ministry.

2. In the cases of expropriation provided for under articles 96 and 97, the approval of the project shall be equivalent to the declaration of public use.

Article 99
Compensation for Expropriation of Cultural Property

1. In the case of expropriation provided for by article 95, compensation shall consist of the

fair price that the property would have in a free contract of sale within the State.

2. Payment of compensation shall be made in accordance with the modalities established by the general provisions for expropriation for public use.

Article 100
Reference to General Laws

1. In the cases of expropriation governed by articles 96 and 97, the general provisions for expropriation for public use shall apply, insofar as they are compatible.

TITLE II
ENJOYMENT AND ENHANCEMENT

Chapter I
Enjoyment of Cultural Property

Section I
General Principles

Article 101
Institutions and Places of Culture

1. For the purposes of this Code, museums, libraries and archives, archaeological parks and areas, and monumental complexes are deemed institutions and places of culture.

2. The following definitions apply:

    a) "museum" shall mean a permanent facility which acquires, conserves, arranges and exhibits cultural property for the purposes of education and study;

    b) "library" shall mean a permanent facility which gathers and conserves an organised collection of books, materials and information, written or published on any kind of support, and ensures consultation for the purposes of promoting reading and study;

    c) "archive" shall mean a permanent facility which collects, inventories, and conserves original documents of historical interest and ensures consultation for purposes of study and research;

    d) "archaeological area" shall mean site characterised by the presence of remains of a fossil nature or of artefacts or prehistoric or ancient structures;

    e) "archaeological park" shall mean a land area characterised by important archaeological evidence and the presence of historical, landscape or environmental values, organised as an open-air museum;

    f) "monumental complex" shall mean a collection of a number of structures which may have been built in different periods, and which over time have, as a whole, acquired autonomous artistic, historical or ethno-anthropological importance.

3. The institutions and places indicated in paragraph 1 which belong to government bodies

are designated for public enjoyment and offer a public service.

4. The exhibition and consultation facilities as well as the places indicated in paragraph 1 which belong to private individuals and are open to the public offer a private socially useful service.

Article 102

Enjoyment of Publicly Owned Institutions and Places of Culture

1. The State, the Regions, other territorial government bodies and any other public body and institution shall ensure the enjoyment of the properties present in the institutions and places indicated in article 101, in compliance with the fundamental principles established by this Code.

2. In the respect of the principles indicated in paragraph 1, regional legislation shall govern the enjoyment of the properties present in the institutions and places of culture not belonging to the State or for which the State has transferred use on the basis of the laws in force.

3. The enjoyment of public cultural properties outside the institutions and places indicated in article 101 shall be ensured in accordance with the provisions of the present Title and compatibly with the implementation of the institutional purposes to which the aforesaid properties are designated.

4. For the purposes of co-ordinating, harmonising and increasing enjoyment in relation to the publicly owned institutions and places of culture, the State, and, on its behalf, the Ministry, the Regions and other territorial government bodies shall define agreements in this sphere, with the procedures set out in article 112. Where no agreement exists, each public body must guarantee the enjoyment of the properties under its jurisdiction.

5. By means of the agreements indicated in paragraph 4, the Ministry may also transfer jurisdiction of cultural institutions and places to the Regions and other territorial government bodies, on the basis of the principle of subsidiarity, for the purpose of ensuring adequate enjoyment and enhancement of the properties located therein.

Article 103

Access to Cultural Institutions and Places

1. Access to public cultural institutions and places may be free of charge or by admission fee.

The Ministry, the Regions and other territorial government bodies may stipulate agreements for co-ordinating access to them.

2. Access to libraries and public archives for purposes of reading, study and research is free of charge.

3. In cases where access involves an admission fee, the Ministry, the Regions and the other territorial government bodies shall determine:

   a) the cases of free access and free admission;

   b) ticket categories and the criteria for establishing their relative prices. The ticket price shall include the costs deriving from the stipulation of the agreements provided for in letter c);

   c) the modalities for the issue, distribution and sale of admission tickets and for the collection of the corresponding fee, which may also be carried out through agreements with public bodies and private persons. New computer technologies may be utilised for handling admission tickets, with the possibility of advance sales and sales by third parties with which agreements have been established.

   d) the percentage of ticket sales proceeds which may be assigned to the National Institute for Social Assistance and Pensions (Ente Nazionale di assistenza e previdenza) for painters, sculptors, musicians, writers and playwrights.

4. Any special rates for admission must be regulated so as not to create unjustified discriminations against the citizens of other European Union Member States.

Article 104
Enjoyment of Privately Owned Cultural Property

1. The following may be subject to public access for cultural purposes:

   a) immovable cultural properties indicated in article 10, paragraph 3, letters a) and d), which are of exceptional interest;

   b) the collections declared under article 13.

2. The exceptional interest of the immovable properties indicated in paragraph 1, letter a) shall be declared by an act of the Ministry, after consultation with the proprietor.

3. Visiting procedures shall be established by agreement between the proprietor and the superintendent, who shall notify the Municipality or the Metropolitan Area in which the properties are located.

4. The provisions in article 38 shall remain in force.

Article 105
Rights of Use and Public Enjoyment

1. The Ministry and the Regions shall, within the sphere of their competence, ensure that the rights of use and enjoyment which the public has acquired over the things and properties subject to the provisions of the present Part are respected.

Section II
Use of Cultural Property

Article 106
Individual Use of Cultural Property

1. The Ministry, the Regions and other territorial government bodies may grant the use of cultural properties - committed to their care - to individual applicants, for purposes which are compatible with their original cultural designation.
2. For properties which are committed to the care of the Ministry, the superintendent shall establish the fee to be paid and adopt the relative procedures.

Article 107
Instrumental and Temporary Use and Reproduction of Cultural Property

1. The Ministry, the Regions and other territorial government bodies may permit the reproduction as well as the instrumental and temporary use of the cultural properties committed to their care, without prejudice to the provisions in paragraph 2 and those with regard to copyright.
2. The reproduction of cultural properties is generally forbidden when it consists in producing casts from the originals of works of sculpture or of works in relief in general, regardless of the material from which such works are made. Casts from already existing copies of the originals are ordinarily permitted, with the authorisation of the superintendent. The procedures for reproducing casts are regulated by ministerial decree.

Article 108

Concession Fees, Payment for Reproduction, Security Deposits

1. Concession fees and payments connected to the reproduction of cultural properties are established by the authority to whose care the property is committed, also taking into account:

   a) the nature of the activities to which concession of use refers;

   b) the means and modalities for producing the reproduction;

   c) the use the spaces and property will be put to and for what period of time;

   d) the use and purpose for which the reproductions are made, as well as the economic benefits which will accrue to the applicant.

2. The fees and payments shall as a rule be paid in advance.

3. No fee is owed for reproductions requested by private individuals for personal use for purposes of study, or by public bodies for purposes of enhancement. The applicants shall nevertheless reimburse the administration granting concession for any costs incurred.

4. In cases where the activities granted in concession may harm the cultural properties, the authorities to whose care the properties are committed shall establish the amount of security deposit, which may be made through a bank or insurance surety. For the same reasons, the security deposit is also required in cases of exemption from payment of fees.

5. The security deposit is returned when it has been ascertained that the property granted in concession has not suffered damage and that expenses incurred have been reimbursed.

6. The minimum amounts of the fees and payments for use and reproduction of the property shall be established by a provision on the part of the administration granting concession.

Article 109

Catalogue of Photographic Images and of Films of Cultural Property

1. When the concession concerns the reproduction of cultural property for purposes of collections and catalogues of photographic images and films in general, the concession provision shall prescribe:

   a) the deposit of an original duplicate of each film or photograph;

   b) the restitution, after use, of the original colour photograph with the relevant code.

Article 110
Cash Receipts and Division of Proceeds

1. In the cases provided for in article 115, paragraph 2, the proceeds deriving from the sale of tickets for admission to cultural institutions and sites, as well as concession fees and payments for the reproduction of cultural property, shall be paid to the government bodies to which the institutions, sites or individual properties belong or to whose care they are committed, in conformity with the respective public accounting provisions.

2. Where institutions, sites or properties belonging to or committed to the care of the State are concerned, the proceeds indicated in paragraph 1 shall be paid to the provincial section of the State treasury. Payment may also be deposited into a postal current account registered to the aforesaid treasury, or into a current account opened by each cultural institution or site officer at a credit institution. In this last hypothesis the banking institution shall deposit the amounts received into the section of the provincial treasury of the State, not more than five days after receipt. The Ministry for the Economy and Finance shall re-assign the sums received to the competent base budget units for the Ministry's expense budget, according to the criteria and measures established by the same Ministry.

3. The proceeds from the sale of tickets for admission to institutions and sites belonging to or committed to the care of the State are designated for the realisation of works for the safety and conservation of the aforesaid sites, pursuant to article 29, as well as to the expropriation and purchase of cultural properties, which may also be carried out by means of the exercise of pre-emption.

4. The proceeds from the sale of tickets for admission to the institutions and sites belonging to or committed to the care of other government bodies are designated for the increase and enhancement of the cultural patrimony.

Chapter II
Principles of Enhancement of the Cultural Heritage

Article 111
Enhancement Activities

1. The activities for the enhancement of the cultural heritage consists in the stable constitution and organisation of resources, facilities or networks, or in providing technical skills or financial or instrumental resources, designed for carrying out the functions and pursuing the aims indicated in article 6. Private subjects may concur, co-operate or participate in such activities.

2. Enhancement may be carried out by public or private initiative.

3. Enhancement carried out by public initiative shall conform to the principles of freedom of participation, plurality of participants, continuity of activity, equality of treatment, economic feasibility and management transparency.

4. Enhancement carried out by private initiative is deemed a socially useful activity and its aims of social solidarity are recognised.

Article 112
Enhancement of Publicly Owned Cultural Property

1. The State, the Regions and other territorial government bodies shall ensure the enhancement of the property held in institutions and in the places indicated in article 101, in observance of the fundamental principles established by this Code.

2. In observance of the principles referred to in paragraph 1, regional legislation shall govern the enhancement of properties held in institutions and places of culture not belonging to the State or of those for which the State has transferred use on the basis of the laws in force.

3. The enhancement of publicly owned cultural properties outside the institutions and places referred to in paragraph 1 shall, in accordance with the provisions of this Title, be ensured compatibly with the institutional uses for which the said properties have been designated.

4. For the purposes of co-ordinating, harmonising and supplementing enhancement activities for properties forming the cultural heritage belonging to the government, the State shall, through the Ministry, the Regions and other territorial government bodies, stipulate a-greements on a regional basis, in order to define objectives and establish the timetable and modalities for achieving them. Suitable forms of management, pursuant to article 115, shall be identified through the same agreements.

5. When, within the fixed term, the agreements indicated in paragraph 4 have not been reached among the competent organs, their definition shall be referred back to joint deci-sion of the Ministry, the president of the Region, the president of the Province and the mayors of the Municipalities concerned. Where there is no agreement, each government body must guarantee the enhancement of the properties under its jurisdiction.

6. The State, through the Ministry, the Regions and other territorial government bodies may, within a Unified Conference, define the general guidelines and procedures for har-monising the agreements indicated in paragraph 4 throughout the national territory.

7. Private persons may also participate in the agreements indicated in paragraph 4, and, with the consent of the interested parties, the same agreements may pertain to privately-owned properties.

8. Interested public bodies may also enter into special agreements with cultural or volunteer associations which carry out activities of promotion and dissemination aimed at knowledge of cultural property.

Article 113
Enhancement of Privately Owned Cultural Property

1. Privately initiated activities and facilities for the enhancement of privately owned cultural property may obtain public support from the State, the Regions and other territorial gov-ernment bodies.

2. The extent of the support shall be established by taking into account the importance of the cultural properties to which it refers.

3. The modalities of enhancement shall be established by an agreement to be stipulated with the proprietor, possessor or holder of the property, when the support measures are adopted.

4. The Region and other territorial government bodies may also concur in the enhancement of the properties indicated in article 104, paragraph 1, by participating in the agreements

provided for therein under paragraph 3.

Article 114
Enhancement Quality Control

1. The Ministry, the Regions and other territorial government bodies, with the possible participation of universities, shall establish standard levels of quality for enhancement, which shall be revised periodically.

2. The quality control levels referred to in paragraph 1 shall be adopted with a decree of the Ministry, after agreement is reached within a Unified Conference.

3. The parties which, under article 115, detain management of enhancement activities must ensure observance of the levels established.

Article 115
Forms of Management

1. Enhancement of cultural property undertaken by private initiative are managed directly or indirectly.

2. Direct management is carried out by means of organisational structures within the administrations, which are endowed with suitable scientific, organisational, financial and accounting autonomy, and provided with proper technical staff.

3. Indirect management is carried out by:

   a) direct assignment of such management to institutions, foundations, associations, consortiums, corporations or other entities, which to a prevalent extent are incorporated by the public administration to which the property pertains or in which the said administration holds a major interest;

   b) concession to a third party, on the basis of criteria indicated in paragraphs 4 and 5.

4. The State and the Regions may resort to indirect management in order to ensure an adequate level of enhancement for cultural property. The choice between the two forms of management indicated in letters *a*) and *b*) of paragraph 3 shall be made following a comparative assessment, in terms of efficiency and efficacy, of the aims to be pursued and the relative means, methods and timetables.

5. When, following the comparative assessment referred to in paragraph 4, it is preferable to resort to concession to a third party, the same is provided for through open competition

procedures, on the basis of a comparative assessment of the projects presented.

6. Other territorial government bodies ordinarily resort to indirect management as referred to in paragraph 3, letter *a*) except where, because of the limited extent or of the type of enhancement activity, direct management proves to be economically advantageous or more suitable.

7. By means of prior agreement between the parties having legal title to the activities of enhancement, the assignment or concession provided for in paragraph 3 may be arranged on a shared and joint basis.

8. The relationship between title-holder of the activities and the party to whom they have been entrusted or granted in concession is governed by a services contract, which shall specify, among other things, the qualitative levels of services provided and the professional level of the staff, as well as the powers of direction and control to be detained by the title-holder of the activity or the service.

9. The title-holder of the activity may share in the assets or capital of the parties indicated in paragraph 3, letter a), which participation may also consist in the conferral of use of the cultural property to be enhanced. The effects of the conferral of use shall end, without indemnity, in all cases of the total cessation of sharing on the part of the title-holder of the activity or service, of the discharge of the participating party, or of the cessation, for whatever cause, of the assignment of the activity or the service. The properties granted in use are not subject to specific financial security unless by virtue of their equivalent economic value.

10. The concession in use of the cultural property to be enhanced may be linked to the assignment or concession referred to in paragraph 3. The concession loses efficacy, without indemnity, in any case whatsoever of cessation of assignment or concession of the service or activity.

Article 116
Protection of Cultural Property Conferred or Granted in Use

1. Cultural properties which have been conferred or granted in use under article 115, paragraphs 9 and 10, shall remain to all effects subject to their own legal regulations. The functions of protection shall be exercised by the Ministry, which may also provide for protection at the request of or with regard to the parties on which use of the same properties have been conferred or to which they have been granted.

Article 117
Additional Services

1. Services of cultural assistance and hospitality for the public may be established in the institutions and places of culture indicated in article 101.

2. Included in the services referred to in paragraph 1 are:

   a) publishing and sales services related to catalogues and to catalogue, audio-visual and computer aids, to all other informational material, and to the reproduction of cultural property;

   b) services related to book and archival properties for the provision of reproductions and library lending delivery;

   c) the management of record, slide and museum library collections;

   d) the management of sales outlets and the commercial utilization of the reproduction of cultural properties;

   e) public relations services, including assistance and entertainment for children, information and educational guidance and assistance services, meeting places:

   f) cafeteria, restaurant and cloakroom services;

   g) the organisation of cultural exhibits and events, as well as promotional initiatives.

3. The services referred to in paragraph 1 may be managed in conjunction with cleaning, security and box office services.

4. The management of the aforesaid services shall be effected in the forms provided for by article 115.

5. The fees from the concession of services shall be received and shared out as set out in article 110.

Article 118
Promotion of Study and Research Activities

1. The Ministry, the Regions and other territorial government bodies shall, with the possible participation of universities and of other public and private entities, carry out, promote and support research, studies and other cognitive activities related to the cultural heritage, and may do so jointly.

2. For the purpose of ensuring the systematic gathering and dissemination of the results of

studies, research and other activities referred to in paragraph 1, including cataloguing, the Ministry and the Regions may enter into agreements to create, on the regional or inter-regional level, permanent centres for the study and documentation of the cultural heritage, providing for the participation of universities and other public and private entities.

Article 119
Dissemination of Knowledge about the Cultural Heritage in the Schools

1. The Ministry, the Ministry for Education, Universities and Research, the Regions and other interested territorial government bodies may conclude agreements to spread knowledge of the cultural heritage and promote its enjoyment on the part of students.

2. On the basis of the agreements provided for in paragraph 1, the directors of the institutions and the places of culture referred to in article 101 may, with schools of every type and level belonging to the national educational system, enter into special agreements for the development of didactic programmes, the preparation of audio-visual material and aids, as well as for the education and training of teachers. The programmes, materials and teaching aids shall take into account the specific nature of the applicant school and any particular needs resulting from the presence of disabled students.

Article 120
Sponsorship of Cultural Property

1. Sponsorship of cultural property is defined as any form of contribution in goods or services on the part of private subjects to the planning or carrying out of initiatives of the Ministry, the Regions and other territorial government bodies, or of private subjects, in the field of protection and enhancement of the cultural heritage, with the aim of promoting the name, brand, image, activity or the product of the aforesaid subjects.

2. The promotion referred to in paragraph 1 occurs through the association of the name, brand, image, activity or product with the initiative which forms the object of the contribution, in forms which are compatible with the artistic or historical nature, the appearance and the decorous aspect of the cultural property to be protected or enhanced, and which are to be established under the sponsorship contract.

3. The sponsorship contract shall also define the modalities for the disbursement of funding as well as the forms of supervision, on the part of the disbursing party, over the realisa-

tion of the initiative to which the funding refers.

Article 121
Agreements with Bank Foundations

1. The Ministry, the Regions and the other territorial government bodies may, each within its own sphere of competence and jointly as well, enter into memoranda of understanding with the granting foundations referred to in the provisions for the restructuring and regulation of credit institutions, which by statute pursue socially useful aims in the sector of the arts and cultural heritage and activities, for the purpose of co-ordinating work for the enhancement of the cultural heritage and, within this context, of ensuring the balanced utilisation of the financial resources made available. The government may participate with its own financial resources in order to ensure the pursuit of the aims set out in the memoranda of understanding.

Chapter III
Consultation of Archive Documents and Safeguarding of Confidentiality

Article 122
State Archives and Historical Archives of Public Bodies :
Consultation of Documents

1. The documents kept in the archives of the State and in the historical archives of the Regions, of other territorial government bodies as well as those of any other public body and institution, may be freely consulted, with the following exceptions:
   a) those declared confidential under article 125, relative to the foreign or domestic policies of the State, which may be consulted fifty years after their date;
   b) those containing sensitive information as well as information relative to measures of a penal nature expressly indicated in the laws on the use of personal data, which may be consulted forty years after their date. The term is seventy years if the information is

such as to reveal state of health, sexual experiences or private family relationships.

2. Prior to the expiry of the time limitations indicated in paragraph 1, the documents shall remain accessible in accordance with the regulations on access to administrative documents. The petition for access is dealt with by the administration which held the document before its filing or deposit.

3. Also subject to the provisions of paragraph 1 are privately-owned archives and documents deposited in the archives of the State or in the historical archives of public bodies, or in the same archives which have been donated or sold or left as inheritance or bequest. Depositors and those who donate or sell or leave as inheritance or make a bequest of the documents may also establish a condition of non-consultation of all or part of the documents of the last seventy-year period. Such limitation, like the general limitation established in paragraph 1, does not apply to the depositors, donators, sellers and any other person they designate; nor does the said limitation apply to assignees of the depositors, donators and sellers, when documents related to property are concerned, in which they have an interest by right of purchase.

Article 123
State Archives and Historical Archives of Public Bodies:
Consultation of Confidential Documents

1. The Ministry of the Interior, after acquiring the advisory opinion of the director competent for State Archives and having heard the Commission on questions pertaining to the consultation of confidential archival documents, which has been established within the Ministry of the Interior, may authorise consultation for historical purposes of documents of a confidential nature preserved in the archives of the State, even before expiry of the terms indicated in article 122, paragraph 1. Authorisation is granted, under equal conditions, to each applicant.

2. The documents for which consultation is authorised under paragraph 1 shall maintain their confidential nature and may not be disseminated.

3. Also subject to the provisions of paragraphs 1 and 2 is the consultation for historical purposes of documents of a confidential nature preserved in the historical archives of the Regions, other territorial government bodies, and any other public body and institution. The opinion referred to in paragraph 1 is given by the archival superintendent.

Article 124

Consultation of Current Archives for Historical Purposes

1. Without prejudice to the provisions of the laws in force on access to public administration documents, the State, the Regions and other territorial government bodies shall establish regulations for consultation for historical purposes of their current and deposited archives.
2. Consultation for the purposes of paragraph 1 of current and deposited archives of other public bodies and institutions, shall be regulated by the same bodies and institutions, on the basis of general guidelines established by the Ministry.

Article 125

Declaration of Confidentiality

1. The ascertainment of the existence and the nature of documents which may not be freely consulted indicated in articles 122 and 127 is carried out by the Ministry of the Interior, in agreement with the Ministry.

Article 126

Protection of Personal Data

1. When the owner of personal data has exercised the rights granted to him/her by the laws which govern their use, the documents of the historical archives shall be preserved and may be consulted along with the documentation pertaining to the exercise of the same rights.
2. At the request of the same owner, a freeze may be ordered on personal data which are not of great interest to the public, whenever their use involves a concrete danger of harming the dignity, privacy or personal identity of the individual concerned.
3. The consultation for historical purposes of documents containing personal data is also subject to the provisions of the code on ethics and good conduct established under the laws on the use of personal data.

Article 127
Consultation of Private Archives

1. Private proprietors, possessors or holders by whatever legal right of archives or of single documents declared under article 13 are obliged to permit scholars, who make a justified request through the archival superintendent, to consult the documents in accordance with the procedures agreed upon between the private parties themselves and the superintendent. The related expenses shall be borne by the scholar.

2. Excluded from consultation are the single documents declared to be of a confidential nature under article 125. Documents for which the condition of non-consultation has been ordered under article 122, paragraph 3, may also be excluded from consultation.

3. The provisions referred to in article 123, paragraph 3, and article 126, paragraph 3, shall apply to private archives used for historical purposes, even if they have not been declared in accordance with article 13.

TITLE III
TRANSITIONAL AND FINAL PROVISIONS

Article 128
Notifications Served Under Prior Legislation

1. Cultural properties referred to in article 10, paragraph 3, for which notifications served in accordance with laws no. 364 of 20 June 1909 and no. 778 of 11 June 1922, have not been renewed and registered are subject to the procedure referred to in article 14. Until the conclusion of the same procedure, the said notifications shall in any case remain valid for the purposes of this Part.

2. Notifications served in accordance with articles 2, 3, 5 and 21 of law no. 1089 of 1 June 1939 and the declarations adopted and notified under article 36 of decree no. 1409 of the President of the Republic of 30 September 1963 and under articles 6, 7, 8 and 49 of legislative decree no. 490 of 29 October 1999, shall also remain in effect.

3. In the presence of elements which effectively occurred subsequently or which had not been previously known or had not been assessed, the Ministry may, ex officio or at the request of the proprietor, possessor or holder concerned, renew the procedure of declaration for properties which have been the object of the notifications referred to in paragraph 2, for the purpose of verifying the continuing presence of the premises for the subjection of the same properties to the provisions for protection.

4. Administrative appeal is admissible under article 16 against the decision of denial of the application to renew the procedure of declaration, produced under paragraph 3, or against the final declaration of the same procedure, even when it has been initiated ex officio.

Article 129
Particular Legislative Provisions

1. The laws pertaining to single cities or parts of them, architectonic complexes, national monuments, sites of historical, artistic or archaeological interest shall remain in force.

2. The provisions relating to *ex fideicommissum* artistic collections, issued with law no. 286 of 28 June 1871, law no. 1461 of 8 July 1883, royal decree no. 653 of 23 November 1891 and law no. 31 of 7 February 1892, shall also remain in force.

Article 130
Prior Regulatory Provisions

1. Until the emanation of the decrees and regulations provided for by this Code, the provisions of the regulations approved by royal decrees no. 1163 of 2 October 1911 and no. 363 of 30 January 1913, and any other regulatory provision pertaining to the laws contained in this part, shall remain in force, insofar as they are applicable.

THIRD PART
LANDSCAPE ASSETS

TITLE I
PROTECTION AND ENHANCEMENT

Chapter I
General Provisions

Article 131
Safeguarding of Landscape Values

1. For the purposes of this Code, the term landscape is defined as an integral part of the territory whose characteristics are derived from nature, the history of humanity or from their reciprocal inter-relationships.

2. The protection and enhancement of the landscape shall safeguard the values which it expresses in terms of perceptible identifying manifestations.

Article 132
Co-operation Between Public Administrations

1. Public administrations shall co-operate in the definitions of guidelines and criteria related to activities of protection, planning, reclamation, upgrading and enhancement of the landscape and the management of related works.

2. The guidelines and criteria shall also pursue the aims of safeguarding and re-integrating the values of the landscape environment, with a view to sustainable development as well.

3. For the purpose of disseminating and increasing knowledge about the landscape, the public administrations shall carry out training and educational activities.

4. The Ministry and the Regions shall define the policies for the protection and enhancement of the landscape, also taking into account studies, analyses and proposals made by the National Observatory for Landscape Quality, established by ministerial decree, as well as those made by Observatories established in each Region for the same purpose.

Article 133

International Agreements

1. The activities carried out for the protection and enhancement of the landscape environment shall conform to the obligations and principles of co-operation between States deriving from international agreements.

Article 134

Landscape Assets

1. Landscape assets include the following:
   a) the immovable properties and areas indicated in article 136, identified under articles 138 to 141;
   b) the areas indicated in article 142;
   c) the immovable properties and areas in any case subjected to protection by landscape plans provided for in articles 143 and 156.

Article 135

Landscape Planning

1. The Regions shall ensure that the landscape is suitably protected and enhanced. To this purpose, they shall subject the territory to suitable zoning laws, by approving landscape plans or urban land plans with specific consideration for landscape values, concerning the entire regional territory, both of which shall hereinafter referred to "landscape plans".

2. With particular reference to the assets indicated in article 134, the landscape plan shall define transformations which are compatible with landscape values, initiatives for the reclamation and upgrading of immovable properties and of areas subjected to protection, as well as measures for the enhancement of the landscape, in relation to prospects for sustainable development as well.

Chapter II
Identification of Landscape Assets

Article 136
Buildings and Areas of Notable Public Interest

1. The following are subject to the provisions of this Title by virtue of their notable public interest:

    a) immovable things of outstanding natural beauty or geological singularity;

    b) the villas, gardens and parks not protected by the provisions of the Second Part of this Code, which stand out for their uncommon beauty;

    c) complexes of immovable things which constitute a characteristic aspect having aesthetic and traditional value;

    d) beautiful views considered to be of picturesque quality as well as vantage points and belvederes which are accessible to the public and from which the spectacle of those beauties may be enjoyed;

Article 137
Provincial Commissions

1. A Commission with the task of making proposals for the declaration of notable public interest for the immovable property indicated in letters *a*) and *b*) and the areas indicated in letters *a*) and *d*) of article 136, shall be established for each Province by a Regional measure.

2. The Regional director, the superintendent for architectonic property and the landscape and the superintendent for archaeological property with competence for each area shall, by right, serve on the Commission. The remaining members, who are not to exceed six, shall be appointed by the Region among individuals with particular professional expertise and experience in the protection of the landscape. The Commission shall hear the opinion of the mayors of the interested Municipalities and may consult experts.

Article 138

Recommendation for Declaration of Notable Public Interest

1. On the initiative of the Regional director, of the Region or of other interested territorial government bodies, the Commission indicated in article 137 shall acquire necessary information through the superintendent and Regional and Provincial offices, assess the existence of notable public interest in the immovable properties and areas indicated in article 136, and recommend declaration of notable public interest. The recommendation shall include the grounds for the aforesaid declaration with reference to the historical, cultural, natural, morphological and aesthetic characteristics belonging to the immovable properties and areas which have identifying significance and value for the territory in which they are located and which are perceived as such by the population. The recommendation shall contain the prescriptions, measures and criteria for management indicated in article 143, paragraph 3.

2. The recommendations for declaration of notable public interest are aimed at establishing specific regulations for protection and enhancement, which would be more responsive to the peculiar elements and the value of the specific landscape contexts and would be an integral part of the regulations provided for in the landscape plan.

Article 139

Participation in the Procedures for the Declaration of Notable Public Interest

1. The recommendation of the Commission for the declaration of notable public interest of immovable properties and areas, accompanied by the relative planimetric drawings drawn in a scale suitable to their identification, shall appear for ninety days on the municipal notice board and be deposited for public consultation with the offices of the Municipalities concerned.

2. Notice of the recommendation and its relative publication on the municipal notice board shall be published without delay in at least two dailies of wide circulation in the area concerned, as well as in a daily newspaper with nation-wide circulation and, where these have been established, on the Web-sites of the Region and of other territorial government bodies in whose jurisdiction the immovable properties or the areas to be subjected to protection are located.

3. Within the sixty days following publication of the Commission's recommendation on the municipal notice board, the Municipalities, the Metropolitan areas, the Provinces, associations for the common public interest identified under article 13 of law no. 349 of 8 July 1986 and any other interested parties may present their observations to the Regions, which shall likewise have the power to order a public enquiry.

4. Following fulfilment of the measures referred to in paragraphs 1, 2, and 3, the Region shall, for the immovable properties indicated in letters *a*) and *b*) of article 136, notify the start of the declaration procedure to the proprietor, possessor or holder of the property, and to the Metropolitan Area or Municipality concerned.

5. The notification referred to in paragraph 4 shall include the elements identifying the immovable property, including cadastral elements, as well as the indication of the consequent obligations to be taken on by the proprietor, possessor or holder.

6. Within sixty days of the date of receipt of the notification referred to in paragraph 4, the proprietor, possessor or holder of the immovable property may present observations to the Region.

Article 140
Declaration of Notable Public Interest and Relative Cognitive Measures

1. On the basis of the recommendation of the Commission and having examined the observations and taken into account the result of any public enquiry, the Region shall emanate the provision of declaration of notable public interest of the immovable properties indicated in letters *a*) and *b*) and of the areas indicated in letters *c*) and *d*) of article 136.

2. The provision of declaration of notable public interest of the immovable properties indicated in letters *a*) and *b*) of article 136 shall likewise be notified to the proprietor, possessor or holder, deposited in the Municipality, and recorded in the land registers by the Region.

3. The provisions of declaration of notable public interest are published in the *Official Gazette* of the Italian Republic and in the Official Bulletin of the Region.

4. A copy of the *Official Gazette* shall be displayed on the notice board of all the Municipalities concerned for the period of ninety days. A copy of the declaration and the relative planimetric drawings shall be deposited for public consultation with the offices of the Municipalities concerned.

Article 141
Ministerial Measures

1. When the Commission fails to carry out its assessments within the term of sixty days from the request made under article 138, or when the Regional provision of declaration of notable public interest is not in any case emanated within the period of one year from the aforesaid request, the Regional director may request the Ministry to proceed instead.

2. Having received a copy of any documentation which may have been acquired by the provincial Commission, the competent Ministerial organ shall carry out the preliminary investigation for the purpose of formulating the recommendation for the declaration of notable public interest.

3. The Ministry shall forward the recommendation to the Municipalities concerned so that they may fulfil the obligation set out in article 139, paragraph 1, and it shall directly fulfil the obligations indicated in article 139, paragraphs 2, 4 and 5.

4. The Ministry shall assess the observations presented under article 139, paragraphs 3 and 6, and shall make provision by decree. The decree of declaration of notable public interest shall be notified, deposited, registered and published in the forms provided for by article 140, paragraphs 2, 3 and 4.

5. The provisions set out in the preceding paragraphs shall also apply to recommendations for the integration of existing provisions for declaration of notable public interest, with reference to the contents indicated in article 143, paragraph 3, letters *e*) and *f*).

Article 142
Areas Protected by Law

1. Until the landscape plan is approved under article 156, the following are in any case subject to the provisions of this Title by virtue of their landscape interest:
   a) coastal territories including a swath of land to a depth of 300 metres from the waterline, and also land elevated over the sea;
   b) territories conterminous with lakes, including a swath of land to a depth of 300 metres from the waterline and also land elevated over the lakes;
   c) the rivers, streams and water courses indicated in the lists provided for in the consolidated law on provisions for waters and electric power plants, approved with royal

decree no. 1775 of 11 December 1933, and the relative banks or base foundations of embankments for a swath of 150 metres each;

d) mountains for the part exceeding 1,600 metres above sea level as regards the Alpine chain and 1,200 metres above sea level as regards the Apennines and the islands;

e) glaciers and glacial cirques;

f) parks and national or regional reserves as well as the external protection areas of the parks;

g) territories covered with forests or woods, even if marked and damaged by fire, and areas subject to reforestation constraints, as defined by article 2, paragraphs 2 and 6, of legislative decree no. 227 of 18 May 2001;

h) areas assigned to agricultural universities and zones designated for civic uses;

i) marshlands included in the list provided for by decree no. 448 of the President of the Republic of 13 March 1976;

j) volcanoes;

k) zones of archaeological interest identified at the time this Code comes into force.

2. The provisions of paragraph 1 shall not apply to areas which on 6 September 1985 were:

a) defined in urban planning instruments as zones A and B;

b) defined in the urban planning instruments under ministerial order no. 1444 of 2 April 1968, with reference to only the parts included in the multiyear implementation programmes, as zones other than those indicated in letter *a*) and, in municipalities without such instruments, as zones situated in the built-up centres whose perimeters were fixed pursuant to article 18 of law no. 865 of 22 October 1971.

3. The provisions of paragraph 1 do not apply to places listed therein under letter *c*) which, in whole or in part, can be considered irrelevant for landscape purposes, and which as such have been entered in a special list compiled and made public by the Region concerned. The Ministry may, with a measure adopted under the procedures provided for by article 141, nevertheless confirm the landscape importance of the aforementioned assets.

4. The regulations deriving from the actions and measures indicated in article 157 shall in any case remain in force.

Chapter III
Landscape Planning

Article 143
Landscape Plan

1. On the basis of natural and historical characteristics and in relation to the level of relevance and integrity of the landscape values, the plan shall organise the territory into homogenous areas, from those of high landscape value to those which have been significantly compromised or degraded.

2. The plan shall assign corresponding objectives regarding landscape environment values to each area in function of the different levels of landscape values recognised. In particular, landscape quality objectives provide for:

   a) the maintenance of the characteristics, constituting elements and morphologies, also taking into account architectonic typologies, as well as construction materials and techniques;

   b) the preparation of lines of urban and construction development that are compatible with the different value levels recognised and which are such that they do not diminish the landscape value of the territory, with particular attention to the safeguarding of sites included in UNESCO's world heritage list, and of agricultural areas;

   c) the reclamation and upgrading of the buildings and areas subject to protection which have been compromised or degraded, with the aim of recovering pre-existing values or of creating new landscape values which are consistent with and integral to the previous ones.

3. The landscape plan shall contain descriptive and prescriptive content and include recommendations and proposals. Its development shall include the following phases:

   a) a survey of the entire land area, through the analysis of its historical, natural and aesthetic characteristics and their inter-relationship, and the consequent definition of the landscape values to be protected, reclaimed, upgraded and enhanced;

   b) analysis of the dynamics of land transformation through the identification of risk factors and elements of landscape vulnerability, comparison with other land programming and planning and protection actions;

c) identification of landscape areas and the relative aims of landscape quality;

d) definition of general and operative prescriptions for protection and use of the land included in the defined areas;

e) definition of measures for the conservation of the distinctive features of areas protected by law and, where necessary, definition of management criteria and work for landscape enhancement to be carried out on buildings and areas declared to be of notable public interest;

f) identification of work to be carried out for the reclamation and upgrading of areas that have been significantly compromised or degraded;

g) identification of the measures necessary to ensure that work changing the aspect of the territory be harmonised with the landscape context, with actions and investments for the sustainable development of the areas concerned being under the obligation to refer to the aforesaid measures;

h) identification, under article 134, letter *c*), of any categories of buildings or areas, different to those indicated in articles 136 and 142, to be subjected to specific safeguarding and use measures.

4. The landscape plan shall, in relation to the different typologies of projects and works transforming the territory, distinctly identify the areas in which such works and projects are permitted on the basis of verification of the compliance with the prescriptions, measures and management criteria established in the landscape plan under paragraph 3, letters *d*), *e*), *f*) and *g*), and those for which the landscape plan also defines binding parameters for the specific previsions to be introduced into land planning instruments when harmonisation and adjustment is effected under article 145.

5. The plan may likewise identify:

a) the areas, protected under article 142, in which the realisation of projects and works permitted, in consideration of the level of excellence of the landscape values or the advisability of assessing impact on the planning scale, in any case requires the prior granting of the authorisation referred to in articles 146, 147 and 159;

b) the areas, to which actions and measures emanated under articles 138, 140, 141 and 157 do not pertain, and in which, instead, projects and works may be carried out on the basis of verification of conformity with the provisions of the landscape plan and of the urban planning instrument, carried out during the building permit procedure and with the modalities set out by the relative regulations, and which do not require the authorisation referred to in articles 146, 147 and 159:

c) the areas which have been significantly compromised or degraded in which reclamation and upgrading work does not require the authorisation referred to in articles 146, 147 and 159.

6. The entry into force of the provisions set out in paragraph 5, letter *b*), shall be made conditional on the approval of the urban planning instruments adjusted to the landscape plan under article 145. The aforesaid authorisation shall entail the modification of the effects deriving from the provisions referred to in articles 157, 140 and 141, and from the inclusion of the area in the categories listed in article 142.

7. The plan may make the entry into force of the provisions permitting works and projects under paragraph 5, letter b), conditional on the positive outcome of a period of monitoring which verifies effective conformity with the provisions in force pertaining to the transformations of the territory carried out.

8. The plan in any case provides that in the areas referred to in article 5, letter *b*), sample checks be carried out on the work done and that ascertainment of a significant level of violation of the provisions in force shall determine the re-introduction of the obligation of authorisation referred to in articles 146, 147 and 159, with regard to the municipalities in which violations have been ascertained.

9. The landscape plan shall also identify priority for projects for the conservation, reclamation, upgrading, enhancement and management of the regional landscape indicating the instruments to be used, including incentive measures.

10. The Regions, the Ministry and the Ministry of the Environment and Land Protection may enter into agreements for the joint development of landscape plans. The agreement shall establish the time limit within which the joint plan will be developed, as well as the time limit within which the Region shall approve the plan. When the joint development of the plan is not followed by a Regional provision, the plan shall be approved in its stead by Minister's decree, after consultation with the Minister of the Environment and Land Protection.

11. The agreement referred to in paragraph 10 shall likewise establish premises, procedures, and a timetable for the periodical revision of the plan, with particular reference to supervening provisions emanated under articles 140 and 141.

12. When the agreement referred to in paragraph 10 is not entered into, or when it is not followed by the joint development of the plan, the provisions of paragraphs 5, 6, 7 and 8 shall not apply.

Article 144
Advertising and Participation

1. The procedures for the approval of landscape plans shall ensure concerted government action, participation of interested parties and of associations created for the protection of common public interests, identified under article 13 of law no. 349 of 8 July 1986, and a wide variety of forms of advertising.

2. When from the application of article 143, paragraphs 3, 4 and 5 a modification of the effects of the actions and provisions referred to in articles 157, 140 and 141 ensues, the coming into force of the relative provisions of the landscape plan is conditional on the fulfilment of the forms of advertising indicated in article 140, paragraphs 3 and 4.

Article 145
Co-ordination of Landscape Planning with other Planning Instruments

1. Pursuant to article 52 of legislative decree no. 112 of 31 March 1998, the Ministry shall identify the fundamental lines for the organisation of the national territory as regards the protection of the landscape, with the aim of defining planning direction.

2. Landscape plans provide for measures of co-ordination with land and sector planning instruments, and with national and regional economic development instruments.

3. The provisions of the landscape plans referred to in articles 143 and 156 are compulsory for the urban planning instruments of the Municipalities, Metropolitan areas and the Provinces, have immediate prevalence over any non-conforming provisions contained in urban planning instruments, establish safeguarding regulations which may be applied until urban planning instruments conform, and are likewise binding for sector intervention. As regards protection of the environment, the provisions of landscape plans shall in any case prevail over the provisions contained in planning instruments.

4. Within the time-limit established in the landscape plan and in any case not more than two years after its approval, the Municipalities, Metropolitan Areas, Provinces and managing bodies of protected natural areas shall conform and adjust land and urban planning instruments to the provisions of the landscape plans, introducing, when necessary, additional conforming provisions which, in light of the specific characteristics of the territory, will prove useful in best ensuring protection of the landscape values identified in the plans.

The limitations to property ensuing from such provisions shall not be eligible for indemnity.

5. The Regions shall regulate the procedures for conformation and adjustment of the urban planning instruments to the provisions of landscape planning, ensuring the participation of the Ministerial organs in the same procedures.

Chapter IV
Supervision and Management of Properties Subject to Protection

Article 146
Authorisation

1. The proprietors, possessors or holders by whatever legal right of immovable property and areas to which pertain the actions and measures listed in article 157, or the recommendation formulated pursuant to articles 138 and 141, or which are protected under article 142, or subject to protection by the provisions of the landscape plans, may not destroy them, or introduce modifications which may harm the landscape values which are to be protected.

2. In order to obtain preventive authorisation, the proprietors, possessors or holders by whatever legal right of the properties indicated in paragraph 1, shall be obliged to submit the plans of the works they intend to carry out, accompanied by the required documentation, to the Region or the local body to which the Region has delegated the relative competence.

3. Within six months of the coming into force of the present legislative decree, the documentation necessary for the verification of the compatibility of the proposed works with landscape values shall be defined by decree of the President of the Council of Ministers, in agreement with the State-Regions Conference.

4. The application for authorisation of work shall indicate the current state of the property concerned, the elements of existing landscape values, the impact of the proposed changes on the landscape and the mitigating and compensatory elements necessary.

5. In examining the request for authorisation, the competent administration shall verify the

conformity of the work with the prescriptions contained in the landscape plans and shall ascertain:

a) compatibility with respect to the landscape values recognised in the constraint order;

b) congruity with the management criteria of the building or area;

c) consistency with the objectives of landscape quality.

6. Having ascertained landscape compatibility of the work and acquired the opinion of the Commission for the Landscape, the administration shall, within the term of forty days from receipt of the application, forward the recommendation for authorisation, accompanied by the project plan and the relative documentation, to the competent Superintendency, notifying the parties concerned. This latter notification shall constitute notification of the start of the relative procedure, pursuant to and for the purposes of law no. 241 of 7 August 1990. Should the administration verify that the documentation attached does not correspond to the documentation requested in paragraph 3, it shall ask for the necessary additional documentation; in such case, the aforementioned term is suspended from the date of the request until receipt of the documentation. Should the administration deem it necessary to acquire documentation additional to that established in paragraph 3, or to carry out ascertainment, the term shall be suspended, once only, from the date of request until receipt of the documentation, or from the date of notification of the necessity of ascertainment to the date of carrying out the same, for a period which in any case may not exceed thirty days.

7. The Superintendency shall communicate its opinion within the peremptory term of sixty days from receipt of the recommendation referred to in paragraph 6. Should the term expire without receipt of the above communication, the administration shall in any case rule with regard to the request for authorisation.

8. Authorisation shall be issued or denied by the competent administration within the term of twenty days from receipt of the superintendent's opinion and shall constitute a distinct action and the premise for concession or other titles legitimising the construction work. Work may not start if authorisation has not been issued.

9. Should the term referred to in paragraph 8 expire without a decision being taken, power is granted to the parties concerned to request authorisation from the Region, which may also respond through an commissioner appointed for the purpose within the term of sixty days from the date of receipt of the request. Should it be deemed necessary to acquire additional documentation or to carry out ascertainment, the term shall be suspended once only until the date of receipt of the requested documentation or until the date on which

ascertainment is carried out. In cases where the Region has not delegated competence to local bodies to issue landscape authorisation, the request for authorisation shall be made instead to the competent Superintendency.

10. Landscape authorisation:

a) becomes efficacious after twenty days have elapsed from its emanation;

b) shall be forwarded without delay to the Superintendency which had given its opinion during the procedure, and, along with the opinion, to the Region and the Province and, where these exist, to the mountain community and to the park authority in whose territory the building or area under a constraint order is located;

c) may not be issued under any curative statute subsequently to the completion, even if partial, of the works.

11. Landscape authorisation may be challenged with appeal to the Regional administrative court or with extraordinary appeal to the President of the Republic by the environmental associations created to protect common public interests identified under article 13 of law no. 349 of 8 July 1986 and by any other public or private entity which has an interest in doing so. A ruling with regard to the appeal shall be issued, even if after its presentation or during the appeal process, the party appealing declares that it withdraws appeal or that it no longer has an interest in it. The decisions and orders issued by the Regional administrative tribunal may be challenged by any party having the right to appeal against a landscape authorisation, even if that party did not lodge the appeal in the first instance.

12. In every Municipality, a list shall be established in which the date of issue of each landscape authorisation is indicated, with a brief description of the relative property in question and indication of whether it was issued contrary to the opinion of the superintendent. The list shall be updated at least every seven days and may be freely consulted. A copy of the list shall be forwarded on a quarterly basis to the Region and the Superintendency, for the purpose of exercising the functions of supervision pursuant to article 155.

13. The provisions of the preceding paragraph shall also apply to the instances concerning mining activities of search and extraction.

14. The provisions of this article do not apply to authorisation for farming activities in quarries and peat bogs. For such activities the powers of the Ministry of the Environment and Land Protection shall remain in effect pursuant to the laws pertaining to such matters, which shall be exercised taking into account the assessment expressed by the competent Superintendency as regards landscape profiles.

Article 147
Authorisation for Works To Be Carried Out by State Administrations

1. When the request for authorisation provided for under article 146 concerns works to be carried out by State administrations, including service accommodation for military personnel, the authorisation shall be issued following a conference of services pursuant to articles 14 ff. , of law no. 241 of 7 August 1990 and subsequent modifications and additions.

2. For work projects which are in any case subject to environmental impact assessment pursuant to article 6 of law no. 349 of 8 July 1986 and which are to be carried out by State administrations, the authorisation prescribed by paragraph 1 shall be issued according to the procedures established in article 26.

3. The modalities for the joint and preventive assessment of the works of national defence which affect buildings and areas subject to landscape protection shall be identified within six months from the date on which this Code comes into force, by decree of the President of the Council of Ministers, upon recommendation of the Ministry and in agreement with the Ministry of Defence and the other State administrations concerned.

Article 148
Landscape Commission

1. Within one year of the coming into force of this Code, the Regions shall take action to establish the Commission for the Landscape within the local bodies to which competence for landscape authorisation has been delegated.

2. The Commission shall be composed of individuals with particular and qualified experience in the protection of the landscape.

3. The Commission shall express an obligatory opinion with regard to the granting of authorisations provided for under articles 146, 147 and 159.

4. The Regions and the Ministry may enter into agreements which establish the modalities of participation of the Ministry in the activities of the Commission for the Landscape. In such case, the opinion referred to in article 146, paragraph 7, shall be expressed in that session according to the modalities established in the agreement, with the application of the provisions of article 146, paragraphs 10, 11 and 12 remaining in effect.

Article 149

Works Not Subject to Authorisation

1. Without prejudice to the application of article 143, paragraph 5, letter *b*) and of article 156, paragraph 4, the authorisation prescribed by article 146, article 147 and article 156 is in any case not required in relation to:

   a) works for ordinary and extraordinary maintenance, of consolidation and of restoration for purposes of conservation which do not alter the condition of the sites and the exterior appearance of the buildings;

   b) works related to the exercise of agricultural, forestry and pastoral activities which do not involve the permanent alteration of the condition of the sites with building structures and other civil works, and on condition that these are works and activities which do not alter the hydro-geological system of the territory.

   c) the cutting of the vegetation cover, and for works of forestation, reforestation, reclamation, fire prevention and conservation to be carried out in the woods and forests indicated in article 142, paragraph 1, letter *g*), on condition that these are provided for and authorised by the laws pertaining to the matter.

Article 150

Interdiction and Suspension of Works

1. Independently of the publication on the municipal notice board provided for by articles 139 and 141, of the notification prescribed by article 139, paragraph 4, the Region or Ministry shall have the power to:

   a) interdict the execution of works without authorisation or which in any case are capable of harming the property;

   b) order the suspension of works begun, even when the interdiction established in letter *a*) has not been applied.

2. The interdiction or suspension of work on buildings or areas which have not yet been declared to be of notable public interest shall cease to have efficacy if within the term of ninety days the recommendation of the Commission referred to in article 138 or the recommendations of the Ministerial organ provided for under article 141 have not been published on the municipal notice board, or if the notification provided for under article 139,

paragraph 4 has not been received by the parties concerned.

3. The provision for interdiction or suspension of works impinging on a landscape property for which landscape planning foresees reclamation or upgrading measures ceases to have efficacy if within the term of ninety days the Region has not informed the parties concerned of the prescriptions to be observed in the execution of the works in order not to compromise planning implementation.

4. The provisions indicated in the preceding paragraphs shall also be notified to the Municipality concerned.

Article 151

Reimbursement of Expenses following Suspension of Works

1. For works on environmental assets which have not previously been the object of the provisions referred to in articles 138 and 141, or which have not previously been declared to be of notable public interest, and suspension of which has been ordered without the preventive interdiction order referred to in article 150, paragraph 1, the party concerned may obtain the reimbursement of expenses incurred until notification of suspension. The works already carried out shall be demolished at the expense of the authority which ordered the suspension.

Article 152

Works Subject to Particular Prescriptions

1. In the case of opening up of roads and quarries and in the case of conduits for industrial plants and of pilings within and in view of the areas indicated at letters *c*) and *d*) of article 136, or in proximity to the buildings indicated in letter *a*) and *b*) of the same article, the Region shall have the power to prescribe distances, measures and variations to the work projects in the process of being carried out, which, taking into due account the economic utility of the works already completed, shall serve to prevent harm to the properties protected by this Title. The Ministry shall have the same power, which it shall exercise after prior consultation with the Region.

Article 153
Advertising Hoardings

1. Within and in the proximity of the landscape assets indicated in article 134, it is forbidden to collocate hoardings and other advertising means without prior authorisation by the competent administration identified by the Region.

2. Along the roads located within and in proximity of the assets indicated in paragraph 1, it is forbidden to collocate hoardings or other advertising means, except with the authorisation issued pursuant to article 23, paragraph 4, of legislative decree no. 285 of 30 April 1992 and subsequent modifications, with the prior favourable opinion of the competent administration identified by the Region regarding the compatibility of the collocation or of the type of advertising means with the landscape values of the buildings and areas subject to protection.

Article 154
Colour of Building Facades

1. The competent administration identified by the Region may order that, in the areas contemplated in letters *c*) and *d*) of article 136, the facades of the buildings whose colour jars with the beauty of the whole be given a different colour which is more in harmony with that beauty.

2. The provision of paragraph 1 shall not apply to buildings referred to in article 10, paragraph 3, letters *a*) and *d*), declared under article 13.

3. For buildings which fall within the areas of archaeological interested listed in article 136, letter *c*) or in article 139, paragraph 1, letter *m*), the administration shall as a precautionary measure consult the competent Superintendencies.

4. In case of non-fulfilment on the part of proprietors, possessors or holders of the buildings, the administration shall proceed to ex officio execution.

Article 155
Supervision

1. The functions of supervision of landscape assets protected by this Title are to be exercised

by the Ministry and the Regions.

2. The Regions shall monitor compliance with the provisions contained in the present legislative decree on the part of the administrations they have identified for the exercise of the competences pertaining to landscape matters. Non-compliance or persistent inactivity in the exercise of such competences shall entail the activation of substitutive powers.

Chapter V

First Application and Transitional Provisions

Article 156

Verification and Adjustment of Landscape Plans

1. Within four years of the coming into force of the present legislative decree, the Regions which have drawn up the plans provided for in article 149 of legislative decree no. 490 of 29 October 1999 shall verify conformity between the provisions of the aforementioned plans and the provisions of article 143 and, when such conformity is lacking, they shall proceed to the necessary adjustments.

2. Within one hundred and eighty days of the coming into force of this Code, the Ministry, in agreement with the State-Regions Conference, shall prepare a general scheme of agreement with the Regions establishing methodologies and procedures for the survey, analyses, census and cataloguing of the buildings and areas subject to protection, including techniques for their cartographical representation and the features most suitable to ensuring the inter-operability of computer systems.

3. The Regions and the Ministry may enter into agreements to regulate the carrying out of joint activities for the verification and adjustment of land plans, on the basis of the general scheme of agreement referred to in paragraph 2. The agreement shall establish the term within which the Region shall approve the adjusted plan. When upon completion of activities no Regional provision follows, the plan shall be approved in its stead by Ministerial decree.

4. If, from verification and adjustment, in application of article 143, paragraphs 3, 4 and 5, a modification ensues of the effects of the actions and provisions referred to in articles

157, 140 and 141, the coming into force of the relative provisions of the landscape plan shall be conditional to fulfilment of the forms of advertising indicated in article 140, paragraphs 3 and 4.

5. When the agreement set out in paragraph 3 is not entered into, or when it is not followed by joint verification and adjustment of the plan, the provisions of paragraphs 5, 6, 7 and 8 of article 143 shall not apply.

Article 157

Notifications Served, Lists Compiled, Provisions and
Actions Issued Under Pre-existing Laws

1. Without prejudice to the application of article 143, paragraph 6, of article 144, paragraph 2, and of article 156, paragraph 4, the following shall maintain efficacy to all intents and purposes:

   a) the notification of important public interest of natural or panoramic beauties, served on the basis of law no. 778 of 11 June 1922;

   b) lists compiled under law no. 1497 of 29 June 1939;

   c) the provisions for declaration of notable public interest issued under law no. 1497 of 29 June 1939;

   d) the provisions for the recognition of the areas of archaeological interest issued pursuant to article 82, fifth paragraph, of decree no. 616 of the President of the Republic of 24 July 1977, with the addition of article 1 of decree law no. 312 of 27 June 1985, converted with modifications into law no. 431 of 8 August 1985;

   e) the provisions for declaration of notable public interest issued pursuant to legislative decree no. 490 of 29 October 1999;

   f) the provisions for recognition of the areas of archaeological interest issued pursuant to legislative decree no. 490 of 29 October 1999.

2. The provisions of this Part shall also apply to buildings and areas regarding which, on the date of the coming into force of this Code, the recommendation was formulated or the perimeter defined for the purposes of the declaration of notable public interest or of recognition as area of archaeological interest.

Article 158

Regional Provisions for Implementation

1. Until special Regional provisions for the implementation of this Code are emanated, the provisions of the regulations approved with royal decree no. 1357 of 3 June 1940 shall remain in effect, insofar as they are applicable.

Article 159

Procedure for Provisional Authorisation

1. Until the approval of landscape plans, under 156 or article 143, and the consequent adjustment of the urban planning instruments is effected pursuant to article 145, the competent administration for granting the authorisation provided for under article 146, paragraph 2, shall give immediate notification of the authorisations granted to the Superintendency, forwarding the documentation produced by the interested party as well as the results of any verifications carried out. Notification shall be sent simultaneously to the parties concerned, for which said notification shall constitute notification of start of procedure, pursuant to and for the intents and purposes of law no. 241 of 7 August 1990.

2. The competent administration may produce a report describing the verifications indicated in article 146, paragraph 5. Authorisation shall be granted or denied within the peremptory term of sixty days from the relative request and shall in case constitute a separate and distinct action and the premise for the building permit or other titles authorising building activity. The works cannot be started without authorisation. In the case of a request for additional documentation or verifications the term shall be suspended once only until the date of receipt of the requested documentation or until the date when verification is carried out. The provisions established in article 6, paragraph 6-bis, of ministerial decree no. 495 of 13 June 1994 shall apply.

3. The Ministry may in any case, by means of a justified provision, annul the authorisation within the sixty days following receipt of the relevant and complete documentation.

4. When the term indicated in paragraph 2 expires with no action taken, the interested parties may submit a request for authorisation to the competent Superintendency, which shall take a decision within the term of sixty days from the date of receipt of request. The application, accompanied by the prescribed documentation, is presented to the competent

Superintendency and the competent administration is notified. In cases where additional documentation or verifications are requested the term shall be suspended once, only until the date of receipt of the requested documentation or until the date verifications are carried out.

5. For landscape assets which on the date in which this Code comes into force are the object of provisions adopted under article 1-*quinquies* of decree law no. 312 of 27 June 1985, converted with modifications into law no. 431 of 8 August 1985 and published in the *Official Gazette* prior to 6 September 1985, the authorisation set out in paragraph 1 and in articles 146 and 147 may be granted only after approval of the landscape plans.

FOURTH PART
SANCTIONS

TITLE I
ADMINISTRATIVE SANCTIONS

Chapter I
Sanctions Relative to the Second Part

Article 160
Order to Restore Places to Original State

1. If a cultural property is harmed as a result of violations of the protection and conservation obligations established by the provisions of Chapter III of Title I of the Second Part, the Ministry shall order the transgressor to carry out the work necessary to restore the property to its original state at his/her own expense.

2. When the works to be ordered pursuant to paragraph 1 have urban planning-building importance the start of procedure and the final provision shall also be notified to the Metropolitan area or Municipality concerned.

3. In case of non-compliance with the order issued pursuant to paragraph 1, the Ministry shall carry out the order ex officio at the expense of the transgressor. The collection of the relative expenses shall be effected in the forms established in the regulations on the compulsory collection of State property revenues.

4. When restoration to original state is not possible, the transgressor must pay to the State an amount which is equal to the value of the thing lost or to the reduction in the value of the thing.

5. If the assessment of the amount, made by the Ministry, is not accepted by the party obliged to pay, the same sum shall be determined by a commission composed of three members, one of which shall be appointed by the Ministry, one by the party obliged to pay and a third by the president of the court. The relative costs shall be advanced by the party obliged to pay.

Article 161
Damage to Things Found

1. The measures established in article 160 shall also apply to those who cause damage to the things referred to in article 91, in violation of the obligations indicated in articles 89 and 90.

Article 162
Violations Relating to Collocation of Advertising

1. Whosoever collocates hoardings or other advertising means in violation of the provisions set out in article 49 shall be punishable with the sanctions established in article 23 of legislative decree no. 285 of 30 April 1992 and subsequent modifications and additions.

Article 163
Loss of Cultural Property

1. If, as the result of violation of the obligations established by the provisions of Section I of Chapter IV and Section I of Chapter V, a cultural property is no longer traceable or proves to have been taken out of the national territory, the transgressor shall be obliged to pay to the State a sum equal to the value of the property.

2. If the offence can be charged to more than one person, the persons shall be obliged to pay the sum jointly and severally.

3. If the assessment of the sum made by Ministry is not accepted by the party obliged to pay, the same sum shall be determined by a commission composed of three members, one of which shall be appointed by the Ministry, one by the party obliged to pay and a third by the president of the court. The relative costs shall be advanced by the party obliged to pay.

4. The assessment of the commission may be challenged in case of error or manifest inequity.

Article 164
Violations Relating to Jural Acts

1. Transfers, agreements and legal transactions in general, performed in violation of the prohibitions established by the provisions of Title I of the Second Part, or in non-compliance of the conditions and modalities prescribed therein, shall be null and void.

2. The power of the Ministry to exercise pre-emption pursuant to article 61, paragraph 2 shall stand.

Article 165
Violations of the Provisions Pertaining to International Circulation

1. Apart from the cases of complicity in a crime provided for in article 174, paragraph 1, whosoever transfers abroad the things or properties indicated in article 10, in violation of the provisions set out in Sections I and II of Chapter V of Title I of the Second Part, shall be punishable with administrative sanction consisting in the payment of a sum ranging from € 77.50 to € 465.00.

Article 166
Failure to Submit Exportation Documents

1. Whosoever effects the exportation of a cultural property beyond the territory of the European Union pursuant to EEC regulations and fails to submit to the competent export office 3 copies of the forms provided for in (EEC) Commission regulation no. 752/93 of 30 March 1993, in application of the EEC regulation, shall be punishable with administrative sanction consisting in the payment of a sum ranging from € 103,50 to € 620.00.

Chapter II
Sanctions Relative to the Third Part

Article 167
Order to Restore to Original State or to Pay Compensation

1. In case of violation of the obligations and orders set out in Title I of the Third Part, the transgressor shall, if the administrative authority responsible for landscape environment protection shall deem it more opportune in the interest of the protection of the properties indicated in article 134, be obliged to restore the cultural property to its original state at his/her own expense or pay a sum equivalent to the greater amount between the damage caused or the profit derived through the transgression. The sum shall be determined on the basis of an official assessment.

2. With the restoration to original state order the transgressor shall be assigned a term for complying with the order.

3. In case of non-compliance, the administrative authority responsible for landscape protection shall proceed ex officio through the prefect and make the bill of costs enforceable.

4. The sums received as a result of the application of paragraph 1 shall be utilised for safeguarding purposes, works for reclamation of landscape values and the upgrading of deteriorated areas.

Article 168
Violations Relating to Hoardings

1. Whosoever collocates hoardings or other advertising means in violation of the provisions referred to in article 153 shall be punishable with the sanctions set out in article 23 of legislative decree no. 285 of 30 April 1992 and subsequent modifications.

TITLE II
PENAL SANCTIONS

Chapter I
Sanctions Relative to the Second Part

Article 169
Unlawful Works

1. The following shall be punishable by imprisonment for a period of six months to one year and by a fine ranging from € 775.00 to € 38,734.50:

   a) whosoever without authorisation demolishes, removes, modifies, restores or carries out works of any kind on the cultural properties indicated in article 10;

   b) whosoever, without the authorisation of the superintendent, proceeds to detach frescoes, escutcheons, graffiti, inscriptions, tabernacles or other ornaments decorating buildings, whether or not they be displayed to public view, even when no declaration under article 13 has been made;

   c) whosoever carries out, in cases of absolute urgency, temporary works indispensable to avoiding substantial damage to the properties indicated in article 10, without immediately notifying the superintendent or without submitting for authorisation, in the briefest time possible, the project design for the definitive works.

2. The same punishment established in paragraph 1 shall apply in cases of non-compliance with an order to suspend works issued by the superintendent pursuant to article 28.

Article 170
Unlawful Use

1. Whosoever designates the cultural properties indicated in article 10 for a use that is incompatible with their historical or artistic nature or which is harmful to their conservation or integrity shall be punishable with imprisonment for a period ranging from six months

to one year and a fine ranging from € 775.00 to € 38,734.50.

Article 171
Unlawful Collocation and Removal

1. Whosoever fails to collocate cultural properties belonging to the subjects established in article 10, paragraph 1 in their designated place and in the manner indicated by the superintendent shall be punishable by imprisonment for a period ranging from six months to one year and a fine ranging from € 775.00 to € 38,734.50.

2. Subject to the same punishment is the holder who fails to notify the competent superintendent of the removal of cultural properties to another locality, due to a change in place of abode, or the holder who fails to comply with the prescriptions issued by the superintendent in order to avoid damage to the same properties during transport.

Article 172
Non-compliance with the Prescriptions of Indirect Protection

1. Whosoever fails to comply with the prescriptions issued by the Ministry pursuant to article 45, paragraph 1 shall be punishable by imprisonment for a period ranging from six months to one year and a fine ranging from € 775.00 to € 38,734.50.

2. Non-compliance with the precautionary measures contained in the action referred to in article 46, paragraph 4, is punishable under article 180.

Article 173
Violations Pertaining to Alienation

1. The following are punishable with imprisonment for a period of up to one year and fine ranging from € 1,549.50 to € 77,469.00 :
   a) whosoever, without the prescribed authorisations, transfers cultural properties indicated in article 55 and 56;
   b) whosoever, being under the obligation to present declaration of the deeds of transfer or of the detention of cultural properties, within the term indicated in article 59, fails to fulfil the aforesaid obligation;
   c) the transferor of a cultural property subject to the right of pre-emption who effects de-

livery of the thing pending the term set out in article 61, paragraph 1.

Article 174
Unlawful Exit and Exportation

1. Whosoever transfers abroad things of artistic, historical, archaeological, ethno-anthropological, bibliographical, documental or archival interest, as well as the things indicated in article 11, paragraph 1, letters f), g), and h), without certificate of free circulation or export licence, shall be punishable by imprisonment for a period of one to four years or with a fine ranging from € 258.00 to € 5,165.00.

2. The punishment established in paragraph 1 shall likewise apply to whosoever, upon expiry of term, fails to return to national territory cultural properties for which temporary exit or exportation was authorised.

3. The judge shall order confiscation of the things, except when these belong to a person extraneous to the crime. Confiscation shall take place in accordance with the regulations of the customs laws pertaining to contraband.

4. If the offence is committed by a person who carries out activities of sale to the public or of exhibition for the purposes of sale of objects of cultural interest, the sentence is followed by the prohibition established under article 30 of the penal code.

Article 175
Violations Relating to Archaeological Research

1. The following are punishable by imprisonment of up to a year and a fine ranging from € 310.00 to € 3,099.00:

   a) whosoever carries out archaeological searches or, in general, works for the discovery of things indicated in article 10 without concession, or fails to comply with the prescriptions established by the administration.

   b) whosoever, being under such obligation, fails to declare within the term prescribed by article 90, paragraph 1, the things indicated in article 10, found fortuitously, or fails to provide for their temporary conservation.

Article 176

Unlawful Appropriation of Cultural Property Belonging to the State

1. Whosoever appropriates cultural property indicated in article 10 belonging to the State under article 91 shall be punishable by imprisonment for a term of up to three years and with a fine ranging from € 31.00 to € 516.50.

2. Punishment shall be imprisonment for a period of one to six years and a fine ranging from € 103.00 to € 1,033.00 if the offence is committed by a person who has obtained the search concession provided for in article 89.

Article 177

Collaboration in the Recovery of Cultural Property

1. The punishment applicable for the crimes set out in articles 174 and 176 shall be reduced by one to two thirds when the offender offers collaboration that is decisive or at any rate of substantial importance for the recovery of properties unlawfully removed or transferred abroad.

Article 178

Forgery of Works of Art

1. The following shall be punishable by imprisonment for a period of three months to four years and with a fine ranging from € 103.00 to € 3,099.00:

   a) whosoever, for purposes of gain, counterfeits, alters or reproduces a work of painting, sculpture or graphic art, or an antique object or an object of historical or archaeological interest;

   b) whosoever, even if he/she did not participate in the counterfeiting, alteration or reproduction, puts on sale, or holds for purposes of sale, or introduces into the territory of the State for such purpose, or in any case puts into circulation, as authentic, counterfeited, altered or reproduced samples of works of painting, sculpture, graphic art or antique objects, or objects of historical or archaeological interest;

   c) whosoever, knowing them to be false, authenticates works or objects, indicated in letters a) and b) which have been counterfeited, altered or reproduced;

d) whosoever, through other declarations, evaluations, publications, affixation of stamps or labels or by any other means, certifies as authentic or contributes to the certification as such of works or objects indicated in letters *a*) and *b*) which have been counterfeited, altered or reproduced, knowing them to be false.

2. If the offences are committed in the exercise of a commercial activity punishment shall be increased and conviction shall be followed by the prohibition established under article 30 of the penal code.

3. Conviction for offences set out in paragraph 1 shall be published in three daily newspapers with national circulation to be designated by the judge and published in three different localities. Article 36, paragraph 3, of the penal code shall apply.

Article 179
Non-punishable Cases

1. The provisions of article 178 shall not apply to whosoever reproduces, holds, puts on sale or otherwise distributes copies of works of painting, sculpture or graphic art, or copies or imitations of antique objects or objects of historical or archaeological interest which are expressly declared to be inauthentic when exhibited or sold, by means of a written annotation on the work or on the object or, when this is not possible because of the nature or size of the copy or imitation, by means of a declaration issued upon exhibition or sale. Nor do the provisions apply to artistic restorations which do not reconstruct the original work in a determinant manner.

Article 180
Non-compliance with Administrative Measures

1. Except in cases where the offence constitutes a more serious crime, whosoever fails to comply with an order issued by the authority responsible for the protection of cultural properties in accordance with this Title shall be punished with the penalties set out in article 650 of the penal code.

Chapter II
Sanctions Relative to the Third Part

Article 181
Works Carried Out Without Authorisation or Contrary To Its Provisions

1. Whosoever, without the prescribed authorisation or contrary to it, carries out works of any kind on landscape assets shall be punishable with the penalties provided for in article 20 of law no. 47 of 28 February 1985.
2. The judgment convicting the guilty party shall rule that the sites be restored to their original state at the party's expense. A copy of the judgement shall be forwarded to the Municipality in whose territory the violation has been committed.

FIFTH PART
INTERIM PROVISIONS, ABROGATION
AND COMING INTO EFFECT OF LAWS

Article 182
Transitional Measures

1. Article 7, paragraph 1, of ministerial decree no. 294 of 3 August 2000, as substituted by article 3 of ministerial decree no. 420 of 24 October 2001, shall continue to apply restrictively to those who, as of the date of this law coming into effect, are enrolled in State university degree courses or schools of restoration therein established.

2. The provisions set out in article 7, paragraph 2, letters *a*), *b*) and *c*), of decree no. 294 of 2000, as substituted by article 3 of decree no. 420 of 2001 shall remain in effect. The provisions set out in article 7, paragraph 2, letters *a*) and *c*) of decree no. 294 of 2000, as substituted by article 3 of decree no. 420 of 2001, shall also apply to those who, on the date when such latter decree came into force, were enrolled, even if not yet in possession of a diploma, in a State or Regional school for restoration established therein until the 2002-2003 academic year.

3. Within sixty days of this Code coming into effect, the Regions and other territorial government bodies shall adopt the necessary provisions for adjustment to the prescription set out in article 103, paragraph 4. In the case of non-fulfilment, the Ministry shall proceed to act in their stead, pursuant to article 117, fifth paragraph, of the Constitution.

Article 183
Final Provisions

1. The provisions set out in articles 13, 45, 141, 143, paragraph 10, and 156, paragraph 3, are not subject to preventive control pursuant to article 3, paragraph 1, of law no. 20 of 14 January 1994.

2. The implementation of articles 5 and 44 shall not entail new and greater burdens for the public purse.

3. Service on the commissions established by this Code is intended to be proffered free of charge, and such service shall in any case not entail new or greater burdens for the public purse.

4. The costs ensuing from the exercise on the part of the Ministry of the powers set out in articles 34, 35 and 37 shall be taken on within the limitations of the budget allocation for the relative items of expenditure.

5. The sureties provided by the State in the implementation of article 48, paragraph 5, are listed in an annex to the budgetary previsions of the Ministry of the Economy and Finance, pursuant to article 13 of law no. 468 of 5 August 1978. In the case of discussion of the said surety the Ministry shall forward the pertinent report to Parliament.

6. The laws of the Republic may not introduce forms of derogation to the principles of this legislative decree except through the express modification of its provisions.

7. This Code shall come into effect on the first day of May 2004.

Article 184
Abrogated Laws

1. The following provisions are abrogated:

—law no. 1089 of 1 June 1939, article 40, in the text last substituted by article 9 of law no. 237 of 12 July 1999;

—decree no. 1409 of the President of the Republic of 30 September 1963, restrictively: to article 21, paragraphs 1 and 3, and paragraph 2, in the text, respectively, modified and substituted by article 8 of legislative decree no. 281 of 30 July 1999; to articles 21-bis and 22, paragraph 1, in the text, respectively, integrated and modified by article 9 of the same legislative decree;

—decree no. 3 of the President of the Republic of 14 January 1972, restrictively to article 9;

—legislative decree no. 285 of 30 April 1992, restrictively to article 23, paragraph 3 and the first sentence of paragraph 13-ter, integrated by article 30 of law no. 472 of 7 December 1999;

—law no. 127 of 15 May 1997, restrictively to article 12, paragraph 5, in the text modified by article 19, paragraph 9, of law no. 448 of 23 December 1998; and paragraph 6, first sentence;

—law no. 352 of 8 October 1997, restrictively to article 7, as modified by articles 3 and 4 of law no. 237 of 12 July 1999 and by article 4 of law no. 513 of 21 December 1999;

—legislative decree no. 112 of 31 March 1998, restrictively to articles 148, 150, 152 and 153;

—law no. 237 of 12 July 1999, restrictively to article 9;

—legislative decree no. 281 of 30 July 1999, restrictively to article 8, paragraphs 2 and

9;

—legislative decree no. 490 of 29 October 1999 and subsequent modifications and additions;

—decree no. 283 of the President of the Republic of 7 September 2000;

—legislative decree no. 196 of 30 June 2003, restrictively to article 179, paragraph 4;

—law no. 172 of 8 July 2003, restrictively to article 7.

Approved, *Minister for Cultural Heritage and Activities*
URBANI

ANNEX A

(Provided for by articles 63, *paragraph* 1; 74, *paragraphs* 1 *and* 3; 75, *paragraph* 3, *letter a)*

A. Categories of cultural property:

1. Archaeological finds dating back more than one hundred years and found in:

   a) terrestrial and marine excavations and discoveries;

   b) archaeological sites:

   c) archaeological collections.

2. Elements, that are an integral part of artistic, historical or religious monuments and are the result of dismemberment of monuments which date back more than one hundred years.

3. Paintings and pictures other than those belonging to categories 4 and 5, entirely created by hand on any base and with any material (1).

4. Watercolours, gouaches and pastels, entirely painted by hand on any base.

5. Mosaics, other than those of categories 1 and 2, entirely made by hand with any material (1) and drawings made entirely by hand on any base.

6. Original engravings, prints, serigraphs and original lithographs and their relative matrices, as well as original posters (1).

7. Original works of statuary art or sculpture and copies obtained with the same procedures as the original (1), other than those in category 1.

8. Photographs, films and relative negatives (1).

9. Incunabula and manuscripts, including geographical maps and musical scores, singly or in collections (1).

10. Books over a hundred years old, singly or in collections.

11. Printed geographical maps dating back more than two hundred years.

12. Archives and supports, including elements of any nature dating back more than fifty years.

13. *a*) Collection and samples from zoological, botanical, mineralogical and anatomical collections:

   b) Collections of historical, paleontological, ethnographical or numismatic interest

14. Means of transport dating back more than seventy-five years.

15. Other antique objects not contemplated by categories 1 to 14, dating back more than fifty years.

Cultural properties which fall into categories 1 to 15 are governed by this Consolidated Text only if their value is equal to or exceeds the values indicated in letter B.

B. **Values applicable to the categories indicated in letter A (in euros).**

   1) of any value

      1. Archaeological finds

      2. Dismemberment of monuments

      9. Incunabula and manuscripts

      12. Archives

   2) 13,979.50

      5. Mosaics and drawings

      6. Engravings

      8. Photographs

      11. Printed geographical maps

   3) 27,959.00

      4. Watercolours, gouaches and pastels

   4) 46,598.00

      7. Statuary art

      10. Books

      13. Collections

      14. Means of transport

      15. Other objects

   5) 139,794.00

      3. Oil paintings

Compliance with the conditions relative to the values must be ascertained when the request for restitution is presented.

(1) Dating back more than fifty years and not belonging to the author.

Approved , Minister for Cultural Heritage and Activities
URBANI

NOTES

Notice :

The text of the notes published herein was written by the administration competent for each matter pursuant to article 10, paragraph 3 of the consolidated text of the provisions for the enactment of laws, the emanation of decrees of the President of the Republic, and the official publications of the Italian Republic, approved by decree no. 1092 of the President of the Republic of 28 December 1985, for the sole purpose of facilitating the reading of the legal provisions to which the note refers. The value and efficacy of the legislative acts recorded herein remain inviolate.

For EEC directives, essential particulars of publication are furnished in the *Official Gazette* of the European Communities (OGEC).

Notes to the premises :

—Articles 76, 87, 117 and 118 of the Constitution of the Italian Republic, published in the extraordinary edition of the *Official Gazette* of the Italian Republic no. 298 of 27 December 1947, as modified by constitutional law no. 3 of 18 October 2001, published in *Official Gazette* no. 248 of 24 October 2001, establish:

≪Art. 76. – The exercise of the legislative function may not be delegated to the Government without the determination of principles and directive criteria and only for a restricted period of time and for definite purposes.

Art. 87. – The President of the Republic is the head of state and represents national unity.

He/she may send messages to the Chambers.

He/she announces the election of the new Chambers and fixes the dates of their first meetings.

He/she authorises the presentation to the Chambers of draft laws initiated by he Government.

He/she enacts the laws and emanates the decrees having the force of law, and regulations.

He/she announces popular referendums in the cases established by the Constitution.

He/she appoints, in the cases established by law, the functionaries of the State.

He/she accredits and receives diplomatic representatives, ratifies International treaties, with the prior authorisation, when necessary, of the Chambers.

He/she detains command of the Armed Forces, presides over the Supreme Council of Defence constituted in accordance with the law, declares state of war deliberated by the Chambers.

He/she presides over the Superior Council of Magistrates.

He/she may grant pardons and commute sentences.

He/she confers the honours of the Republic.

Art. 117. – Legislative power shall be exercised by the State and the Regions in the respect of the Constitution, as well as the constraints deriving from European Community regulations and international obligations.

The State shall have exclusive legislation in the following matters:

a) foreign policy and international relations of the State; relations of the State with the European Union; right to asylum and legal status of citizens of States which do not belong to the European Union;

b) immigration;

c) relations between the Republic and religious denominations;

d) defence and the Armed Forces; security of the State; arms, munitions and explosives;

e) currency, protection of savings and financial markets; protection of competition; monetary system; tax and accounting system of the State; equalisation of financial resources;

f) organs of the State and relative electoral laws; State *referenda*; election of the European Parliament;

g) administrative regulation and organisation of the State and the national government bodies;

h) public order and safety, with the exception of the local administrative police;

i) citizenship, marital status and birth and death registry offices;

j) trial jurisdiction and regulations; civil and penal system; administrative justice;

k) determination of essential levels of services concerning civil and social rights which must be ensured throughout the national territory;

l) general regulations on education;

m) social security;

n) electoral legislation, government organs and fundamental functions of Municipalities, Provinces and Metropolitan Areas;

o) customs, protection of national borders and international disease prevention;

p) weights, measures and determination of time; statistical and electronic co-ordination of State, Regional, and local administration data; intellectual property;

q) protection of the environment, the ecosystem and cultural property.

Matters of concurrent legislation include those relative to: international relations and relations with the European Union of the Regions; foreign trade; job security and safety; education, without prejudice to the autonomy of scholastic institutions remaining, and with the exception of vocational education and training; professions; scientific and technological research and support for innovation in the productive sectors; safeguarding of health; food and nutrition; sports regulations; public safety; management of the territory; civil ports and airports; major transportation and navigation networks; communications regulations; national production, transportation and distribution of energy; complementary and supplementary social security; harmonisation of public budgets and co-ordination of public finances and the tax system; enhancement of the cultural and environmental heritage and promotion and organisation of cultural activities; savings banks, rural savings banks, credit institutions of a regional nature; land and agricultural credit institutions of a regional nature. In matters of concurrent legislation, the legislative power belongs to the Regions, except for the determination of the fundamental principles, reserved to the legislation of the State.

The Regions shall have legislative powers with reference to any matter not expressly reserved to the legislation of the State.

The autonomous Regions of Trento and Bolzano shall, in matters under their competence, participate in the decisions aimed at the formation of European Community regulatory instruments and provide for the implementation and execution of international accords and instruments of the European Union, in compliance with the rules of procedure established by the laws of the State, which govern the modalities for the exercise of substitutive powers in cases of non-compliance.

Law-making powers shall belong to the State in matters of exclusive legislation, except in cases of delegation to the Regions. Law-making powers shall belong to the Regions in all other matters. The Municipalities, the Provinces and the Metropolitan areas shall have law-making powers with regard to the regulation of the organisation and the exercise of the functions attributed to them.

Regional laws shall remove any obstacle which prevents full equality between men and women in social, cultural and economic life and shall promote equal opportunity between women and men for elected office.

Regional law shall ratify the agreements of a Region with other regions in order to improve the exercise of their functions, and may also do so with the identification of common bodies.

In matters under its competence, the Region may conclude accords with other States and agreements with territorial bodies within other States in the cases and forms governed by the laws of the State.

Art. 118. – The administrative functions are assigned to the Municipalities, except in cases where, in order to ensure their unified exercise, these are conferred on Provinces, Metropolitan areas, Regions and the State, on the basis of the principles of subsidiarity, differentiation and appropriateness.

The Municipalities, Provinces and Metropolitan Areas are the title-holders of their own administrative functions and those conferred upon them by State or Regional law, according to their respective competences.

State law governs forms of co-ordination between the State and the Regions in matters set out in letters *b*) and *h*) of the second paragraph of art. 117, and also governs forms of agreement and co-ordination between the State and the Regions in matters of cultural heritage protection.

The State, Regions, Metropolitan areas, Provinces and Municipalities shall promote autonomous initiative on the part of the citizens, both as individuals and in association, for carrying out activities of general interest, on the basis of the principles of subsidiarity ≫.

—Article 14 of Law no. 400 of 23 August 1988, containing "Rules and Regulations for Government Activities and the Regulations of the Presidency of the Council of Ministers", published in the ordinary supplement to *Official Gazette* no. 214 of 12 September 1988 establishes the following:

≪Art. 14 (*Legislative decrees*). –

1. The legislative decrees adopted by the Government under article 76 of the Constitution shall be emanated by the President of the Republic with the denomination of "legislative decree" and with the indication, in the preamble, of the law of delegation, of the resolution of the Council of Ministers and of the other fulfilments of the procedure prescribed by the delegation law.

2. The emanation of the legislative decree must occur within the term fixed by the delegation law; the text of the legislative decree adopted by the Government shall be forwarded to the President of the Republic, for emanation, at least twenty days before the expiry date.

3. If the enabling statute refers to a plurality of distinct matters which may be dealt with separately, the Government may exercise it by means of several successive instruments for one or more of the aforementioned matters. With regard to the final term established by the law of delegation, the Government shall periodically inform the Chambers on the criteria it is following in the organisation of the exercise of the legislative power.

4. In any case, when the term established for the exercise of legislative power exceeds two years, the Government must ask for the opinion of the Chambers on the schemes for the delegated decrees. The opinion shall be expressed by the permanent Commissions of the two Chambers competent for each matter within sixty days, indicating specifically any provisions which are deemed not to correspond to the directives of the law of delegation. In the thirty days following, the Government, having examined the opinion, shall send back the texts, with observations and any changes, to the Commissions for a final opinion which must be expressed within thirty days ≫.

—Legislative decree no. 368 of 20 October 1988, containing: "Creation of the Ministry for Cultural Heritage and Activities, pursuant to article 11 of Law no. 59 of 15 March 1997", is published in *Official Gazette* no. 250 of 26 October 1998.

—Legislative decree no. 490 of 29 October 1999, containing "The Consolidated Text of the Legislative Provisions for Cultural Heritage and Activities, in accordance with art. 1 of law no. 352 of 8 October 1997" is published in the ordinary supplement to *Official Gazette* no. 302 of 27 December 1999.

—Art. 10 of law no. 137 of 6 July 2002 containing "Enabling Statute for the Reform of the Organisation of the Government and of the Presidency of the Council of Ministers, and of Public Bodies", published in *Official Gazette* no. 158 of 8 July 2002, as modified by art. 1-bis of law decree no. 24 of 18 February 2003, published in *Official Gazette* no. 40 of 18 February 2003 and converted, with modifications, into law no. 82 of 17 April 2003, published in *Official Gazette* no. 92 of 19 April 2003, establishes:

– Art. 10 (*Enabling Statute for the Re-organisation and Codification of Cultural and Environmental Assets*, *Entertainment*, *Sports*, *Literary Property and Copyright*). –

1. With the enabling statute referred to in art. 1, as regards the Ministry for Cultural heritage and Activities, remaining in force, the Government is empowered to adopt, within eighteen months of the date of the coming into force of the present law, one or more legislative decrees for the re-organisation and, restrictively to letter a), the codification of the legislative provisions for:

   a) cultural and environmental assets;

   b) cinematography;

   c) theatre, music, dance and other forms of live entertainment;

   d) sport;

   e) literary property and copyright;

2. The legislative decrees referred to in paragraph 1 shall, without determining new or greater burdens for public purse, adhere to the following guiding principles and criteria:

   a) compliance with articles 117 and 118 of the Constitution;

   b) compliance with European Community regulations and international agreements;

   c) improvement of the effectiveness of measures concerning the cultural heritage and activities, including the aim of bringing about best possible use of the resources granted and increase in revenues; clear indication of public policy in the sector, in order to also achieve a significant and transparent budget accounting system; streamlining and abbreviation of procedures; conformity of the procedures to the new computer technologies;

   d) with reference to the matter referred to in letter *a*) of paragraph 1: update the tools for identification, conservation and protection of cultural and environment assets, also through the creation of foundations open to participation by Regions, local bodies, bank foundations, private and public associations, without establishing further restrictions to private property, nor abrogation of current instruments and, in an case, in complete respect of international agreements, above all as regards the circulation of cultural property; re-organise services offered, which may also be effected by means of concession to parties other than the State, by establishing foundations open to participation by Regions, local bodies, bank foundations, public and private associations, in line with the provisions set out in letter *b-bis*) of paragraph 1 of art. 10 of legislative decree no. 368 of 2 October 1998, and subsequent modifications; adapt the regulations for public tenders concerning cultural properties, modifying the thresholds for using the different procedures to identify contractors so as to permit the participation of firms of artisans of proven specialisation and experience, redefining the levels of planning necessary for awarding contracts, defining the awarding criteria and foreseeing the possibility of variations beyond the percentage limits ordinarily established, in relation to objective characteristics and the needs of protection and conservation of cultural property; redefine the modalities for the formation and functioning of the advisory organisms which intervene in the procedures for granting funding and facilitations to cultural bodies and institutions, for the purpose of a precise definition of the responsibilities of the technical organs, according to the principle of separation between administration and policy and with particular attention to profiles of incompatibility; identify forms of collaboration, during the procedures process, between the administrations for cultural heritage and activities and defence, for the realisation of works for military defence;

e) with reference to matters set out in letters *b*) and *c*) of paragraph 1: rationalise the advisory organisms and their relative functions, in ways which may include suppression, merging of and reduction in the number of organisms and their components; streamline the procedures for paying out funding and redefine the modalities for the creation and functioning of the organisms which participate in the procedures for the identification of associations and individuals that may receive funding and the quantification of such funding; reform the organisational structure of the organisms and the bodies in the sector; revise the system of checks and balances on the use of resources assigned and the effects produced by the measures;

f) with reference to the matter set out in letter *d*) of paragraph 1: harmonise the legislation with the general principles which inspire the States belonging to the European Union as regards doping; re-organise the tasks of the Sport Credit Institute (Istituto per il credito sportivo), ensuring that the Regions and autonomous local bodies are represented in the organs as well; guarantee funding instruments to private subjects;

g) with reference to the matter set out in letter *e*) of paragraph 1; reorganise, in the respect of the guiding principles and criteria indicated in article 14, paragraph 1, letter *b*) of law no. 59 of 15 March 1997, the Italian Society of Authors and Publishers (SIAE), whose statute must ensure an adequate presence of authors, publishers and other creative individuals in the organs of the Society and maximum transparency in the sharing out of the proceeds from the levy of copyrights among those entitled to them; harmonise the legislation relative to the production and dissemination of digital and multimedia content and software with the general principles followed by the European Union in matters pertaining to copyright and related rights.

3. The legislative decrees referred to in paragraph 1 explicitly indicate the provisions which have been substituted or abrogated, with the exception of the application of article 15 of the provisions on the law in general in the premise to the civil code. The legislative decrees referred to in paragraph 1 are adopted, after consultation with the Unified Conference referred to in article 8 of legislative decree no. 281 of 28 August 1997, with the prior opinion of the Parliamentary Commissions competent in each matter, which shall be expressed within the term of sixty days of receipt of the relative request. Upon expiration of such term, the legislative decrees may in any case be adopted.

4. Provisions which are corrective and supplementary to the legislative decrees referred to in paragraph 1 may be adopted, respecting the same guiding principles and criteria and with the same procedures referred to in the present article, within two years of the date of their coming into force.

Notes to art. 1:

—Art. 9 of the Constitution of the Italian Republic, published in the extraordinary edition of *Official Gazette* no. 298 of 27 December 1947, establishes:
<< Art. 9. − The Republic shall promote the development of culture and scientific and technological research.
It shall protect the landscape and the historical and artistic heritage of the Nation. >>

—For the text of art. 117 of the Constitution of the Italian Republic, see note to the premise.

Note to art. 4:

—For the text of art. 118 of the Constitution of the Italian Republic, see note to the premise.

Notes to art. 9:

—Art. 12 of the Accord signed at Rome on 18 February 1984, which introduces modifica-

tions to the Lateran Treaty of 11 February 1929 between the Italian Republic and the Holy See, ratified and implemented with law no. 121 of 25 March 1985, published in the ordinary supplement to *Official Gazette* no. 85 of 10 April 1985, establishes:
≪Art. 12. –

1. The Holy See and the Italian Republic, within their respective spheres, shall collaborate for the protection of the historical and artistic heritage. For the purpose of harmonising the application of Italian law with exigencies of a religious nature, the competent organs of the two Parties shall agree upon suitable provisions for the safeguarding, enhancement and enjoyment of cultural properties of religious interest belonging to ecclesiastical bodies and institutions. The conservation and consultation of the archives of historical interest and of the libraries of the same bodies and institutions shall be fostered and facilitated on the basis of agreements between the competent organs of the two Parties.

2. The Holy See shall continue to have at its disposal the Christian catacombs located on Roman soil and other parts of the Italian territory along with the consequent burden of their custody, maintenance and conservation, surrendering the use of the other catacombs. In compliance with the laws of the State and notwithstanding any rights of third parties, the Holy See may proceed to necessary excavations and to the transferral of sacred relics ≫.

– **Art. 8 of the Constitution of the Italian Republic, published in** *Official Gazette* – **extraordinary edition** – **no. 298 of 27 December 1947, establishes:**
≪Art. 8. – All religious denominations shall be equally free before the law.
Religious denominations other than the Catholic denomination shall have the right to organise themselves according to their own statutes, insofar as the same are not contrary to Italian laws.
Their relations with the State shall be governed by law on the basis of agreements with the relative agencies of representation ≫.

Note to art. 12:

—Art. 27 of decree law no. 269 of 30 September 2003, containing: "Urgent Provisions for Promoting Development and for the Correction of Public Accounts", published in the ordinary supplement to *Official Gazette* no. 229 of 2 October 2003 and converted, with modifications, into law no. 326 of 24 November 2003, published in the ordinary supplement to *Official Gazette* no. 274 of 25 November 2003, establishes:
≪Art. 27 (*Verification of Cultural Interest of Immovable Government Property*). –

1. The immovable and movable things belonging to the State, the Regions, the Provinces, Metropolitan Areas, Municipalities and to any other public body or institution, referred to in art. 2 of legislative decree no. 490 of 29 October 1999, shall be subject to the provisions for the protection of the cultural heritage until such time as the verification referred to in paragraph 2 is carried out.

2. The verification of the existence of artistic, historical, archaeological or ethno-anthropological interest in the things referred to in paragraph 1, shall be carried out by Superintendencies, ex officio or upon request by the parties to whom the things belong, on the basis of guidelines of a general nature established by the Ministry for Cultural Heritage and Activities.

3. When in the things subjected to verification the interest referred to in paragraph 2 is not found to exist, the same things are excluded from the application of the provisions for protection set out in legislative decree no. 490 of 1999.

4. The negative outcome of the verification of things belonging to the State, the Regions and other territorial government bodies, shall be notified to the competent offices so that they may order their release from State ownership, when there are no other reasons of public interest to be assessed on the part of the Ministry concerned.

5. [*paragraph suppressed by the law of conversion*].

6. The properties in which artistic, historical, archaeological or ethno-anthropological interest has been found to exist, in accordance with the general guidelines referred to in paragraph 2, shall remain definitively subject to the provisions for protection. Positive ascertainment shall constitute declaration pursuant to articles 6 and 7 of the Consolidated Text referred to in legislative decree no. 490 of 1999 and shall be registered in the ways provided for by art. 8 of the aforesaid Consolidated Text.

7. The provisions of the present article shall apply to the things referred to in paragraph 1 even when the subjects to whom they belong change their legal status in any way.

8. Upon the first application of the present article, the competent branch of the State Property Agency shall, within thirty days of the emanation of the decree referred to in paragraph 9, forward to the Regional Superintendency, the lists of the buildings owned by the State or belonging to State property for which verification is to be carried out, accompanied by descriptive information sheets containing the cognitive data relative to the individual buildings.

9. The criteria for the preparation of the lists and the manner in which the descriptive information sheets are to be compiled, as well as the procedures for the transmission of the

aforesaid lists and descriptive information sheets, which may also occur through the agency of other administrations concerned, shall be established by decree by the Ministry for Cultural Heritage and Activities, to be emanated in accord with the State Property Agency and with the Directorate General of Public Works and State Property of the Ministry of Defence for real estate assets in use by the administration of defence within thirty days of the coming into force of the present decree law.

10. On the basis of the investigation carried out by the competent Superintendencies and on the basis of the opinion formed by the aforesaid Superintendencies, the regional Superintendency shall, within the peremptory term of thirty days from the request, conclude the process of verification as regards the existence of cultural interest in the building in question with a reasoned provision and shall notify the requesting agency, within sixty days of receipt of the relative descriptive information sheet. Non-notification within the comprehensive term of one hundred and twenty days from receipt of the information sheet shall be deemed equivalent to a negative verification outcome.

11. The descriptive information sheets for buildings owned by the State with a positive verification outcome, along with the measure referred to in paragraph 10, are collected in a computer archive accessible to both administrations, for the purposes of monitoring real estate assets and of planning measures according to their respective institutional competences.

12. For buildings belonging to the Regions and other territorial government bodies, as well as those owned by other public bodies and institutions, the process of verification shall be initiated upon request on the part of the interested bodies, which along with the application shall provide the descriptive information sheets for each building. The provisions of paragraphs 10 and 11 shall be applied to procedures thus initiated.

13. The procedures for enhancement and divestment provided for by paragraphs 15 and 17 of art. 3 of law decree no. 351 of 25 September 2001, converted, with modifications, from law no. 410 of 23 November 2001, as well as from paragraphs 3 to 5 of art. 80 of law no. 289 of 27 December 2002, shall also apply to real estate assets referred to in paragraph 3 of the present article, as well as to those identified under paragraph 112 of art. 3 of law no. 662 of 23 December 1996, and subsequent modifications, and of paragraph 1 of art. 44 of law no. 448 of 23 December 1998. In art. 44 of law no. 448 of 23 December 1998, and subsequent modifications, paragraphs 1-*bis* and 3 are suppressed.

13-*bis*. The State Property Agency, in concert with the Directorate General of Public Works and State Property of the Ministry of Defence, shall identify real estate assets in use by the administration of defence which are no longer useful for institutional purposes and are to be included in divestment programmes for the purposes referred to in art. 3, paragraph 112, of law no. 662 of 23 December 1996, and subsequent modifications >>.

Note to art. 14:

—Art. 2 of law no. 241 of 7 August 1990, containing: "New Rules and Regulations for Administrative Procedures and Right of Access to Administrative Documents", published in *Official Gazette* no. 192 of 18 August 1990 establishes:

<< Art. 2. –

1. Where the procedure is the obligatory consequence of an application or must be initiated ex officio, the public administration is obliged to conclude it through the adoption of a special measure.

2. The public administrations shall, for each type of procedure, determine the term within which it is to be concluded, insofar as the said term has not already been directly established by law or regulation. Such term begins with the ex officio start of the procedure or from receipt of the request if the procedure is initiated by another party.

3. When the public administrations do not act pursuant to paragraph 2, the term shall be for a period of thirty days.

4. The decisions adopted pursuant to paragraph 2 shall be made public in accordance with the provisions of the single regulations >>.

Note to art. 16:

—The decree of the President of the Republic no. 1199 of 24 November 1971, containing: "Simplification of Administrative Appeal Procedures", is published in *Official Gazette* no. 13 of 17 January 1972.

Notes to art. 29

—Art. 17 of law no. 400 of 23 August 1988, containing: "Regulation of Government Activity and Rules for the Presidency of the Council of Ministers", published in the ordinary supplement to *Official Gazette* no. 214 of 12 September 1988, as modified by art. 74 of legislative decree no. 29 of 3 February 1993 published in the ordinary supplement to

Official Gazette no. 30 of 6 February 1993, and by art. 11 of law no. 25 of 5 February 1999, published in the ordinary supplement to *Official Gazette* no. 35 of 12 February 1999; and supplemented by art. 13 of law no. 59 of 15 March 1997, published in the ordinary supplement to *Official Gazette* no. 63 of March 1997, establishes:

≪Art. 17 (*Regulations*) −

1. Following resolution by the Council of Ministers, and consultation of the Council of State which must give its opinion within ninety days from the request, regulations may be emanated by decree of the President of the Republic to govern the following:

    a) the enforcement of laws and legislative decrees, as well as European Community regulations;

    b) the implementation and integration of laws and legislative decrees containing rules and regulations of principle, excluding those pertaining to matters reserved to Regional competence;

    c) matters in which no regulations exist by law or by acts having force of law, on condition that matters which are in any case reserved for legal regulation are not concerned;

    d) the organisation and functioning of public administrations according to the provisions dictated by law;

    e) [*suppressed*].

2. By decree of the President of the Republic, following resolution of the Council of Ministers and consultation with the Council of State, regulations shall be emanated for the regulation of matters, not covered by absolute reservation of law provided for by the Constitution, for which the laws of the Republic, authorising the exercise of the regulatory powers of the Government, shall determine the general rules regulating the matter and order the abrogation of laws in force, with the effect of the regulatory laws coming into force.

3. Regulations for matters under the competence of the Ministry or of an authority subordinated to the Ministry may be adopted by ministerial decree when the law expressly confers such power. For matters under the competence of more than one Ministry, such regulations may be adopted by inter-ministerial decree, on condition that proper authorisation is provided by law. Ministerial and inter-ministerial regulations may not dictate rules contrary to the regulations emanated by the Government. They must be notified to the President of the Council of Ministers before emanation.

4. The regulations referred to in paragraph 1 and ministerial and inter-ministerial regula-

tions, which must carry the denomination of "regulation", are adopted following the opinion of the Council of State, subject to approval and registration by the Court of Audits and published in the *Official Gazette*.

4-*bis*. The organisation and regulation of the Ministry offices shall be determined, with regulations emanated pursuant to paragraph 2, at the recommendation of the competent Minister in agreement with the President of the Council of Ministers and with the Minister of the Treasury, and in the respect of the principles established by legislative decree no. 29 of 3 February 1993, and subsequent modifications, with the contents of and in compliance with the following criteria:

a) re-organisation of the offices directly collaborating with the Ministers and the Undersecretaries of State, establishing that such offices have exclusive support competence for the policy direction organ and for the lines of communication between the policy organ and the administration;

b) identification of the offices at the general, central and peripheral management levels, through diversification between structures with final functions and instrumental functions and their organisation for homogenous functions, according to criteria of flexibility eliminating duplication of functions;

c) establishment of instruments for the periodical verification of organisation efficiency and results;

d) periodical indication and revisions of the consistency of staff plans;

e) provision for ministerial decrees of a non-regulatory nature for the definition of tasks of managerial staff within the general management offices >>.

—**Art. 9 of legislative decree no. 368 of 20 October 1998, containing: "Institution of the Ministry for Cultural Heritage and Activities, pursuant to art. 11 of law no. 59 of 15 March 1997", published in *Official Gazette* no. 250 of 26 October 1998, establishes:**
<< Art. 9 (Schools of training and study). –

1. Schools of specialised training and study operate in the following institutes: Istituto Centrale di Restauro (Central Institute for Restoration); Opificio delle pietre dure (Semiprecious Stones Workshop); Istituto centrale per la patologia del libro (Central Institute for Damaged Books).

2. The Institutes referred to in paragraph 1 organise training and specialisation courses, and may avail themselves of the collaboration of universities and other institutions and Italian and foreign bodies, and may, in their turn, participate in and contribute to the initiatives of such institutions and bodies.

3. The regulations regarding the courses offered by the schools, admission requirements and criteria for the selection of the teaching staff are established by ministerial regulations adopted, under article 17, paragraph 3, of law no. 400 of 23 August 1988, by decree of the Minister, in agreement with the Presidency of the Council of Ministers – Civil Service Department and with the Minister of the Treasury, Budget and Economic Planning. Branches of schools previously established may be established by decree of the Minister.

4. The re-organisation of the schools referred to in art. 14 of decree no. 1409 of the President of the Republic of 30 September 1963 shall be carried out with a regulation adopted with the modalities referred to in paragraph 3 >> .

—Art. 4 of legislative decree no. 281 of 28 August 1997, containing: "Definition and Enlargement of the Functions and Tasks of the Permanent Conference for Relations between the State, the Regions and the Autonomous Provinces of Trento and Bolzano and Unification, in matters and tasks of common interest, of the Regions, Provinces and Municipalities with the State-Cities Conference and Local Autonomies", published in *Official Gazette* no. 202 of 30 August 1997, establishes:

<< Art. 4 (*Accords between the Government, Regions and Autonomous Provinces of Trento and Bolzano*). –

1. The Government, the Regions and the Autonomous Provinces of Trento and Bolzano may, in the application of the principle of fair collaboration and in the pursuit of objectives for the efficacious functioning, economy and effectiveness of administrative action, may conclude accords within the State-Regions Conference, for the purpose of co-ordinating the exercise of respective competences and of carrying out activities of common interest.

3. The accords shall be concluded with the expression of assent on the part of the Government and of the Presidents of the Regions and of the Autonomous Provinces of Trento and Bolzano. >>

Note to art. 41:

—For the text of art. 17 of law no. 400 of 23 August 1988 see note to art. 29.

Note to art. 46:

—For the text of art. 2 of law no. 241 of 7 August 1990, see note to art. 14.

Note to art. 53:

—Art. 822 of the civil code, approved by royal decree no. 262 of 16 March 1942, published in the extraordinary edition of *Official Gazette* no. 79 of 4 April 1942, establishes:
<<Art. 822 (*Government Property*). – Belonging to the State and part of State property are seashores, beaches, harbours and ports; rivers, streams, lakes and other waters defined as public in the laws pertaining to the matter; and the works designated for national defence.

The following are likewise part of government property, when they belong to the State: roads, motorways and railways; aerodromes; aqueducts; buildings recognised as having historical, archaeological and artistic interest in accordance with the laws on the matter, the collections of museums, picture galleries, archives, libraries; and finally other properties which by law are subject to the system of laws regulating public property >> .

Note to art. 69:

—For decree no. 1199 of the President of the Republic of 24 November 1971, see note to art. 16.

Note to art. 73:

—Council Regulation (EEC) no. 3911/92, of 9 December 1992, on the exportation of cultural properties, is published in *Official Gazette* – 2nd special series – no. 17 of 1st March 1993; it was amended by Council Regulation (EC) no. 2469/96, of 16 December 1996, published in *Official Gazette* – 2nd special series – no. 16 of 27 February 1997 and by Council Regulation (EC) no. 974/01, of 14 May 2001, published in *Official Gazette* – 2nd special series – no. 57 of 23 July 2001.

—Council Directive 93/7/EEC, of 15 March 1993, concerning the "Return of Cultural Objects Unlawfully Removed from the Territory of a Member State", is published in *Official Gazette* – 2nd special series – no. 54 of 12 July 1993; it was modified by Directive 96/100/EC of the European Parliament and Council, of 17 February 1997, published in *Official Gazette* – 2nd special series – no. 45 of 16 June 1997 and by Directive 2001/38/ EC of the European Parliament and Council, of 5 June 2001, published in *Official Gazette*

– 2nd special series – no. 71 of 10 September 2001.

Note to art. **74:**

—For Council Regulation (EEC) no. 3911/92, of 9 December 1992, see note to art. 73.

Note to art. **75:**

—Art. 30 of the Treaty which establishes the European Economic Community, ratified and made enforceable by law no. 1203 of 14 October 1957, published in *Official Gazette* no. 317 of 23 December 1957, substituted and renumbered by art. 6 of the Treaty of Amsterdam, ratified and made enforceable with law no. 209 of 16 June 1998, published in the ordinary supplement to *Official Gazette* no. 155 of 6 July 1998, establishes:
≪Art. 30 [36] – The provisions of articles 28 [30] and 29 [34] shall not preclude the prohibitions or restrictions on import, exports or goods in transit justified on grounds of public morality, public policy or public security; the protection of the health and life of humans animals or plants; the protection of national treasures possessing artistic, historic or archaeological value; or the protection of industrial and commercial property. Such prohibitions or restrictions shall not, however, constitute a means of arbitrary discrimination or a disguised restriction on trade between Member States ≫.

—For Council Regulation (EEC) no. 3911/92, of 9 December 1992, see note to art. 73.

Note to art. **76:**

—For Council directive 93/7/EEC, of 15 March 1993, see note to art. 73.

Note to art. **77:**

—Art. 163 of the civil procedures code, approved by royal decree no. 1443 of 28 October 1940, published in the ordinary supplement to *Official Gazette* no. 253 of 28 October 1940, as modified by art. 7 of law no. 581 of 14 July 1950, published in the ordinary supplement to *Official Gazette* no. 186 of 16 August 1950, and by art. 7 of law no. 353 of 26 November 1990, published in the ordinary supplement to *Official Gazette* no. 281 of 1 December 1990, establishes:

<< Art. 163 (*Contents of the Summons*). – The application shall be made through a summons to appear at a fixed hearing.

The president of the court [*tribunale*] shall, at the beginning of the judicial calendar year, by decree approved by the first president of the appellate court, establish the days of the week and the times of the hearings designated exclusively for the first appearance of the parties in the court.

The summons must contain:

1) the indication of the court before which application is made;

2) the name, surname and the residence of the plaintiff; the name, surname, residence or domicile or home of the defendant and of the persons who respectively represent or assist them. If the plaintiff or defendant, is a corporate entity, a non-recognised association or a committee, the summons must contain its denomination or the company name, with the indication of the organ or office which is to represent it in court;

3) the determination of the thing which is the object of the application;

4) the exposition of the facts and elements which by law constitute the reasons for the application, with relative conclusions;

5) the specific indication of the means of evidence of which the plaintiff intends to avail him/herself and in particular of the documents he/she wishes to provide;

6) the name and surname of the attorney and indication of the power of attorney when the latter has already been issued;

7) the indication of the day of the hearing; summons to the defendant to appear twenty days before the hearing indicated pursuant to and in the forms established by art. 166, or ten days before in case of abridgement of time, and to appear, in the hearing indicated, before the judge designated under art. 168-bis, with the warning that the appearance after the aforesaid terms constitutes forfeiture under art. 167.

The summons, undersigned in accordance with art. 125, shall be delivered by the party or by the attorney to the court officer, who shall notify it in accordance with articles 137 following >>.

Note to art. 84:

—For Council Regulation (EEC) no. 3911/92, of 9 December 1992, see note to art. 73.

—For Council Directive 93/7/EEC, of 15 March 1993, see note to art. 73.

Note to art. 87:

—The final document of the diplomatic conference for the adoption of the UNIDROIT draft convention on the international return of stolen or unlawfully exported cultural property, with annex, produced in Rome, 24 June 1995, was ratified and made enforceable with law no. 213 of 7 June 1999, published in *Official Gazette* no. 153 of 2 July 1999.

Note to art. 91:

—For the text of art. 822 of the civil code, see note to art. 53.

—Art. 826 of the civil code, approved by royal decree no. 262 of 16 March 1942, published in the extraordinary edition of *Official Gazette* no. 79 of 4 April 1942, establishes:
<< Art. 826 (*Property of the State, the Provinces and the Municipalities*). – The things belonging to the State, the Provinces and the Municipalities, which are not of the kind indicated in the preceding articles, constitute the property of the State or, respectively, of the Provinces or Municipalities.
Forming part of the inalienable property of the State are the forests, which under the laws pertaining to the matter constitute the forest property of the State; mines, quarries and peat bogs when free use is denied to the proprietor of the land; the things possessing historical, archaeological, paleo-ethnological, paleontological and artistic interest, regardless of by whom and in what way they were discovered in the subsoil; the property constituting the furnishings of the Presidency of the Republic, and of barracks, armaments, military aircraft, and warships.
Forming part of the inalienable property of the State or, respectively, of the Provinces and Municipalities, according to which they belong, are the buildings designated to house public offices, with their furnishings, and other property designated for public service >>.

Note to art. 92:

—For the text to art. 17 of law no. 400 of 23 August 1988, see note to art. 29.

Note to art. 128:

—Law no. 364 of 20 June 1909, "which establishes and fixes regulations for the inalienability of antiquities and fine arts", is published in *Official Gazette* no. 150 of 28 June 1909.

—Law no. 778 of 11 June 1922 containing: "Measures for the protection of natural beauties and buildings of particular historical interest", is published in *Official Gazette* no. 148 of 24 June 1922.

—Articles 2, 3, 5 and 21 of law no. 1089 of 1 June 1939, concerning the "Protection of things possessing artistic and historical interest", published in *Official Gazette* no. 184 of 8 August 1939, establish:

≪Art. 2. – Likewise subject to the present law are immovable things which, because of their reference to political or military history, to literature, art and culture in general, have been recognised to possess particularly important interest and as such have formed the object of notification, in administrative form, of the Minister for National Education.

At the request of the Minister, the notification shall be recorded in the Land Register and shall have efficacy with regard to each successive proprietor, possessor or holder of the thing by whatever legal right.

Art. 3. – The Minister for National Education shall notify in administrative form private proprietors, possessors or holders by whatever legal right of the things indicated in art. 1 which possess particularly important interest.

Where buildings by nature or appurtenance are concerned, the provisions established in the second paragraph of the preceding article shall apply.

The list of movable property, for which notification of particularly important interest has been served, shall be conserved in the Ministry of National Education and copies of the same shall be deposited in the Préfectures of the Kingdom.

Any interested person may consult the list.

Art. 5. – The Minister for National Education, following consultation with the National Council on Education, the Sciences and Arts, may proceed to notification of the collections or series of objects which, by tradition, renown and particular environmental characteristics, as a whole possess exceptional artistic or historical interest.

The notified collections and series may not, by virtue of any legal right, be dismembered without the authorisation of the Minister for National Education.

Art. 21. – The Minister for National Education shall have the power to prescribe distances, measures and other provisions in order to prevent harm to the integrity of the immovable things subject to the provisions of the present law, or to their perspective or natural light, or to prevent that conditions of their setting or their decorous aspect be altered.

The exercise of such power shall be independent of the application of building regulations or enforcement of town plans.

The prescriptions established on the basis of the present article must, at the request of the Minister, be recorded in the Land Register and shall have efficacy for each successive proprietor, possessor or holder, by whatever legal right, of the thing to which the aforesaid prescriptions refer ≫.

—Art. 36 of decree no. 1409 of the President of the Republic of 30 September 1963 containing: "Provisions pertaining to the Organisation and Personnel of the Archives of the State", published in *Official Gazette* no. 285 of 31 October 1963, establishes:

≪Art. 36 (*Declaration of Notable Historical Interest*). − It is the task of the archival superintendents to declare, with a justified order to be notified under administrative procedure, the notable historical interest of archives or of single documents of which private individuals are the proprietors, possessors or holders, by whatever legal right.

Private individuals may, within the term of sixty days, appeal against the orders of the superintendents to the Minister for Internal Affairs who, following consultation with the Committee of the Superior Council of Archives, shall rule on the appeal ≫.

—Articles 6, 7, 8 and 49 of legislative decree no. 490 of 29 October 1999, containing: "Consolidation Text of the Legislative Provisions pertaining to matters of Cultural and Environmental Property, under the provisions of art. 1 of law no. 352 of 8 October 1997", published in the ordinary supplement to *Official Gazette* no. 302 of 27 December 1999, establish:

≪Art. 6 (*Declaration*). −

1. Without prejudice to the provisions of paragraph 4, the Minister shall declare the particularly important interest possessed by the things indicated in art. 2, paragraph 1, letter *a*), belonging to subjects other than those indicated in art. 5, paragraph 1.

2. The Minister shall likewise declare the particularly important interest possessed by the things indicated in art. 2, paragraph 1, letter *b*), the exceptional interest possessed by the collections or series of objects indicated in article 2, paragraph 1, letter *c*) and the notable historical interest possessed by the things indicated in article 2, paragraph 4, letter *c*).

3. The effects of the declaration are established by art. 10.

4. The Region locally competent shall declare the particularly important interest possessed by the things indicated in art. 2, paragraph 2, letter *c*) under private ownership. In the case of inaction on the part of the Region, the Ministry shall proceed under the provisions of art. 9, paragraph 3, of decree no. 3 of the President of the Republic of 14 January 1972.

Art. 7 (*Declaration proceeding*). –

1. The Minister shall start the declaration proceeding provided for by art. 6 either directly or on the recommendation of the superintendent, which recommendation may also be requested by the Region, the Province or the Municipality, and shall notify the proprietor, possessor or holder.

2. Notification shall include the identifying elements of the property and its assessed value resulting from the initiating action or the recommendation, the indication of the effects foreseen under paragraph 4, as well as the indication of the time limit, which in any case may not be less than thirty days, for the presentation of observations and comments.

3. When the proceeding regards real estate complexes, the notification shall also be forwarded to the Municipality concerned.

4. The notification shall, as a precautionary measure, entail the application of the provisions provided for in Section I of Chapter II and in Section I of Chapter III of this Title.

5. The effects indicated in paragraph 4 shall cease upon expiry of the term of declaration proceeding which the Ministry shall establish under the provisions of art. 2, paragraph 2 of law no. 241 of 7 August 1990.

6. The Regions shall apply the provisions indicated in the preceding paragraphs in the exercise of the functions indicated in art. 6, paragraph 4.

Art. 8 (Notification of Declaration). –

1. The declaration provided for in art. 6 shall be notified to the proprietor, possessor or holder of the things concerning which it was formulated.

2. Where things subject to the advertising of real estate are concerned, the declaration shall, at the request of the Ministry, be recorded in the land registries and shall have efficacy for every successive proprietor, possessor or holder by whatever right.

3. The declarations adopted by the Regions under the provisions of art. 6, paragraph 4, shall be forwarded to the Ministry.

Art. 49 (Prescriptions of Indirect Protection). –

1. The Ministry, which may also act upon the recommendation of the superintendent, shall have the power to prescribe distances, measures and other rules and regulations aimed at preventing harm to the immovable things subject to the provisions of this title, and at avoiding damage to the perspective or natural light or alterations to conditions of their setting or their decorous aspect.

2. The exercise of such power shall be independent of the provisions of building codes and urban planning instruments.

3. Notification of the start of proceedings shall be carried out in accordance with the modalities set out in art. 2, paragraph 2, or, when the number of assignees makes personal notification impossible or proves particularly onerous, through suitable means of advertising. For personal notification, the administration shall have the power to adopt precautionary measures.

4. The prescriptions dictated on the basis of this article shall be recorded in the land registries and shall have efficacy for every successive proprietor, possessor or holder, by whatever legal right, of the thing to which the aforesaid prescriptions refer.

5. In the case of real estate complexes, the provision of art. 7, paragraph 3 shall also apply to the notification >> .

Notes to art. 129:

—Law no. 286 of 28 June 1871 "which extends to the Province of Rome articles 24 and 25 of the interim provisions for the implementation of the Civil Code", is published in *Official Gazette* no. 174 of 28 June 1871.

—Law no. 1461 of 8 July 1883, "which provides for the conservation of galleries, libraries and other collections of art and antiquities", is published in *Official Gazette* no. 162 of 12 July 1883.

—Royal decree no. 653 of 23 November 1891, "which approves the regulation for the implementation of art. 4 of law no. 286 (2nd series) of 28 June 1871, and of law no. 1461 (3rd series) of 8 July 1883", is published in *Official Gazette* no. 285 of 5 December 1891.

—Law no. 31 of 7 February 1892, "which contains provisions for galleries, libraries and collections of art and antiquities", is published in *Official Gazette* no. 32 of 8 February 1892.

Notes to art. 130:

—Royal decree no. 1163 of 2 October 1911, containing " Regulations for State Archives", is published in *Official Gazette* no. 260 of 8 November 1911.

—Royal decree no. 363 of 30 January 1913, containing the "Regulation for the Implementation of law no. 364 of 20 June 1909 and law no. 688 of 23 June 1912, for Antiquities and Fine Arts", is published in *Official Gazette* no. 130 of 5 June 1913.

Note to art. **139:**

—Art. 13 of law no. 349 of 8 July 1986, containing: "Establishment of the Ministry of the Environment and Provisions in matters pertaining to Environmental Damage", published in the ordinary supplement to *Official Gazette* no. 162 of 15 July 1986, establishes:
≪ Art. 13. –

1. The associations of environmental protection on a national level and those present in at least five Regions shall be identified by decree of the Ministry of the Environment on the basis of programme aims and democratic internal regulations established by their statutes, as well as continuity of action and its external relevance, with the prior opinion of the National Council for the Environment, to be expressed within ninety days of request. When the aforesaid term expires with no opinion being expressed, the Minister of the Environment shall decide.

2. For the sole purpose of obtaining the short list of three members indicated in the preceding art. 12, paragraph 1, letter *c*) for the preliminary composition of the National Council for the Environment, the Minister shall, within thirty days of the coming into force of the present law, carry out a preliminary identification of the associations on the national level and of those present in at least five Regions, according to the criteria set out in the preceding paragraph 1, and shall inform Parliament ≫.

Notes to art. **142:**

—Royal decree no. 1775 of 11 December 1933, containing the "Consolidation of the Statutory Provisions on Waters and Electrical Systems" is published in *Official Gazette* no. 5 of 8 January 1934.

—Art. 2 of legislative decree no. 227 of 18 March 2001, containing "Orientation and Modernisation of the Forestry Sector, under the provisions of art. 7 of law no. 57 of 5 March 2001", published in the ordinary supplement to *Official Gazette* no. 137 of 15 June 2001, establishes:
≪Art. 2 (*Definition of woods and of wood arboriculture*). –

1. For the effects of the present legislative decree and of any other provision in force in the territory of the Republic the terms woods, forest and woodland are equalised.

2. Within twelve months of the coming into force of the present legislative decree the Re-

gions shall establish the definition of wood for the territory within their jurisdiction and:

a) the minimum values of width, extension and cover necessary for an area to be considered a wood;

b) the size of clearings and vacant areas which interrupt the continuity of a wood;

c) the cases in point which because of their particular nature are not to be considered woods.

3. The following are deemed woods:

a) lands encumbered with the obligation of reforestation for the purposes of protecting the hydro-geological system of the territory and air quality, safeguarding water resources, conserving biodiversity, protecting the landscape and the environment in general;

b) forest areas temporarily deprived of tree and bush cover as a result of forestry uses, biotic and non-biotic adversities, accidental events, fire;

c) clearings and all other surfaces with an area under 2000 square metres which interrupt the continuity of the wood;

4. The definition referred to in paragraphs 2 and 6 shall be applied for the purposes of identification of areas covered by woods referred to in art. 146, paragraph 1, letter *g*), of legislative decree no. 490 of 20 October 1999.

5. With the term arboriculture for wood is meant the cultivation of trees, in non-wooded lands, for the sole purpose of producing wood and biomass. Cultivation is reversible upon expiry of the growth cycle.

6. In default of the emanation of the Regional provisions referred to in paragraph 2 and where a different definition has not been established by the Regions themselves, woods are considered to be the lands covered by arboreal forest vegetation, whether or not it be associated with shrub vegetation of natural or artificial origin, in any stage of development, chestnut woods, corkwood plantations and Mediterranean brushwood, and excluding public and private gardens, trees lining streets, chestnut woods under cultivation and plantations of fruit trees and of arboriculture for wood referred to in paragraph 5. The aforesaid plant formations and the lands on which they grow must have an area under 2000 square metres and an average width of not less than 20 metres and cover of not less than 20 percent, with measurement being carried out on the external base of the trunks. The definition of cork-tree wood stands as referred to in law no. 759 of 18 July 1956. Likewise considered woods are the lands encumbered with the obligation of reforestation for the purposes of hydro-geological protection of the territory and air quality, safeguard-

ing the water supply, conserving biodiversity, protecting the landscape and environment in general, as well as the clearings and all other surfaces with an area of less than 2000 square metres which interrupt the continuity of the wood >>.

—Decree no. 448 of the President of the Republic of 13 March 1976, containing: "Implementation of the Convention on Wetlands of International Importance, above all as the Habitat of Water-birds, signed at Ramsar on 2 February 1971", is published in *Official Gazette* no. 173 of 3 July 1976.

—Ministerial decree no. 1444 of 2 April 1968, containing: "Mandatory Limits for Building Density, Height, Distance between Structures and Maximum Ratios between Areas Designated for Residential and Industrial Uses and Public Spaces or Spaces Reserved for Collective Activities, Public Green Areas or for Parking, to be Observed for the Purposes of the Formation of New Urban Planning Instruments or the Revision of Those Already in Existence, pursuant to art. 17 of law no. 765 of 6 August 1967" is published in *Official Gazette* no. 97 of 16 April 1968.

—Art. 18 of law no. 865 of 22 October 1971, containing "Planning and Co-ordination of Public Residential Building; Regulations on Expropriation for Public Use; Modifications and Additions to law no. 1150 of 17 August 1942; law no. 167 of 18 April 1962 and law no. 847 of 29 September 1964; and Expenditure Authorisation for Extraordinary Works in the Residential Building Sector, Benefiting from Facilitations and Agreements", published in *Official Gazette* no. 276 of 30 October 1971, establishes:

<< Art. 18 . – Within the term of six months from the date of entry into force of this law, the Municipalities shall, for the purposes of the application of the preceding art. 16, proceed to the delimitation of the built-up centres with a resolution adopted in the City Council. When such resolution is pending, the Municipality shall, with Council approval, declare whether or not the area falls within the built-up centres, for the effects of the expropriation procedure being carried out.

The boundaries of the built-up centre shall, for each centre or inhabited area, be defined by the continuous perimeter which includes all the built-up areas continuously and with parcels of land enclosed. Scattered settlements and external areas may not be included in the perimeter of the built-up areas, even when they are affected by the process of urbanisation. When the term established in the first paragraph of this article expires with no action taken, the Region shall establish the boundaries of the built-up centres. >>

Note to art. 144:

For the text of art. 13 of law no. 349 of 8 July 1986 see note to art. 139.

Note to art. 145:

—Art. 52 of legislative decree no. 112 of 31 March 1998, containing "Conferral of Administrative Functions and Tasks of the State to the Regions and Local Bodies, in Implementation of Chapter I of law no. 59 of 15 March 1997", published in the ordinary supplement to *Official Gazette* no. 92 of 21 April 1998, establishes:
<< Art. 52 (*Tasks of National Relevance*). —

1. Under art. 1, paragraph 4, letter c), of law no. 59 of 15 March 1997, tasks which have national relevance are those related to the identification of the fundamental lines of the organisation of the national territory with reference to natural and environmental values, the protection of the land, and the territorial organisation of infra-structural networks and of the works under State competence, as well as the system of the Cities and the Metropolitan Areas, and also for the purposes of developing the "Mezzogiorno" area and economically depressed areas of the country.

2. Within the competence of the State fall relations with international bodies and coordination with the European Union referred to in art. 1, paragraph 4, letter e), of law no. 59 of 15 March 1997, on matters pertaining to urban policy and land planning.

3. The tasks referred to in paragraph 1 of the present article shall be exercised by means of agreements established in the Unified Conference.

4. In art. 81, first paragraph, of decree no. 616 of the President of the Republic of 24 July 1977, letter a) is abrogated.

Note to art. 146:

—Law no. 241 of 7 August 1990 containing: "New Provisions on matters pertaining to Administrative Procedure and Right of Access to Administrative Documents", is published in *Official Gazette* no. 192 of 18 August 1990.

—For the text of art. 13 of law no. 349 of 8 July 1986, see note to art. 139.

Note to art. 147:

—Articles 14, 14-bis, 14-ter and 14-*quater* of law no. 241 of 7 August 1990, containing "New Provisions on matters pertaining to Administrative Procedure and Right of Access to Administrative Documents", published in *Official Gazette* no. 192 of 18 August 1990, establish:

≪Art. 14. —

1. When it is advisable to carry out a contemporaneous examination of the various public interests involved in an administrative procedure, the proceeding administration shall as a rule convene a Conference of Services.

2. The Conference of Services shall always be convened when the proceeding administration must acquire agreements, concerted action, permits or waivers, or the consent, however denominated, of other public administrations, and, having formally requested the same, fails to obtain them, within fifteen days of the start of proceedings.

3. The Conference of Services may also be convened for the contemporaneous examination of interests involved in several connected administrative procedures, regarding the same activities or results. In such cases, the Conference shall be convened by the administration or, with prior informal agreement, by one of the administrations responsible for the prevalent public interest. For public works, art. 7 of law no. 109 of 11 February 1994 and subsequent modifications shall continue to apply. The Conference may be convened at the request of any other administration involved.

4. When activities in the private sector are subordinated to consent, however denominated, falling within the competence of several government administrations, the Conference of Services shall be convened, also at the request of the interested administration, by the administration with competence for the adoption of the final provision.

5. In cases where public works are granted in concession, the Conference of Services shall be convened by the grantor within fifteen days, without prejudice to the provisions of Regional laws with regard to environmental impact assessment.

Art. 14-*bis*. —

1. The Conference of Services may be convened for projects of particular complexity, at the reasoned and documented request of the interested party, before the presentation of a definitive application or project, for the purpose of verifying the conditions that must exist upon presentation in order to obtain the necessary permits. In such cases the Confer-

ence shall rule within thirty days of the date of the request and the relative costs shall be charged to the applicant.

2. In procedures dealing with the realisation of public works and with public interest, the Conference of Services shall express its opinion on the preliminary project for the purpose of establishing the conditions for obtaining for the definitive project the agreements, opinions, concessions, authorisations, licences, permits or waivers, however denominated, required by the laws in force. At the same time, the administrations responsible for environmental and landscape-territorial protection, for the protection of the historical and artistic heritage and of health, shall give their opinion, with regard to the interests protected by each, on the project solutions chosen. When, on the basis of the available documentation, no elements emerge which in any case preclude the realisation of the project, the aforesaid administrations shall, within forty-five days, indicate the conditions and elements necessary to obtain the deeds of permit when the definitive project is presented.

3. In cases where environmental impact assessment is requested, the Conference of Services shall express its opinion within thirty days of the conclusion of the preliminary phase in the definition of the contents of the environmental impact study, according to the provisions pertaining to environmental impact assessment. If such conclusion fails to occur within ninety days of the request referred to in paragraph 1, the Conference of Services shall in any case express its opinion within the next thirty days. Within such Conference, the authority responsible for environmental impact assessment shall indicate the conditions for the development of the project and of the environmental impact study. In this phase, which is an integral part of the environmental impact assessment procedure, the aforesaid authority shall examine the main alternatives, including the zero alternative, and, on the basis of the available documentation, shall verify the existence of any elements of incompatibility, which may also relate to the planned location of the project, and, when such elements do not exist, shall indicate within the Conference of Services, the conditions necessary to obtain the necessary deeds of permit when the definitive project is presented.

4. In the cases referred to in paragraphs 1, 2 and 3, the Conference of Services shall express its opinion on the basis of the documents in its possession and the indications furnished on this occasion may be modified with grounds or added to only in the presence of significant elements which emerged in subsequent stages of the procedure, including those resulting from the observations of private persons on the definitive project.

5. In the case referred to in paragraph 2, the sole party responsible for the procedure shall

forward to the administrations concerned the definitive project, drawn up on the basis of the conditions indicated by the same administrations during the Conference of Services on the preliminary project, and shall convene the Conference between the thirtieth and sixtieth day following submission of the definitive project. In the case of government contract for the procurement of goods and services or granting of a concession for public works, the administration awarding the contract or concession shall convene the Conference of Services on the basis of the preliminary project only, in accordance with the provisions of law no. 109 of 11 February 1994 and subsequent modifications.

Art. 14-*ter*. −

1. The Conference of Services shall take decisions relative to the organisation of its work on the basis of a majority vote of the members present.

2. The administrations concerned must receive notice of the convocation of the first meeting of the Conference of Services at least ten days before the relative date, and such notice may be sent through electronic mail. Within the next five days, the administrations convened may, when it is impossible for them to attend, request that the meeting be held at a different date; in such cases, the proceeding administration shall negotiate a new date, which must in any case be within ten days of the first date.

3. In the first meeting of the Conference of Services, or in any case in the meeting immediately following the forwarding of the application or the definitive project pursuant to art. 14-bis, the participating administrations shall determine the term for the adoption of the final decision. The work of the Conference may not exceed ninety days, excepting the provisions of paragraph 4. When such terms have expired with no action taken, the proceeding administration shall take action pursuant to paragraphs 2 ff., of art. 14-*quater*.

4. In cases where environmental impact assessment is requested, the Conference of Services shall express its opinion after having acquired the assessment. If the environmental impact assessment fails to occur within the term established for the adoption of the relative provision, the administration responsible shall express its opinion within the Conference of Services, which shall conclude within thirty days following the aforesaid term. Nevertheless, when the majority of participants in the Conference of Services requests it, the term of thirty days referred to in the preceding sentence is extended by another thirty days when there is an evident need for further preliminary studies.

5. In procedures for which a decision has already been taken concerning environmental impact assessment, the provisions referred to in paragraph 3 of art. 14-*quater*, as well as those referred to in article 16, paragraph 3, and article 17, paragraph 2, shall apply only

to the administrations responsible for safeguarding public health.

6. Each administration summoned shall participate in the Conference of Services through a single representative authorised, by the responsible organ, to give the binding expression of the wishes of the administration regarding all the decisions that fall within the competence of the same.

7. Consent shall be deemed to be granted by the administration whose representative has not definitively expressed the wishes of the administration represented and has not, within the term of thirty days from the date of receipt of the concluding decision of the proceeding, notified the proceeding administration, of its reasoned dissent, or when it has not, within the same term, contested the concluding decision of the Conference of Services.

8. During the sitting of the Conference of Services, the proponents of the application or the designers of the project may be asked, once only, for clarifications or additional documentation. If the latter are not furnished during the aforesaid sitting, the provision shall then be examined, within the following thirty days.

9. The final provision conforming to the favourable conclusive decision of the Conference of Services shall, to all intents and purposes, substitute any authorisation, concession, permit or waiver or deed of permit, however denominated, under the competence of the participating administrations, or of the administrations which were in any case invited to participate, in the aforesaid Conference.

10. The final provision concerning works subjected to environmental impact assessment shall be published by the proponent, along with the abstract of the aforesaid environmental impact assessment, in the *Official Gazette*, or the Regional Bulletin in the case of a Regional environmental impact assessment, and in a nationally circulated daily newspaper. The terms for any judicial appeal on the part of interested parties shall lapse from the date of publication in the *Official Gazette*.

Art. 14-*quarter*. –

1. The dissent of one or more administration representatives, regularly summoned to the Conference of Services must, on pain of inadmissibility, be expressed during the Conference of Services, must be adequately motivated, may not refer to related issues which are not the object of the Conference itself, and must contain the specific indications of the design modifications necessary for assent.

2. If one or more administrations have, during the Conference, expressed dissent on the proposal of the proceeding administration, the latter, within the peremptory time-limits indicated in art. 14-*ter*, paragraph 3, shall take the concluding decision of the proceed-

ing on the basis of the majority of the positions expressed during the Conference of Services. The decision shall be immediately enforceable.

3. Should motivated dissent be expressed by an administration charged with environmental and landscape-territorial protection, protection of the historical-artistic heritage or the safeguarding of public health, the decision shall be remitted to the Council of Ministers, when the dissenting administration or the proceeding administration is a State administration, or to the competent governing organs of the territorial bodies, in other cases. The Council of Ministers or the governing organs of the territorial bodies shall deliberate within thirty days, except when, in assessing the complexity of the preliminary investigation, the President of the Council of Ministers or the President of the Regional Council or the President of the Province or the Mayor decide to extend such time limit for a further period not to exceed sixty days.

4. When dissent is expressed by a Region, the decisions under the competence of the Council of Ministers provided for in paragraph 3 shall be taken with the participation of the President of the Regional Council concerned, to whom an invitation is sent to participate in the meeting for this purpose, in order to be heard with no voting right.

5. In the event that the work is subjected to environmental impact assessment and in the case of a negative decision, art. 5, paragraph 2, letter c-*bis*) of law no. 400 of 23 August 1988, introduced by art. 12, paragraph 2 of legislative decree no. 303 of 30 July 1999 shall apply. >>

—**Art. 6 of law no. 349 of 8 July 1986, containing, "Establishment of the Ministry of the Environment and Laws pertaining to Environmental Damage", published in the ordinary supplement to** *Official Gazette* **no. 162 of 15 July 1986, establishes:**
<<Art. 6. –

1. Within six months of the coming into force of this law, the Government shall present to Parliament the draft law pertaining to the implementation of the European Community directives on environmental impact.

2. Until such time as the European Community directives on environmental impact are implemented into law, the technical regulations and the categories of works capable of producing significant modifications to the environment and to which shall apply the provisions referred to in paragraphs 3, 4 and 5 which follow, shall be identified by decree of the President of the Council of Ministries, following resolution by the Council of Ministers, adopted on the recommendation of the Minister of the Environment, after consultation with the Scientific Committee referred to in article 11 which follows, in accordance

with European Community Council directive no. 85/337 of 27 June 1985.

3. The project designs for the works referred to in the preceding paragraph 2 shall, before their approval, be communicated to the Minister of the Environment, to the Minister for Cultural and Environmental Heritage and to the Region concerned at the local level, for the purposes of environmental impact assessment. The notification shall contain the indication of the location of the work, the specification of liquid and solid waste, emission and introduction of pollution in the atmosphere and of noise emissions produced by the work, the description of the devices to be used for the elimination or resolution of damage to the environment and for environmental monitoring. The announcement of the notification served must be published, by the principal, in the daily newspaper most widely circulated in the Region whose area is concerned, as well as a nationally circulated daily.

4. After consulting the Region concerned and in accord with the Ministry for the Cultural and Environmental Heritage, the Minister of the Environment shall express a decision on environmental compatibility within the ninety days following, upon expiry of which the procedure for approval of the project design shall continue its course, except when the Council of Ministers decides to extend the term in cases of particular importance. For works affecting areas subject to ordinances of cultural or landscape protection the Minister of the Environment shall take a decision in agreement with the Minister for the Cultural and Environmental Heritage.

5. When the Ministry responsible for carrying out the work does not wish to conform to the assessment of the Ministry of the Environment, the question shall be remitted to the Council of Ministers.

6. In the event that, in carrying out the works referred to in paragraph 3, the Minister of the Environment perceives behaviour contrasting with the opinion on environmental compatibility expressed pursuant to paragraph 4, or such behaviour as is in any case likely to compromise the fundamental exigencies of ecological and environmental equilibrium, he shall order the suspension of the works and remit the question to the Council of Ministers.

7. The powers of the Ministry for the Cultural and Environmental Heritage shall stand in matters under its competence.

8. The Minister for the Cultural and Environmental Heritage in the case provided for in art. 1-*bis*, paragraph 2 of decree-law no. 312 of 27 June 1985, converted with modifications into law no. 431 of 8 August 1985, shall exercise the powers referred to in articles 4 and 82 of decree no. 616 of the President of the Republic of 24 July 1977, in accord with the Minister of the Environment.

9. Any citizen, in conformity with the laws in force, may present petitions, observations or opinions, in written form, on the work subject to environmental impact assessment, within the time limit of thirty days from the announcement of the notification of the project, to the Ministry of the Environment, the Ministry for the Cultural and Environmental Heritage and to the Region concerned >> .

Note to art. 153:

—Art. 23, paragraph 4, of legislative decree no. 285 of 30 April 1992, containing the "New Highway Code", published in the ordinary supplement to *Official Gazette* no. 114 of 18 May 1992, as modified by article 13 of legislative decree no. 360 of 10 September 1993, published in the ordinary supplement to *Official Gazette* no. 217 of 15 September 1993, by art. 30 of law no. 472 of 7 December 1999, published in the ordinary supplement to *Official Gazette* no. 294 of 16 December 1999 and by art. 1 of decree law no. 151 of 27 June 2003, published in the *Official Gazette* no. 149 of 30 June 2003, and converted with modifications into law no. 214 of 1st August 2003, published in *Official Gazette* no. 186 of 12 August 2003, establishes:
<< Art. 4. The collocation of hoardings and other means of advertising along the roads or in view of the same is in all cases subject to authorisation by the body owning the road in conformity with the current laws. Within the built-up centres, competence belongs to the Municipality, without prejudice to the preventive technical waiver of the owning body if the road belongs to the State, the Region or the Province >> .

Note to art. 156:

—Article 149 of legislative decree no. 490 of 29 October 1999 containing: "Consolidation Text of the Legislative Provisions pertaining to Cultural and Environmental Property, in accordance with art. 1 of law no. 352 of 8 October 1997", published in the ordinary supplement to *Official Gazette* no. 302 of 27 December 1999, establishes:
<< Art. 149 (*Landscape Planning*). –

1. The Regions shall subject the territory, including environmental assets indicated in art. 146, to specific regulations for environmental use and enhancement, by drawing up landscape plans or urban land plans having the same purpose of safeguarding the values of the landscape and the environment.

2. Landscape planning prescribed in paragraph 1 is voluntary for the vast localities indicated

in letters c) and d) of art. 139 included in the lists set out in art. 140 and by art. 144.

3. In the event that the Regions fail to fulfil the provisions set out in paragraph 1, the provisions set out in art. 4 of decree no. 616 of the President of the Republic of 24 July 1977, as modified by art. 8 of law no. 59 of 15 March 1997, shall be followed.

4. Without prejudice to the provisions of art. 164, the Minister, in agreement with the Minister of the Environment and with the Region, may adopt measures for the reclamation and upgrading of the assets protected under this title, whose values have in any case been compromised >>.

Note to art. 157:

—For law no. 778 of 11 June 1922, see note to art. 128.

—Law no. 1497 of 29 June 1939 concerning the "Protection of Natural Beauties", is published in *Official Gazette* no. 241 of 14 October 1939.

—Art. 82 of decree no. 616 of the President of the Republic of 24 July 1977, containing: "Implementation of the Enabling Clause referred to in Art. 1 of Law no. 382 of 22 July 1975", published in the ordinary supplement to *Official Gazette* no. 234 of 29 August 1977, as supplemented by art. 1 of decree law no. 312 of 27 June 1985, published in *Official Gazette* no. 152 of 29 June 1985, and converted with modifications, into law no. 431 of 8 August 1985, published in *Official Gazette* no. 197 of 22 August 1985, establishes:

<< Article 82 (**Environmental Assets**). – The administrative functions exercised by the central and peripheral organs of the State for the protection of natural beauties as regards their identification, protection and relative sanctions shall be delegated to the Regions.

The enabling clause regards, among other things, the administrative functions concerning:

a) the identification of natural beauties, without prejudice to the power of the Minister for the Cultural and Environmental Heritage to, following consultation with the National Council for the Cultural and Environmental Heritage, add to the lists of natural beauties approved by the Regions;

b) the granting of authorisations and permits for their modification;

c) the opening up of roads and quarries;

d) the installation of hoardings or other means of advertising;

e) the adoption of preventive measures, even when these assets are not included in the relative lists;

f) the adoption of measures for demolition and the imposition of sanctions;

g) the powers of the central and peripheral State organs inherent to the Provincial Commissions provided for in art. 2 of law no. 1497 of 29 June 1939 and in art. 31 of decree no. 805 of the President of the Republic of 3 December 1975;

h) the authorisation provided for by law no. 1097 of 29 November 1971, for the protection of the Euganeian Hills (Colli Euganei)

Notifications of the notable public interest possessed by natural and panoramic beauties served on the basis of law no. 1497 of 29 June 1939 may not be revoked or modified without the advice of the National Council for the Cultural Heritage.

The Minister of the Cultural and Environmental Heritage may prohibit works or order their suspension, when they harm environmental assets which may be defined as natural beautifies, even if they are not included in the lists.

The following are subject to landscape constraint orders pursuant to law no. 1497 of 29 June 1939:

a) coastal territories included within a swath of land 300 metres in depth from the waterline, including elevated land overlooking lakes;

b) areas conterminous with lakes included within a swath of land 300 metres in depth from the waterline, including elevated land overlooking lakes;

c) rivers, streams and water courses registered in the lists referred to in the consolidated text of the legal provisions for waters and electricity plants, approved by royal decree no. 1775 of 11 December 1933, and the relative shores or base foundations of the embankments for a swath of land of 150 metres each;

d) mountains for the part exceeding 1600 metres above sea level for the Alpine chain and 1200 metres above sea level for the Apennine chain and the islands;

e) glaciers and cirques;

f) national or regional parks and reserves, as well as the areas of protection external to the parks;

g) areas covered by forests and woods, even if swept or damaged by fire, and those under a reforestation constraint order;

h) areas assigned to agricultural universities and zones encumbered for civic uses;

i) wetlands included in the list referred to in decree no. 448 of the President of the Republic of 13 March 1976;

j) volcanoes;

k) areas of archaeological interest.

The constraint order referred to in the preceding paragraph does not apply to zones A, B and

— restrictively to the parts included in the multiyear implementation plans — to other zones, as defined in the urban planning instruments pursuant to ministerial decree no. 1444 of 2 April 1968, and, in Municipalities lacking such instruments, to the built-up centres with perimeters defined under art. 18 of law no. 865 of 22 October 1971.

Subject to landscape constraint as well are the assets referred to in no. 2) of art. 1 of law no. 1497 of 29 June 1939, even in the zones referred to in the preceding paragraph.

In the woods and forests referred to in letter g) of the fifth paragraph of the present article, the following are permitted: the cutting of cultivated vegetation, forestation, reforestation, and work for reclamation, fire prevention and conservation provided for and authorised on the basis of laws in force pertaining to the matter.

The authorisation referred to in art. 7 of law no. 1497 of 29 June 1939, must be granted or denied within the peremptory term of sixty days. The Regions shall immediately inform the Minister for the Cultural and Environmental Heritage of the authorisations granted and shall contemporaneously forward the relative documentation. When the aforesaid term expires without action taken, the interested parties may, within thirty days, request authorisation from the Minister for the Cultural and Environmental Heritage who shall take a decision within sixty days of the date of receipt of the aforesaid request. The Minister for the Cultural and Environmental Heritage may, in any case, annul, with a reasoned provision, the Regional authorisation within the sixty days following the relative notification.

Whenever the request for authorisation concerns works to be carried out by the State administrations, the Minister for the Cultural and Environmental Heritage may, in any case, within sixty days, grant or deny the authorisation referred to in art. 7 of law no. 1497 of 29 June 1939, even when such granting or denial differs from the Regional decision.

For the activities of search and extraction referred to in royal decree no. 1443 of 29 July 1927, the authorisation of the Ministry for the Cultural and Environmental Heritage, provided for by the preceding ninth paragraph, shall be granted following consultation with the Minister of Industry, Commerce and Crafts.

The authorisation referred to in art. 7 of law no. 1497 of 29 June 1939 is not required for works of ordinary and extraordinary maintenance, consolidation, and conservational restoration which do not alter the state of the sites and the exterior aspect of the buildings, nor is it necessary for carrying out agricultural, forestry or pastoral activities which do not permanently alter the condition of the sites for building structures or other civil works, and on condition that the activities and works are such that they do not alter the hydro-geological system of the territory.

The tasks of supervision with regard to the constraints referred to in the fifth paragraph of the present article are also exercised by the organs of the Ministry for the Cultural and Environmental Heritage >>.

—For legislative decree no. 490 of 29 October 1999, see note to the premises.

Note to art. 158:

—Royal decree no. 1357 of 3 June 1940, containing the "Regulation for the Application of Law no. 1497 of 29 June 1939", is published in *Official Gazette* no. 234 of 5 October 1940.

Note to art. 159:

—For law no. 241 of 7 August 1990, see note to art. 146.

—Ministerial decree no. 495 of 13 June 1994, containing the "Regulation concerning Provisions for Implementation of Articles 2 and 4 of Law no. 241 of 7 August 1990, regarding the Time limits and Officials Responsible for the Procedures", published in the ordinary supplement to *Official Gazette* no. 187 of 11 August 1994, as modified by art. 3 of ministerial decree no. 165 of 19 June 2002, published in *Official Gazette* no. 180 of 2 August 2002, establishes:

<<Article 6 (*Procedural Time Limits*). –

1. The time limits for the conclusion of the procedures refer to the date of adoption of the provision, or, in the case of provisions valid only upon declared receipt, to the date on which the recipient receives notification.

2. When during the procedure certain phases, apart from the cases provided for by articles 16 and 17 of law no. 241 of 7 August 1990, fall within the competence of administrations other than the administration for the cultural and environmental heritage the time limit for the proceeding shall be understood to include the period of time necessary for the completion of the aforesaid phases. To this end, the administrations concerned shall, within sixty days of the coming into force of the present regulation, together verify the adequacy or inadequacy of the time limits established, within the context of the final deadline, for the completion of the phases themselves. When verification demonstrates the inadequacy of the final time limit, the Ministry for the Cultural and Environmental Heritage shall proceed, within the prescribed regulatory form, to vary the term, unless the same is established by law.

3. The time limits referred to in paragraphs 1 and 2 constitute maximum time limits and their expiry does not exonerate the administration from the obligation of acting with the greatest promptness, without prejudice to any other consequence of non-compliance with the time limit.

4. In cases where review of the actions of the proceeding administration is of a preventive nature, the period of time relative to the integration phase of the enforceability of the provision is not calculated for the purposes of the time limit for the conclusion of the proceeding. In a footnote to the action subject to review, the administration responsible for the proceeding shall indicate the organ responsible for the aforesaid review and the time limits, where established, within which the same must be exercised.

5. When not otherwise established, the same time limits indicated for the main procedures shall apply for the modification of orders previously emanated.

6. When the law establishes that the application of the interested party shall be deemed to be rejected or approved following the lapse of a determined period of time from the presentation of the application itself, the time limit established by law or by regulation for the constitution of silence-rejection or silence-consent shall likewise constitute the time limit within which the administration must adopt its decision. When the law establishes new cases or new time limits for silence-consent or silence-rejection, the time limits contained in the annexed tables are deemed to be integrated or modified accordingly.

6-*bis*. When, during the preliminary investigation, it becomes necessary to obtain clarifications or to acquire additional elements for judgement, or to proceed to verifications of a technical nature, the party responsible for the proceeding shall immediately inform those indicated in art. 4, paragraph 1, as well as, where advisable, the administration which has forwarded the additional documentation. In such case, the time-limit for the conclusion of the proceeding shall be interrupted, once only and for a period not exceeding thirty days, from the date of notification and shall begin to lapse again upon receipt of the documentation or the acquisition of the results of the technical verifications. >>

—Art. 1-*quinquies* of decree law no. 312 of 27 June 1985, containing: "Urgent Provisions for the Protection of Areas of Particular Environmental Interest. Supplement to art. 82 of decree no. 616 of the President of the Republic of 24 July 1977", published in *Official Gazette* no. 152 of 29 June 1985 and converted, with modifications, into law no. 431 of 8 August 1985, published in *Official Gazette* no. 197 of 22 August 1985, establishes:
<< Art. 1-*quinquies*. –

1. The areas and properties identified under art. 2 of ministerial decree of 21 September

1984 published in *Official Gazette* no. 265 of 26 September 1984, are included among those in which, until the adoption by the Regions of the plans referred to in the preceding article 1-bis, is prohibited any modification of the organisation of the territory, as well as any construction work, with the exclusion of the works of ordinary and extraordinary maintenance, static consolidation and conservational restoration which do not alter the condition of the sites and the exterior aspect of the buildings >>.

Note to art. 162:

—For the text of art. 23 of legislative decree no. 285 of 30 April 1992, see note to art. 153.

Note to art. 166:

—For Council Regulation (EEC) no. 3911/92 of 9 December 1992, see note to art. 71.

—Commission Regulation (EEC) no. 752/93 of 30 March 1993, containing "Application Provisions for Council Regulation (EEC) no. 3911/92, relative to the Exportation of Cultural Property" is published in *Official Gazette* — 2nd special series — no. 39 of 20 May 1993; it was modified by Commission Regulation (EC) no. 1526/98 of 16 July 1998, published in *Official Gazette* — 2nd special series — no. 87 of 5 November 1998.

Note to art. 168:

—For the text to art. 23 of legislative decree no. 285 of 30 April 1992, see note to art. 153.

Note to art. 180:

—Art. 650 of the penal code, approved by royal decree no. 1398 of 19 October 1930, published in the ordinary supplement to *Official Gazette* no. 251 of 26 October 1930, establishes:

<<Art. 650 (*Failure to Comply with Provisions of the Law*). — Whosoever fails to comply with a provision legally established by law for reasons of justice or public safety or public order or hygiene, shall, if the offence does not constitute a more serious crime, be punishable with arrest of up to three months and with a fine of up to four hundred thousand lire >>.

Note to art. 181:

—Art. 20 of law no. 47 of 28 February 1985, containing: "Provisions for the Control of Urban Planning and Building, Sanctions, Salvage and Curability of Building Works", published in the ordinary supplement to *Official Gazette* no. 53 of 2 March 1985, as modified by article 7-bis of decree law no. 146 of 23 April 1985, published in *Official Gazette* no. 97 of 24 April 1985 and converted, with modifications, into law no. 298 of 21 June 1985, published in *Official Gazette* no. 146 of 22 June 1985, establishes:

≪Article 20 (*Penal Sanctions*). – Unless the offence constitutes a more serious crime and with administrative sanctions remaining in force, the following sanctions are applicable:

a) a fine of up to 20 million lire for failure to comply with the laws, prescriptions and implementation modalities established by the present law, by law no. 1150 of 17 August 1942, and subsequent modifications and additions, insofar as they are applicable, as well as by building regulations, urban planning instruments and concessions;

b) arrest of up to two years and a fine from 10 million to 100 million lire in cases of execution of works in total non-conformity with or in absence of concession or the continuance of the same in spite of a suspension order;

c) arrest of up to two years and a fine from 30 million to 100 million lire in the case of illegal parceling of land for building purposes, as established by the first paragraph of art. 18. The same punishment shall also apply in cases of construction in zones subject to historical, artistic, archaeological, landscape or environmental constraint orders, which are in essential variance with, in total variance with or in absence of concession.

The provisions referred to in the preceding paragraph substitute those referred to in art. 17 of law no. 10 of 28 January 1977 ≫.

Note to art. 182:

—Art. 7 of ministerial decree no. 294 of 3 August 2000, containing: "Regulation concerning the Identification of Qualifications of Professionals carrying out Restoration and Maintenance Work on Movable Properties and on the Decorated Surfaces of Architectonic Properties", published in *Official Gazette* no. 246 of 20 October 2000, as substituted by ministerial decree no. 420 of 24 October 2001, published in *Official Gazette* no. 280 of 1 December 2001, establishes:

<< Article 7 (*Restorer of Cultural Properties*). –

1. For the purposes of the present regulation, as well as the purposes referred to in article 224 of decree no. 554 of the President of the Republic of 21 December 1999, by restorer of cultural properties is meant the person who has attained a diploma from a State school of restoration referred to in article 9 of legislative decree no. 368 of 20 October 1998, with a programme of studies lasting not less than four years, or a specialised university degree in the conservation and restoration of the historical-artistic heritage.

2. By restorer of cultural properties is likewise meant the person who on the date of the coming into force of the present regulation:

   a) has attained a diploma from a State or Regional school of restoration lasting not less than two years and has carried out restoration activities on the properties themselves, directly and on his/her own or as a permanent employee or under a continuous contract with direct responsibilities in the technical management of the work, with regular execution of the work certified by the authority responsible for the protection of the property or of the decorated surface, for a period of time which is at least double that of the school period lacking, and in any case not less than two years;

   b) has carried out restoration work on the aforesaid properties, directly and on his/her own or as a permanent employee or under a continuous contract with direct responsibilities in the technical management of the work, for not less than eight years with regular execution of the work certified by the authority responsible for the protection of the properties on which restoration work has been done;

   c) has attained a diploma from a State or Regional school of restoration lasting not less than two years or has carried out restoration work on movable properties or decorated surfaces for a period equalling at least four years, directly and on his/her own or as a permanent employee or under a continuous contract with direct responsibilities in the technical management of the work, with regular execution of the work certified by the protection authority, where qualifications have been certified or where a training programme has been completed according to modalities established by decree of the Minister for the Cultural Heritage and Activities, to be adopted by 31 December 2001 >>.

—For the text to art. 117 of the Constitution of the Italian Republic, see note to the premises.

Note to art. **183**:

— For article 3 of law no. 20 of 14 January 1994, containing: "Provisions pertaining to Jurisdiction and Auditing by the Court of Auditors" published in *Official Gazette* no. 10 of 14 January 1994, as modified by art. 2 of decree law no. 543 of 23 October 1996, published in *Official Gazette* no. 249 of 23 October 1996 and converted, with modifications, into law no. 639 of 20 December 1996, published in *Official Gazette* no. 299 of 21 December 1996; by art. 43 of legislative decree no. 80 of 31 March 1998, published in the ordinary supplement to *Official Gazette* no. 82 of 8 April 1998; by art. 27 of law no. 340 of 24 November 200, published in *Official Gazette* no. 275 of 24 November 2000; by art. 49 of law no. 388 of 23 December 2000, published in the ordinary supplement to *Official Gazette* no. 302 of 29 December 2000; and by art. 72 of legislative decree no. 165 of 30 March 2001, published in the ordinary supplement to *Official Gazette* no. 106 of 9 May 2001, establishes:

≪Art. 3 (*Regulations on Auditing by the Court of Auditors*). –

1. The preventive review of legitimacy on the part of the Court of Auditors is exercised exclusively on the following measures not having the force of law:

   a) measures emanated after deliberation by the Council of Ministers;

   b) decisions of the President of the Council of Ministers and decisions of the Ministry with regard to the definition of structural plans, the appointment of management functions and general guidelines for directing and carrying out administrative action,

   c) regulatory measures with external relevance, planning decisions involving expenditures and general actions taken for implementing European community regulations;

   d) decisions of inter-ministerial department committees or the designation of funds and other deliberations emanated on matters referred to in letters *b*) and *c*);

   e) [*abrogated*];

   f) measures for the disposal of State property and real estate assets;

   g) decrees which approve the contracts of State Administrations, excluding public corporations; assets, of any value, excepting those falling within the hypothesis set out in the last paragraph of art. 19 of royal decree no. 2440 of 18 November 1923; government contracts for the procurement of goods and services, for sums exceeding the value in ECU established by European Community regulations for the application of the procedures for the adjudication of the aforesaid contracts; other liabilities contracts, if they are for amounts exceeding one tenth of the above-indicated value.

h) decrees of variations in the State budget, of assessment of balances and of preventive consent of the Ministry of the Treasury for charging current expenditures to the following accounting period;

i) actions for the initiation of which a written order has been issued by the Minister;

j) actions which the President of the Council of Ministers requests be temporarily subject to preventive review or which the Court of Auditors decides to subject, for a determined period of time, to preventive review in relation to situations of widespread and repeated irregularities detected during subsequent inspection;

2. The provisions subjected to preventive review shall acquire efficacy if the competent inspection office does not remit examination to the inspection section within the time limit of thirty days from receipt. The time limit is interrupted if the office requests clarifications or additional elements for judgement. When thirty days have elapsed from receipt of the counter-arguments of the administration, the provision shall acquire efficacy if the office does not remit examination to the inspection section. The inspection section shall rule on the conformity to law within thirty days of the date of the referral of the provisions or from the date of arrival of the elements requested with a judicial order. When this term has elapsed the provisions shall be enforceable.

3. The Sections of the Court of Auditors may in assembly, and with a grounded ruling establish that single actions of substantial financial importance, identified according to categories and State Administrations, be subjected to examination by the Court for a determined period of time. The Court may request a re-examination of the actions within fifteen days of receipt, with enforceability remaining valid. The administrations shall transmit the actions adopted following re-examination to the Court of Auditors which shall advise the Ministry when it detects irregularities.

4. The Court of Auditors shall, even within the accounting period currently in progress, carry out further inspections on the management of the budget and assets of public administrations, as well as extra-budgetary activities and on European Community funding, verifying the legitimacy and the regularity of management, as well as the effectiveness of internal inspections within each administration. It shall also, on the basis of other inspections as well, assess the conformity of the outcomes of administrative activity with the objectives established by law, comparatively assessing costs, means and times for carrying out administrative activities. The Court shall annually define the programmes and reference criteria for the inspection.

5. With regard to Regional administrations, inspection of management concerns the pursuit of the aims established by the laws pertaining to principles and programmes.

6. The Court of Auditors shall, at least annually, report to Parliament and to the Regional Councils on the results of the inspections carried out. The Court's reports shall also be sent to the administrations concerned, for which the Court, at any other time, formulates its observations. The administrations shall inform the Court and the elected organs of the measures adopted as a consequence.

7. Relative to local bodies, the provisions referred to in decree law no. 786 of 22 December 1981, converted, with modifications, by law no. 51 of 26 February 1982, and subsequent modifications and additions, shall remain in force, along with the provisions of law no. 259 of 21 March 1958, with relation to the bodies to which the State ordinarily contributes. The reports of the Court shall also contain assessments on the effectiveness of internal inspections.

8. In exercising the powers set out in the present article, the Court of Auditors may request any document or information from the public administrations and internal inspection organs and may carry out and order direct inspections and assessments. Paragraph 4 of art. 2 of decree law no. 453 of 15 November 1993 shall apply. The Court may request nonterritorial public administrations to re-examine actions which are deemed not to conform with the law. The administrations shall forward the provisions adopted following re-examination to the Court of Auditors, which shall notify the general management organ should irregularities be found. The laws concerning additional inspections established by legislative decree no. 29 of 3 February 1993, and subsequent modifications, and by legislative decree no. 39 of 12 February 1993, as well as by article 166 of law no. 312 of 11 July 1980, shall stand, insofar as they are compatible with the provisions of the present law.

9. For the exercise of the powers of inspection, the procedural rules set out in the consolidated law on the Court of Auditors, approved with royal decree no. 1214 of 12 July 1934, and successive modifications, shall apply, insofar as they are compatible with the provisions of the present law.

10. The inspection section is composed of the president of the Court of Auditors who is its presiding officer, by the presidents of the sections responsible for co-ordination and by all the magistrates who have been assigned inspection tasks. The section is annually divided into four committees of which, in any case, the president of the Court of Auditors and the presidents of the co-ordinating sections are members. The committees have specific competences according to the typology of inspection and matters under inspection

and make decisions with a minimum of eleven voting members. The plenary assembly is presided over by the president of the Court of Auditors and is composed of the co-ordinating section presidents and of thirty-five magistrates assigned inspection tasks, who are identified annually by the Council of the Presidency on the basis of at least three for each section committee and one for each of the inspection sections for the administrations of the special statute Regions and of the autonomous provinces of Trento and Bolzano. The plenary assembly makes decisions with a minimum of twenty one voting members.

10-*bis*. In the plenary meeting the inspection section annually establishes the programme of activities and the tasks and responsibilities of the committees, as well as the criteria for their composition on the part of the president of the Court of Auditors.

11. With the possibility of referral established by art. 24 of the above-mentioned consolidated law on the Court of Auditors as substituted by art. 1 of law no. 161 of 21 March 1953, remaining valid, the inspections section shall rule in every case in which dissent occurs among the competent magistrates with regard to the legitimacy of actions. The magistrate who refers the question to the section is called upon to participate in the section as referee.

12. The magistrates assigned to the additional inspections referred to in paragraph 4 shall work according to the established annual programmes, but they may temporarily abandon these, for motivated reasons, for situations and measures which require timely assessments and verifications, notifying the inspection section.

13. The provisions of paragraph 1 do not apply to the acts and measures emanated with regard to monetary matters, credit, movable property and currency. >>

—Art. 13 of law no. 468 of 5 August 1978, containing: "Reform of Some Regulations on Public Accounting pertaining to the State Budget", published in *Official Gazette* no. 233 of 22 August 1978, establishes:

<< Article 13 (*Government guaranty*). – A list of the principal and subsidiary guarantees given by the State for government bodies and other subjects is included in an annex to the budgetary previsions of the Ministry of the Treasury >>.

Note to art. **184**:

—Law no. 1089 of 1 June 1939, concerning the "Protection of Things Possessing Artistic and Historical interest", is published in *Official Gazette* no. 184 of 8 August 1939.

—Decree no. 1409 of the President of the Republic of 30 September 1963, containing:

"Regulations relative to Organisation and Staff of the State Archives", is published in *Official Gazette* no. 285 of 31 October 1963.

—Decree no. 3 of the President of the Republic of 14 January 1972, containing: "Transfer to Ordinary Statute Regions of Government Administrative Functions for Assistance to Schools and to the Museums and Libraries of Local Bodies and their Relative Staff and Offices", is published in the ordinary supplement to *Official Gazette* no. 15 of 19 January 1972.

—Law no. 127 of 15 May 1997, containing: "Urgent Measures for Streamlining Administrative Activities and Decision-making and Inspection Procedures", is published in the ordinary supplement to *Official Gazette* no. 113 of 17 May 1997.

—Law no. 352 of 8 October 1997, containing: "Provisions for Cultural Properties", is published in the ordinary supplement to *Official Gazette* no. 243 of 17 October 1997.

—Legislative decree no. 112 of 31 March 1998, containing: "Conferral of State Administrative Functions and Tasks to the Regions and Local Bodies, in Implementation of Chapter I of law no. 59 of 15 March 1997", is published in the ordinary supplement to *Official Gazette* no. 92 of 21 April 1998.

—Law no. 237 of 12 July 1999, containing: "Establishment of the Centre for the Documentation and Enhancement of the Contemporary Arts and of New Museums, and Modifications to the Legislation on Cultural Property and Measures for Cultural Activities", is published in *Official Gazette* no. 173 of 26 July 1999.

—Legislative decree no. 281 of 30 July 1999, containing "Provisions pertaining to the Treatment of Personal Data for Historical, Statistical and Scientific Research Purposes", is published in *Official Gazette* no. 191 of 16 August 1999.

—For legislative decree no. 490 of 29 October 1999, see note to the premises.

—Decree no. 283 of the President of the Republic of 7 September 2000, concerning: "Regulation Containing Laws on the Alienation of Immovable Assets belonging to the Historical and Artistic Property of the State", is published in *Official Gazette* no. 240 of 13 October 2000.

—Legislative decree no. 196 of 30 June 2003, containing the "Code on the Protection of Personal Data", is published in the ordinary supplement to *Official Gazette* no. 174 of 29 July 2003.

—Law no. 172 of 8 July 2003, containing: "Provisions for the Reorganisation and Re-launching of Recreational Navigation and Marine Tourism" is published in *Official Gazette* no. 161 of 14 July 2003.